Childhood and Society

Childhood and Society

An Introduction to the Sociology of Childhood

Michael Wyness

First published 2006 by
PALGRAVE MACMILLAN
Houndmills, Basingstoke, Hampshire RG21 6XS and
175 Fifth Avenue, New York, N.Y. 10010
Companies and representatives throughout the world

PALGRAVE MACMILLAN is the global academic imprint of the Palgrave Macmillan division of St. Martin's Press, LLC and of Palgrave Macmillan Ltd. Macmillan® is a registered trademark in the United States, United Kingdom and other countries. Palgrave is a registered trademark in the European Union and other countries.

ISBN-13: 978–0–333–94648–0 hardback
ISBN 10: 0–333–94648–0   hardback
ISBN-13: 978–0–333–94649–7 paperback
ISBN 10: 0-333-94649-9   paperback

This book is printed on paper suitable for recycling and made from fully managed and sustained forest sources.

A catalogue record for this book is available from the British Library.

A catalog record for this book is available from the Library of Congress.

10   9   8   7   6   5   4   3   2   1
15   14   13   12   11   10   09   08   07   06

Printed in China

For Henry George

Contents

List of Figures and Tables

Figures

Tables

Acknowledgements

I would like to thank Catherine Gray, Sheree Keep and Emily Salz at Palgrave for their support and forbearance during the six years that it has taken to finish the book. Jo Moran-Ellis was there at the start; I am grateful for her early input. I also want to thank the anonymous reviewers for their detailed comments on the first draft. I should also like to mention my third year 'Childhood and Society' students who were unwittingly exposed to some of the material. Finally, I owe a deep gratitude to Beth for her love and support. I dedicate this book to our little boy Henry.

MICHAEL WYNESS

Introduction

The study of children and childhood in sociology has come a long way in the last couple of decades. From the almost exclusive focus on children as the objects of socialisation, sociology is now addressing dynamic, social, structural, relational and interpretive dimensions of the state of childhood alongside the status of 'child'. This broadening of the sociological gaze has led to a richness of empirical studies and developments in theoretical and conceptual ideas about children and childhood. There is also a growing recognition that the study of childhood can illuminate wider issues in society and challenge current thinking in social theory and research.

This book sets out to explore a range of approaches that sociologists have employed in researching into and theorising about the lives and social worlds of children, and the phenomenon of childhood. In doing this, it will explore competing positions taken on childhood as a meaning system, as a cultural and historical construct and as a biological and sociostructural state. Key concepts such as social dependence, vulnerability and protection, and socialisation/development will be employed to understand the positioning of children, and will also themselves be critically examined for their analytic contribution to sociological studies. Throughout the book empirical and theoretical work will be drawn on that illustrates the challenges made by the new social studies of childhood which focus on the idea of the child as a social agent. The book will also examine some of the crises that are said to beset childhood: poverty, abuse, child labour, the disappearance of childhood, and reflect too on how a study of childhood can inform sociological thinking relating to other social crises, changes and social problems such as globalisation, criminality and disruption of social order. Finally, the book will consider the practical and methodological implications of the move towards placing children in the centre of the sociological frame from an empirical and practical point of view.

The intention is to acquaint the reader with the key debates in social studies of childhood, and key current concepts such as agency, competence, and citizenship. The reader will be introduced to the significant early work that informed the emergence of a new approach to childhood in sociology, as well as current work which is moving the field forward. In addition, attention will be paid to key developments in sociology and how they relate

1

to the study of children and childhood, such as work on globalisation, late modernity, and the risk society.

The book is divided up into four parts. The key theme running through the first part is the interplay between a deterministic approach, which until recently has dominated our understanding of children and childhood, and the current advances which locate children's actions and meanings in the foreground. The first chapter sets out what I consider to be the new and possibly dominant theoretical framework within the sociology of childhood: social constructionism. An emphasis on meaning and the socially malleable nature of childhood moves us beyond an earlier orthodoxy that foregrounded biological and chronological certainty. The idea of the child as both a socially produced and culturally relative phenomenon will be addressed more critically in Chapter 2 when I explore theories which emphasise the fixed nature of childhood through an emphasis on social structure and categorisation. A structuralist approach locates children within a pre-existing social universe. Other more established social structuralist approaches are examined, such as Marxism and feminism. The aims here are to uncover the relative influences of these approaches on the sociology of childhood and highlight the need to go beyond these dominant sociological 'paradigms' in making sense of children and childhood. The chapter also touches on the extent to which age/generation can have as much explanatory value as more established dimensions of stratification such as social class and gender. Chapters 1 and 2 concentrate on sociological theories of childhood. For the bulk of Chapter 3 the emphasis is shifted towards more general sociological theories. The aim of this chapter is to locate children and childhood and recent social scientific interest in childhood within broader sociological theories of change at local, national and global levels. Theories of late modernity are central here. Attempts are made to locate childhood and children within these theoretical approaches by drawing on late twentieth- and early twenty-first-century processes such as individualisation and globalisation.

In Part Two I continue with the macroglobal approach and examine the idea of children and childhood as a social problem within Western and non-Western cultures. I will contend here that sociologists are becoming increasingly concerned with problems that policy-makers and professionals have making sense of children's position within a taken-for-granted social hierarchy. Chapter 4 examines this problem with reference to the argument that the institution of childhood is in decline. I will illustrate this by drawing on key social problems such as child crime and the street child. I also refer to crisis in terms of children's relationship to technology. Chapter 5 deals with how societies are responding to these problems in terms of strategies of control and surveillance. Here I examine the historical and political processes associated with state-building and their relationship to conceptions of childhood.

What roles do the child protection and criminal justice systems play in our modern understandings of childhood? How are children treated through these systems of regulation? As well as focusing on the political systems that shape our understandings of childhood, in Chapters 4 and 5 I draw on the child-as-actor theme in critically examining the assumptions built into the idea that childhood is in crisis. The analysis thus moves beyond the idea that children are literally and metaphorically out of place by questioning the meaning of 'children's place' and offering an analysis that broadens our understanding of contemporary childhoods.

In the two chapters in Part Three I review the different ways that children are assessed, documented and measured as the objects and projects of social scientists and educationalists. In Chapter 6 I address the influence of socialisation and child development as frames of reference for understanding childhood. Sociologists and psychologists tend to inhabit different meaning systems in terms of theorising and researching social phenomena. Nevertheless, in this chapter I outline the convergent as well as divergent assumptions that these disciplines make about children and childhood through what has been termed a 'dominant framework'. I go on and evaluate this framework in the light of recent work which views children as accomplished social actors. At the same time I assess the implications of these practices for childhood and children. The theme of regulation and control continues in the following chapter on children, schooling and education. I examine the influence of the dominant framework within the education sector and through teaching practice, particularly in primary schools in England and Wales. The chapter also draws on theoretical approaches from the first part of the book in outlining the relationship between childhood and education and the positioning of school pupils within a reformed education system. In the final section I reassess the links between childhood, schooling and education by outlining the sociological significance of truancy and home education.

In the first three parts I concentrate on the way that childhood has been constituted and reconstituted through the dynamic interplay of adult structures and children's agency. In the final part I advance in more substantive terms one of the central ideas of a new sociology of childhood that children themselves, in a variety of ways and with varying degrees of success, are quite instrumental in constituting themselves as social subjects. Chapter 8 is concerned with what we know about the worlds within which children interact with each other. I will address the ways in which children make sense of the social world in and through membership of peer groups and what might be termed childhood cultures. I go on in this chapter to look at the extent to which children are formative in the wider adult society. I will extend the analysis of children's cultures by assessing the impact of technological innovations. In particular, I look at how the advent of information technology is providing children with opportunities to broaden their social relationships. Chapter 9 deals with how sociologists currently grapple with the business of researching children and childhood. Methodological and ethical issues are discussed, along with the idea that children might play a formative role within the research process. The final chapter addresses a key issue that social scientists, policy makers and professionals are presently wrestling with: children's rights and their relationship to the political sphere. I will return to globalisation, one of the key themes discussed earlier, and argue that a rights discourse has to take account of children from quite different cultural backgrounds. In the second half of the chapter the global context will also serve as a framework for comparing children's political involvement in different cultural settings.

On the Age Range

'Age' and age range is one of the contested areas examined throughout the book. In particular my discussion of the boundary between childhood and adulthood in Chapter 1 illustrates the fluid definition of childhood when referring to age-grading. Common practice has been to break childhood down into three periods: early (0–4), middle (5–9) and late (10–14), with adolescence accounting for those aged between 14 and 17. Whilst there is an element of arbitrariness here, when we are writing about children and childhood, I am mainly thinking about those up to around the age of 14. However, in Chapters 4 and 10 we are dealing with legal boundaries which extend the period of childhood up until 18. I am well aware that the United Nations defines childhood as the period from 0 to 18 and an important marker in most Western societies is the inclusion of children into a political community, which tends to take place when they achieve voting rights at 18.

Part One
Childhood and Theory

1

The Social Meaning of Childhood

Introduction

We all have experience of childhood not only as children but also in bringing up children, working with children or simply being members of a society that values childhood. Children are a common part of our physical and social landscape. Our culture and values nowadays are suffused with memories, experiences and symbols of childhood and all things 'childish'. Moreover, we think of childhood as a natural and inevitable phase that we all go through before we reach adulthood. We may be forgiven, then, for taking children and childhood for granted. Given this situation, we are rarely asked what childhood is or how it relates to children. If we are pushed to define childhood, the invocation of 'nature' directs us towards thinking about children's 'natural' biological incapacities. Children are physically smaller and weaker than adults are. Common sense tells us that their size and stature are visible markers of difference. This is an unexceptional observation in itself, for no one would deny that children are not as fully developed biologically as adults. We assume that this smallness becomes increasingly less significant as children move through childhood into adulthood. Childhood is thus commonly associated with this smallness. 'Children' and 'childhood' here are seen as aspects of the same thing, children being the grounded and physical manifestations of childhood. It is then a quick step to deducing childhood from what we commonly experience in society: children. Children's physicality is what also seems to characterise children's minds and identities; throughout most of the twentieth century, at least in Western societies, the idea that children's physical immaturity determines their social identities has been built into our way of thinking such that it assumes the status of fact.

We might concede that childhood is an abstraction, a set of ideas or concepts, which define children's nature and the kinds of relations they have with other members of society. Yet because children and childhood are seen to be, more or less, the same thing, the abstract ideas associated with childhood seem to flow directly from children and their smallness. Our concern in this chapter develops out of debates within the social sciences and more specifically within the sociology of childhood on what it means to talk about childhood as an abstraction. In particular, sociologists and others working in related fields have been challenging the notion that there is a close connection between children's physical immaturity and the cultural and social features that make up childhood. As Postman (1982, p. xi) proposes, 'from a biological point of view it is inconceivable that any culture will forget that it needs to reproduce itself. But it is quite possible for a culture to exist without a social idea of children.' The basic thrust of this chapter, then, is to separate the link made between the physical and abstract features of children. We intend to do this by emphasising the *meaning of childhood*, a bundle of ideas and sentiments that characterise the socially constructed nature of childhood.

In this chapter I introduce childhood as part of the subjective realm by emphasising its malleable, changeable and ultimately contested nature. In the first section of the chapter I address our taken-for-granted ideas about childhood and draw out their social, and by implication context-dependent, contours. I hope to demonstrate through an examination of one key feature of childhood, child's play, that the meaning of childhood cannot simply be taken for granted. In the second and third sections I outline in more substantive terms social constructionism. I start from a more historical perspective and examine the historical construction or development of a modern childhood. This is followed by an exposition of a more radical social constructionism where childhood is produced through discourse. Sociologists abandon any idea that there is anything to childhood other than what we think and say about childhood. Childhood here is a quintessentially cultural phenomenon. In the fourth section I step back from our exposition of social constructionism and examine some of its limitations. In the final section I attempt a synthesis of constructionist and what we might call more universalist approaches to childhood. David Archard's (1993) work is central here: sociologists are correct to stress the influence of culture and the idea of a range of different childhoods. Nonetheless, our starting point must be some very general and more or less given differences between adults and children found in most if not all societies.

The 'Playing-Child' Construction

In a recent theoretical text on childhood, James, Jenks and Prout (1998) whilst not completely rejecting the relationship between biology and culture, paraphrase Ennew and suggest that childhood is characterised by sets of cultural values: 'In the twentieth century ... Western childhood has become a period in the life course characterised by social dependency, asexuality, and the obligation to be happy, with children having the right to protection and training but not to social or personal autonomy' (James, Jenks and Prout 1998, p. 62).

What we have here is a definition of childhood in terms of distinguishable features. It also suggests that these features not only distinguish children from, say, adults, it implies that the *meaning of childhood* may be different depending on our cultural and historical backgrounds.

Let us take one key feature of this construction of childhood, the 'obligation to be happy'. We commonly equate this with children playing. Let us also examine the 'playing-child' in common-sense terms to begin with. We might think of play as a cultural space within which children have fun, explore their imaginations, and learn in a desultory fashion how to get on with others, usually their peers. Play is also seen as a part of childhood in that it is a period of time when children are free from responsibilities. Children play because they have no responsibilities. This lack of responsibility is often taken to mean that children do not work, at least in terms of earning an income or paying income tax. Responsibility here equates with how earning a living generates sets of expectations and obligations, whether it relates to providing for other members of the family or having broader social and moral responsibilities as a citizen. These responsibilities in themselves have been the subject of much debate, not least in the way they have become powerful cultural means of compelling people to work.[1] Nevertheless, the point I wish to make is that we expect adults to provide for children economically and morally by working and earning an income. Being a child and going through the period of childhood means having no economic and moral responsibilities; it means not having to work.

I have characterised childhood in terms of lack of work. In the process I have also offered a definition of adulthood. To simplify things a little:

Childhood = Play
Adulthood = Work

In strengthening the adult/work equation we can point to the numbers of adults excluded from earning a living, some whom are unable to find work. Most of these groups, such as single parents, the unemployed and the sick, are able to claim some sort of income from the state because in other circumstances they would be in a position to work. Furthermore, in some countries the state recognises the financial responsibilities of unemployed adults by providing them with different levels of financial support on the basis of their child-rearing responsibilities. As I said before, when it comes to children there is no expectation that they work. Thus children in their own right cannot claim an income from the state.[2] The grounds for this exclusion are legal, with children under the age of 13 in the United Kingdom excluded from the labour market and with older children limited to a few hours' work a week during specific times of the day. Pressed further, we would probably refer to children's size and immaturity. We assume that laws which prohibit or at least restrict children from working are based on the idea that children are incapable of holding down a job. This in turn stems from their lack of development; their lack of understanding of the world, which would make it difficult for us to think that children could make the right decisions within the workplace. Children's emotional, cognitive and social immaturity is commonly seen to relate to biological growth. As children grow, so do their emotional and social abilities. Thus we assume that when children are old enough to work they are competent enough to work.

In linking childhood to play, play is seen as the opposite of work: a period free of responsibility, where individuals can relax and have fun. Now play in relation to modern childhood can be structured and educational. As we shall see in Chapter 4, some have argued that an excess of structure within play undermines the very idea of childhood. Nevertheless, our common sense distinguishes between play, which is fun, and work, which is more serious, the latter often viewed as something that we adults have to do.

Let us now examine a little more closely the claim that children play and adults work. From an historical perspective we might ask whether children have never worked and have always played. After consulting the work of social historians we would probably answer this question by saying that children have always played and have only recently stopped working (Corsaro 1997, pp. 55–6). Children in the past, particularly those from poor families, had considerable economic responsibilities. In the UK, for instance, it was only in the first few years of the twentieth century that children's economic responsibilities were superseded by compulsory schooling. The 'playing-child' image of childhood is, therefore, a recent construction. Zelitzer (1985) talks about the changing value of childhood in the USA. She refers to children's working responsibilities in the nineteenth century, with parents viewing children as having economic value. This is not to say that parents did not love their children or that they treated them harshly; children were simply included as members of an economically productive unit. As children moved out of the work sphere in the early twentieth century, parents gradually saw their children differently. They became emotionally valuable, with parents placing more importance on their children's social development and happiness. What Zelitzer (1985) is pointing to is a change in value and meaning; she is exploring the idea that childhood might have meant something different in the nineteenth century from what it does today.

From a sociological and anthropological perspective we might ask about children's present-day responsibilities. Is the 'playing-child' image a universal one today? Have all parents followed the American example of protecting their children from the world of economic responsibility by providing for them? In answering this second question we might say that our own childhoods and those of our children in North American and European countries are inadequate guides to the lives of children in many poor developing countries. In subsequent chapters I discuss the problem of 'child labour' and the plight of children who work in Asia, Africa and Latin America. Yet it is evident that many children in the early years of the twenty-first century have considerable economic responsibilities which are prioritised before any time to play. Not only is the 'play-child' construction historically recent, it is culturally specific.[3]

A third question surrounds the 'childish' nature of play: to what extent does the association of childhood with play as fun, imaginative and chaotic compromise children's contributions to society? If play exists within the adult world, it is residual not real, something done after the important business of work. Do we undervalue play because it is associated with childhood or do we compromise childhood because we trivialise play? Play in these terms can be linked with another taken-for-granted feature of childhood: innocence. We can equate innocence with children having insufficient character and social guile to make their way in the world. Childhood here becomes a period where the real world of sexual, economic and public action is suspended until children are old enough to cope. Child's play is synonymous with innocence. As I stated earlier in the chapter, children play because they have no responsibilities. Innocence connotes 'irresponsibility' in that children's moral and social fragility, their vulnerability, precludes them from having responsibilities. Play thus becomes a key feature of the child's world, with the latter sequestered from the adult world through a dominant imperative to nurture and protect. In these terms childhood has a political as well as cultural and historical meaning. By associating play with childhood we are unintentionally marginalising children, treating them as immature and incomplete members of society who require constant adult attention and regulation. In returning to the earlier definition of James, Jenks and Prout (1998), politically children have very few rights, corresponding to the absence of 'social and personal autonomy'.

The Historical Development of Modern Childhood

I have hinted at the idea of childhood as an historical construction. In examining this idea in a little more detail, let us turn to the work of sociologists who take a more historical approach and emphasise the different ways that childhood as a construct has developed over time. I look at three versions: the 'sentiments' school, a more materialist approach, and a social history that concentrates on children rather than childhood.

Ariès and Modern Childhood

Whilst the origin of Ariès's thesis can be traced back to Elias's arguments on the civilising process (Cunningham 1995, p. 5), his work has been rightly acknowledged as one of the earliest challenges to the existing orthodoxy on childhood: its natural and universal status as a stage of development. There is some ambiguity as to whether Ariès is proposing childhood as a modern invention. He refers to the similarities between the Hellenistic and Neolithic periods and the modern period: both were preoccupied with regulating children's lives. He goes on to talk about the 'revival, at the beginning of modern times in education' (p. 396) and by implication the re-emergence of childhood from the sixteenth century onwards. That being said, his focus is the medieval period onwards and the change in senti-ments. His thesis is that during the medieval period, from around the twelfth to the sixteenth century, childhood did not exist as a period within which children were treated either as uniquely different from adults or as nascent individuals who had to be carefully nurtured. There was a distinct lack of sentiment, an indifference to children as a separate sector of the population. In effect, Ariès concludes that our understanding and treatment of children in medieval times indicates the absence of the concept of child-hood.

This indifference was clearly brought out by Ariès in his treatment of the medieval school, which was 'not intended for children: it was a sort of tech-nical school for the instruction of clerics, young and old. ... Thus it welcomed equally and indifferently, children, youths and adults, the preco-cious and the backward' (p. 317). This is in stark contrast to a more familiar picture of the modern classroom drawn by Ariès:

> Today the class, the constituent cell of the school structure, presents certain precise characteristics which are entirely familiar: it corresponds to a stage in the progressive acquisition of knowledge (to a curriculum), to an average age from which every attempt is made not to depart, to a physical, spatial unit, for each age group and subject group has its special premises (and the word 'class' denotes both the container and the contents), and to a period of time, an annual period at the end of which the class's complement changes. (1960, pp. 171–2)

For Ariès the modern image of childhood is crystallised in the shift from the amorphous, disorganised and undisciplined nature of the medieval school to the tightly structured and regulated demands of modern schooling. Ariès focuses on the increasing significance attached to age as an organising principle. First of all, schools were becoming the preserves of children with a gradual narrowing of the age range. Drawing on statistical material, he also contrasts the variegated ages found in year groups in medieval schools with the gradual segregation of children by age, and the emergence of the classroom as a significant organisational unit in French schools in the eighteenth and nineteenth centuries.

The medieval indifference to children was apparent in the way that 'schooling' took place in a range of adult contexts. 'Child' as well as 'adult' students' life in school was characterised by a lack of manners and morals, and violence and licentiousness were common. The need to isolate, protect and discipline children was apparent in the way that schools and classrooms were physically segregated from the rest of the community, with the introduction of colleges from about the seventeenth century. These were 'designed not only for tuition but also for the supervision and care of youth' (p. 169). It is clear that the school as an 'essential institution' was starting to display the characteristics of the modern school with its separate teaching staff and disciplinary codes. It was also starting to become apparent that the classroom was becoming a container or laboratory for the assessment and regulation of children's social and moral development. Discipline gradually became less severe as childhood started to be seen as a sort of social and moral apprenticeship: there was a stronger emphasis on conditioning, in preparing children for their futures as adults. As I shall go on to discuss in following chapters, a key characteristic of modern childhood is its future orientation, the idea that children are nascent individuals with personalities and social and moral predispositions that need to be harnessed and moulded in preparation for adulthood.

Whilst schooling seems to dominate Ariès's analysis of modern childhood, the rise of the private conjugal family plays a significant if subordinate role in the construction of childhood. Ariès's inferential approach identifies the rise in childhood sentiment from the changing nature of family portraits in medieval and modern periods. The child as a focal point for the parental gaze and the central position of children in portraits from the seventeenth century onwards indicates a degree of child-centredness. Yet this goes along with a more implosive trend in family life, with middle and upper classes distancing themselves from community, kin and latterly household servants.

Ariès documents an uneasy relationship between the evolution of the modern school and the privatised family, which reflects many of the concerns that we have today about the relative power exercised by adults within each sphere (see Chapter 5). The school became an important reference point for the development and disciplining of children. Schools were seen as being important for parents because they were relatively close, allowing parents to see their children as much as possible. However, the literature on manners and etiquette that was widely distributed in France in the seventeenth and eighteenth centuries served to limit the power of the school to socialise in that this literature tended to be read by both parents and children within the family. Thus a range of manuals on how to discipline and punish children and how to prepare them for school as well as how adults ought to conduct themselves were circulated within families. And some of this material addressed the children themselves.

Ariès identifies the influence of moralists and pedagogues in the seventeenth and eighteenth centuries. Powerful ideas started to restrict children's access to the community and the adult population. Moreover, these ideas distributed among middle- and upper-class children in the form of manuals on etiquette emphasised both the necessity of their education and the need to protect their innocence. Social class and gender are significant here. The modern sentiments regarding childhood had a limited impact on the poorer sectors of society until well into the nineteenth century. And, as several authors have noted, Ariès's construct of childhood really only applies to boys; girls were excluded from schooling throughout most of the modernising period, continually expected from an early age to have domestic responsibilities (Gittins 1998).

Thus for Ariès two institutional developments are crucial between the seventeenth and the nineteenth century: the introduction of a modern system of schooling and the privatising of family life. Each is significant in the gradual separation and segregation of children from adult society; each reflects modern sensibilities on the child as both the embodiment of innocence and purity and an investment in the future.

Shorter and Motherhood

Edward Shorter's (1976) work is often associated with Ariès in that they are both dealing with sentiments and values relating to family and childhood. Nevertheless, there are significant differences. Shorter's analysis of childhood is more indirect, focusing on the development of the modern nuclear family rather than childhood per se. His analysis covers a shorter, more recent historical period and he takes a more explicitly comparative line than Ariès, drawing on premodern eighteenth-century mothers and twentieth-century modern motherhood. His research base is wider than that of Ariès in that he was (a) trying to incorporate the lives of peasant and working-class mothers as well as the bourgeoisie, (b) drawing on wider European sources as well as France, and (c) making regional comparisons largely between rural and urban situations.

Having said this, the realm of ideas and values is significant for Shorter as it is for Ariès. Shorter's notion of sentiments covers historical shifts in family life in terms of the development of spontaneity and romantic love, and the gradual rise in the 'sacrificial' role of the mother. As with Ariès, Shorter separates nature from culture: he spells out the cultural rather than instinctive importance of 'good mothering'. Rather than there being some innate tendency for mothers to bond with their infants, in the past there was often a lack of care and attention to children's specific needs; there was a general maternal indifference towards infant children. Shorter is arguing that whereas modern mothers put the interests of their children above all else, mothers in the eighteenth century failed what he called the 'sacrifice test'. Shorter thus takes a different and harder line than Ariès with respect to the culpability of eighteenth-century mothers. Whilst Shorter is not explicit about this, maternal indifference is equated with modern-day notions of abuse and neglect, and seen as a determinate factor in the continually high rates of infant mortality during this period. According to Shorter, mothers ignored their babies' cries, were likely to treat them roughly and constrict their movements through swaddling, and often farmed their children out to wet-nurses who were incapable of looking after their children. The net result was often the children's early death, with mothers 'often resigned to (their children's) squalling, usually fatal "convulsions" and "fevers" ' (Shorter 1976, p. 170).

What Shorter is saying here is that this indifference stemmed from an inability to view their children as any different from any other aspect of their lives. There was little sense in which mothers were sacrificial: children were not central or special or in any way a priority in the lives of seventeenth- and eighteenth-century mothers. If we think of childhood in terms of the way parents related to their young children: notions of centring, nurturing and protection, that is if we define childhood in a relational sense, then Shorter is arguing that as well as 'good mothering', childhood did not exist.

Shorter draws on a change in sentiments from about the middle of the eighteenth century among the affluent members of society. This resulted in children gradually being seen as central in the lives of women and families. The influence of thinkers like Rousseau, the rise of romantic love and the circulation of ideas about proper child care all contributed to the development of a discourse on good mothering. Child-rearing practices changed: wet-nurses took a less mercenary approach to their work, 'attaching' themselves to their charges, and there was a gradual decline in their employment as women started to attach themselves to their babies through breast-feeding. These sentiments and practices gradually percolated down to the working classes by the beginning of the twentieth century. Women, then, over time, have had to learn how to be good mothers and, in the process, become aware of children as separate entities in need of love, protection and separate treatment. The construction of a modern Western childhood is thus intimately linked to the historical development of motherhood.

The Rise and Fall of Childhood – A Materialist Analysis

Postman's (1982) thesis provides a material basis to the history of childhood. The 'sentiments school' concentrates on the power of attitudes, moral dispositions and expectations; Postman (1982) refers to their technological underpinnings. Childhood evolved much earlier for Postman than Shorter, between the sixteenth and eighteenth century, owing to the demands that adults made on children to learn to read. This was in turn a consequence of the invention of the printing press, which allowed for the dissemination of the written word. Reading skills were to be learned by children in a sequential and developmental way, thus producing distance between children and adults who had gone through the process and were charged with regulating children's reading. This process was gradually institutionalised through mass schooling. The developmental 'secrets' acquired through learning to read thus served as a literal and metaphorical basis to schooling. Children were located within a system of learning organised around children's age-related, incremental acquisition of knowledge and skills.

Postman's thesis was different from the 'sentiments school' in a second way: he discusses the 'fall' as well as the 'rise' of childhood. I will deal with the former in more detail when I come to discuss the crisis of childhood in Chapter 4. Yet it is worth mentioning this here, for the logic of social constructionism offers us a framework for conceptualising the 'unmaking' as well as the constructing of childhood. Postman views the making and unmaking of childhood in the same way, as a product of technological change. Thus the moral and cultural boundaries that separate children and adults were gradually eroded throughout the second half of the twentieth century owing to the influence of electronic media. The television, in particular, comes in for criticism as a medium that introduces children to 'a world of simultaneity and instancy' (Postman 1982, p. 70). The immediacy of television undercuts the sequential and adult-regulated process of reading and development, flattening the boundaries between adults and children. Thus children through watching television are put on a par with the parents; are exposed to the same images, ideas and risks as their parents. Children thus lose their special qualities as vulnerable, innocent and dependent.

A Social History of Children

So far I have emphasised the construction of childhood in terms of adult sentiments and material factors that subordinate children. I want now to turn briefly to a sociology that foregrounds the activities of children themselves. In this third, broad, historical approach I focus more on children than childhood. Cunningham (1995) refers to this in terms of the 'actualité' of children, a concern for the flesh-and-blood lives of children and the parts they played in relation to their own cultures and in terms of a more central role with adults. A more revisionist history of childhood concentrating on children's roles and voices in the past has to contend with the lack of documentary evidence and the fact that this probably reflects children's lack of standing or involvement in the past (Hendrick 2000). Nevertheless, Corsaro (1997) has been able to draw on several studies of children's lives in the past in order to illustrate the idea that children themselves as well as adults were active in creating their own cultures. Thus Hanawalt's (1993) work on children in medieval London attempts to document the roles that children played in community celebrations and rituals as well as creating their own games. Corsaro also refers to children's lives in early nineteenth-century slave communities in the southern United States. Here white children often played with slave children, with the former often playing the superior roles in their games. Slave children also had important socialising and caring responsibilities with their younger siblings. Finally, Corsaro illustrates the 'agentic' child in historical terms through his case study of the 'newsies'. In the first years of the twentieth century in many American cities, newspaper publishers subcontracted newspaper-selling to the newsies, children in their early teens who stood on street corners and sold the evening paper. Children had to buy the initial supply from the publishers and sell all their papers to make a profit. Corsaro states that they became well known for their entrepreneurial skills on the street and formed their own trade union in a attempt to protect themselves from the intermittent unilateral increase in paper prices.

Radical Social Constructionism

A radical version of social constructionism sees childhood as a product of discourse. Childhood is more completely disembodied here, with little or no tangible substance or essence. Childhood is almost entirely composed of myths, accounts and visual representations. In the key text, *Stories of Childhood* (Stainton-Rogers and Stainton-Rogers 1992), we have a meticulous working-through of the logic of social constructionism. It is worth mentioning that the Stainton-Rogers completely reject any biological basis to childhood. Biology implies a physical essence, a reality that stands outside of any interpretation or text. Reality here can only be produced through discourse or 'stories of childhood, a multiplicity of texts on the young' (p. 7). Thus we do not simply read about childhood or talk about childhood or even theorise about childhood; we bring childhood into being. Human and social endeavour produces ideas, 'facts' and knowledge that constitute childhood. What we have are accounts of childhood and nothing beyond or underneath this. Childhood is a product of discourse: we do not ask what is childhood but from what standpoint and for what purposes do we talk about childhood?

In these terms developmental psychology, which we shall discuss in Chapter 6, offers us a dominant account of childhood. From a constructionist perspective, the academic discipline associated with the study of child development was able to gain a legitimate status as the founder and trustee of the 'truth' about childhood. It has been able to weld together folkloric knowledge about children's essential characters, and concepts akin to the natural sciences. Thus the power of these stories or myths of childhood lie in the plausibility of the idea that human development is a combination of nature and nurture. The seeming validity of this combination develops through a scientific structure of concepts and techniques that generate a discreet and esoteric body of knowledge. Thus child development is both familiar and strange in terms of its resonance. For the Stainton-Rogers what is grounded and truthful is exposed as constructed and mythical. Furthermore, the techniques for uncovering these truths, the measurement and observation of children in 'controlled environments', are seen to be moral and political. Developmental psychology has helped to bring childhood into being. In going back to our introductory comments on the conflation of biology and culture, developmental psychology is a particularly powerful story of childhood because it plausibly accounts for the fixed biological nature of childhood, making it difficult for us to view childhood any differently.

Deconstruction

I will pursue the moral and political nature of the science of childhood in more detail in Chapter 6. The exercise in stepping back and analysing childhood as a cultural product is an exercise in deconstruction. The analysis goes behind the naming of a social phenomenon and examines the interplay of social, political, intellectual and economic forces that bring the phenomenon into being. In turning to another example, the street child, Glauser (1997) asks whose interests are being served by naming the problem 'street children' and for what reasons? His purpose is to lay bare the forces and interests behind the public concern for children on the street, to deconstruct the common-sensical notion that street children, particularly those in developing countries, can be saved through benevolent Western state action. His analysis uncovers a range of competing interests, from those with a liberal Western conscience intent on 'saving' children from the nefarious forces on the street to those who take more extreme punitive actions in freeing the streets from the perceived 'criminogenic' tendencies of vagrant children. Paraphrasing the Stainton-Rogers (1992, ch. 11), what deconstructing the street child does here is to offer a 'concern about concern', to question some of the powerful images of childhood that imply particular courses of action, whether these are generated by the need to control or the need to protect children.

A final example or construction, 'the sexually abused child', concentrates more on the media's ability to generate powerful images of children who suffer at the hands of adults. These images generate particular conceptions of abused children through images and texts. Kitzinger (1997) refers to two characteristics of childhood brought out through this construction, children as innocent and passive. Sexually abused children are depicted as innocent victims with little or no ability to deal with the problem. Their innocence has been 'stolen' or 'betrayed', their passivity constructed in the way that abusers are seen as all-powerful predators attacking their vulnerable victims. What this does, according to Kitzinger (1997), is generate powerful protectionist impulses among the adult population. Powerful stories in the media are often followed by periods where the control of young children is tightened, and among parents there is a deep distrust of strangers within the immediate vicinity of their children.

The case of Megan Kanka exemplifies this point. Megan, a seven-year-old girl from New Jersey was sexually assaulted and murdered by a neighbour who had previously been convicted twice for sexual abuse. The subsequent furore centred on the inability of the family to take preventative action because the law forbade the publication of information about the whereabouts of convicted child sexual abusers. In 1996 the Clinton administration passed what was known as 'Megan's Law', which requires the authorities to release information about the whereabouts of convicted sexual abusers who have been released from prison.

Kitzinger (1997) deconstructs these images of childhood to demonstrate the difficulties they create in tackling the problem of child sexual abuse. First, given that sexual abuse often stems from 'normal' adult/child relations in families and 'caring' institutions, a greater reliance on adults to keep children close, which protectionism implies, may simply open up more opportunities for adults sexually to abuse children. That is, an emphasis on regulation and protection may unintentionally reinforce children's vulnerability. Secondly, to construct innocence as a period of naivety and asexuality is to make it more difficult to think that children themselves can be better equipped to deal with the problem through sex education. Thirdly, to emphasise children's passivity is to marginalise and trivialise any attempts that children might make to fight back. Kitzinger's (1997) deconstruction exposes the protectionist structures that reinforce a dominant construction of childhood, unintentionally making it difficult to deal with the problem of abuse. Deconstructing therefore becomes an exercise in transforming the taken-for-granted into the problematic through the uncovering of power and competing interests, what Foucault (1980) has called 'regimes of truth'.

Pluralism

One of the underpinnings of a radical social constructionism is that childhood presupposes few truths or starting points and that different interests and vantage points produce different ways of seeing the world, what Rex Stainton-Rogers (1989) refers to as 'multiple realities'. If childhood has to be situated within specific discourses, then different discourses generate different childhoods. Hendrick (1997) explicitly draws this out in his historical examination of British childhoods over the past two centuries. The convergence of different forces during different periods produces different understandings of childhood. To take one example: the political, social and economic debate on the introduction of compulsory schooling in the second half of the nineteenth century generated understandings of childhood in terms of schooling and state regulation. Thus all children would experience a proper and natural childhood through schooling; the education, the control and the morality that emanated from school produced a dominant image of the 'schooled child' during this period. According to Hendrick (1997), the schooled child had developed from the 'delinquent child', the product of an earlier period where the political and social concerns revolved around children and crime, children as both vulnerable victims and precocious offenders. The 'schooled child' and the 'delinquent child' are not totally contingent as there was a general trend throughout the latter part of the nineteenth century towards state regulation of children. Nevertheless, childhood is different in the middle and later parts of the nineteenth century because different combinations of adult interests generated different meanings of childhood.

Limits to Social Constructionism

Social constructionism separates the cultural and biological aspects of childhood, with the former taking precedence over the latter. Accentuating ideas, sentiments and meaning rather than the material elements has arguably become the new orthodoxy within the sociology of childhood. At the same time, various authors have taken issue with this approach.

The Physicality and Experience of Childhood

Gittins (1998) takes issue with the radical version of social constructionism because of its overreliance on accounts of childhood. She argues that this approach talks up childhood, seeing it merely as a product of competing discourses. The material aspects of being a child, children's experiences, which would presumably result from dominant constructions such as innocence, naivety and incompetence, are ignored. Whilst children may not always have a language for communicating these experiences, it may be plausible to speculate that living through childhood in an embodied sense generates particular ways of seeing the world. An emphasis on accounts and stories that are strictly segregated from any experiences also implies that the physicality of problems relating to being a child, such as abuse, poverty and, as I mentioned earlier, being on the street, are neglected. Some authors have argued that social problems revolving around children are social constructions, an analysis that focuses our attention on discursive processes through which abuse is placed on the political agenda (Hacking 1991). As well as little attention being paid to the experience of being a child, there is an absence of any consideration of underlying factors that put children in situations where they are more likely to be abused than adults. Once we start questioning the absence of equivalent concepts such as 'adult abuse' or 'adult poverty', we start to think of features that are intrinsic to children rather than any other group within society.

The embodied nature of childhood has also been highlighted through actor network theory (Latour 1993; Prout 2000b). Social constructionism is seen as an innovative but ultimately flawed way of viewing childhood. Rather than counterpoising culture and nature, Prout (2000b) locates children's bodies next to their dominant representations. Thus the discursive and material worlds are part of a more complex assemblage of things that make up the social world. In these terms, children's developing bodies and accounts of childhood that accentuate vulnerability and incompetence are significant, as are a multitude of practices and objects in constituting children's social worlds and adults' understanding of childhood.

The Neglect of Global Universal Features

If childhood is a product of discourse, it is also a product of very specific sets of circumstances. As I outlined earlier, one of the key themes within the sociology of childhood now is that childhood has been pluralised; that is, we can bring into being an infinite number of constructions arising out of an infinite number of discourses. Social constructionism thus cannot deal adequately enough with universal notions such as the children's needs or children's welfare. Woodhead (1990) in the first edition of the James and Prout reader offers a cogent 'deconstruction' of these notions. He argues that 'needs' has become such a dominant part of our common vocabulary that we assume that it contains the facts about what should and should not happen to all children. Woodhead goes on to deconstruct 'needs' by examining its cultural and intellectual underpinnings. In particular, he examines the way that 'needs' in context implies very specific Westernised understandings of child-rearing and family. In the second edition (1997) he draws back from an out-and-out constructionism in arguing that in accentuating the cultural origins of 'needs' we tend to obscure the possibility of uncovering conditions and problems that most children face at a global level. Thus the problems of child neglect and abuse and child labour can be found in almost all societies, making it difficult to avoid questions about immanent aspects of childhood that put children in more exploitable positions. In these terms, viewing childhood as a construct generates a relativistic view of childhood. To tie childhood wholly to the context within which we find it is to imply that there is little that can be said generally about the nature of childhood, what Qvortrup views (1994, p. 5) as 'the preponderance of what is unique over what is common'.

Children as Constructors?

A third question turns on the role that children play within the discourse on childhood. One of the key questions running through the book is the role that children play within society as co-constructors. Are children's lives merely determined by adults or do children, as Corsaro (1997, p. 18) contends, 'negotiate, share and create culture with adults and each other'? Social constructionists assume the former in that adults are the creative source here. It is important to be clear about this point. Social constructionists are primarily concerned with how the idea of childhood develops through the intersection of a variety of *adult* interests. The deconstruction of childhood leads to claims being made about how powerful adult ideas lock children into behaving in particular ways at particular times. These insights have led constructionists to broaden their empirical range and focus more on children's voices being heard within adult discourses. I will refer to this in more detail in future chapters.

One or Several Childhoods?

A final criticism can be levelled at the historical constructionists. The radical constructionists might talk about a dominant construction of childhood, but the reliance on culture and discourse has produced a relativism that implies a range of different childhoods. The sentiments school and the work of Postman, on the other hand, whilst positing the social contours of childhood and implying different childhoods, produce a singular, modern, capitalist model which assumes a kind of universal and natural state. Postman's emphasis on a 'televisual' culture where children now inhabit the same cultural worlds as adults, is an irredeemably American model and arguably not that applicable outside of an American context. Despite persistent critical commentary surrounding his assumptions and methods, Aries presents us with a powerful model of modern childhood.[4] Nonetheless, the fact is, we have only one modern construction of childhood that clearly differentiates the premodern from the modern. The problem is that there is no room for other competing or just different understandings of childhood that existed in both premodern and modern periods. What we are presented with is the historical unfolding of a single dominant conception of childhood.

Archard's Synthesis

In this final section I take note of the problems that a social-constructionist approach generates and attempt what we might call a synthesis. Linda Pollock's (1983) often-referenced critique of Aries is based on the idea that parents are biologically programmed to love their children. Thus medieval parents quite simply could not have been 'indifferent' to their children's needs because they could not have evolved to behave in this way. I want to hold on to a more universal or fixed notion of childhood without resorting to biological reductionism. To restate what I argued earlier, children's biological differences from adults need to be separated from the cultural components of childhood. The idea that children are commonly believed to be morally and culturally weaker or less significant than adults does not necessarily indicate that this incapacity or subordination is based on their physiological or biological weakness. As we have seen, children in different historical and cultural contexts are quite capable of actions that belie their physiological immaturity.

At the same time, we need to be able to identify by some means the cultural significance of childhood by linking key features of childhood to its social and cultural origins. Here we start with David Archard's (1993, pp.

21–8) distinction between *concept* and *conception*. A concept of childhood refers to some sort of unspecified difference between children and adults in society. A conception of childhood specifies more clearly what that difference entails. *The concept* of childhood refers to the principle of difference whereas *a conception* of childhood provides the details as to what that concept means in any given society. The emphasis on the definite and indefinite article is deliberate here. In the first case, the concept leads us to think that there is a structural distinction between child and adult which suggests some sort of universal difference. We are prefiguring the discussion of structuralism in the following chapter, but what we are saying here is that there is only one concept of childhood that is found pretty much in all societies and in most historical periods. Here Archard (1993) is thinking about some agreed and commonly articulated notions of difference between being a child and being an adult. All cultures have mechanisms for distinguishing between children and adults. In the second case, a conception of childhood means that how this universal difference manifests itself is dependent on the various factors that go to make up the culture, the organisation, the structure of any society. Given that societies are different in their make-ups, so we will find different ways of seeing childhood – different conceptions of childhood. For some people the concept of childhood is significant because they seek to emphasise common social or cultural characteristics of children. Linda Pollock's (1983) work would come into this category. For others, and I include myself here, the conception, or should I say conceptions, of childhood are equally significant.

Archard's distinction between concept and conception allows us to ask the question, 'what is childhood?' It assumes that the question is worth asking, that there will be several answers to the question and that these answers will probably be different depending on the historical and cultural vantage point of the curious observer. We might restate the question 'what is childhood?' by asking how we distinguish between different *conceptions* of childhood. When do children become adults and how do societies make judgements as to when children become adults? In addressing these questions a further distinction of Archard's (1993) between *boundaries* and *dimensions* of childhood is instructive. The idea that childhood is part of the 'life course' means that childhood has a beginning and an ending; that is, it is bounded by criteria which mark it off from adulthood.

Adult/child *boundaries* are defined within societies from a series of perspectives or *dimensions*. This refers to the categories and criteria that a society draws on in defining this boundary. We might think of this in terms of the different dimensions of childhood, with each dimension reflecting sets of interests that draw age-related boundaries at different points. For example, medical practitioners, legal experts, philosophers and politicians all have an interest in when childhood ends. With different sets of interests drawing on the boundary at different points along the life course, this creates innumerable problems for anyone outside of a particular culture wanting to define the childhood of that culture (Archard 1993, p. 22). In advanced contemporary societies this has become a contentious issue, with familiar refrains such as the loss of innocence signifying that there is no clear boundary between childhood and adulthood. Any concern about the shortening of childhood may be related to a lack of agreement as to how we collectively know when it ends, rather than any intrinsic difference in children's behaviour and their relations with others. (There will be more on this in Chapter 4.) To some extent this has always been a problem in some Western societies. To take the example of the UK and the issue we referred to earlier of responsibility, children are responsible in a criminological sense at the age of 10, sexually responsible in heterosexual and homosexual terms at 16 and 18, respectively, and responsible in a political sense at 18. These divergent dimensions of childhood are not new; if anything, with the reduction of the age of homosexual consent in the late 1990s from 21 to 18, the dimensions are less divergent.[5] Nevertheless, until the recent public questioning of childhood, we have assumed that there is a clear boundary between childhood and adulthood, what Archard (1993, p. 25) refers to as the boundary having a 'virtual status'. However, despite these contentions, broadly speaking, in Western cultures a mixture of legal, medical and political judgements have been made which suggest that childhood ends between the ages of 16 and 18. In Europe and North America we commonly tend to think that by around the age of 18 children are socially and morally responsible enough to vote, pay income tax and be sexually active.

In other cultures, however, children may make the transition to adulthood once they are physically able to work or judged to be capable of bearing arms. In cultures where economic production involves all members of the community or where physical prowess determines membership to the armed forces, the age at which children make the transition to adulthood is likely to be different from that in Western societies. One contemporary example of this can be found within working-class Mexican families (Blasco 2005). The introduction of compulsory secondary schooling in Mexico in 1993 had the effect of bringing into sharp relief differing conceptions of childhood between developed and developing countries. In Western cultures childhood is characterised by social dependence and economic 'irresponsibility' at least up until the age of 16. Mexican children, on the other hand, spend their teenage years in domestic and paid employment. Blasco (2005) is careful to distinguish between middle- and working-class Mexican children. Nevertheless, the introduction of compulsory schooling compromised the productive role of working-class Mexican children, forcing them to stay at school and extending their childhoods well into their teenage years.

Conclusion

We need to distinguish between tying children's social experiences to their biological growth and viewing children's biological and cultural development as parallel and inter-related features of what it is to be a child. In the first case, there are far fewer opportunities for viewing children as competent and full members of society. Biology is fixed and as children are biologically inferior so are their social positions. In the latter case, biology and culture work in tandem to exclude children, with the former being drawn on as the grounds for children's social exclusion. In this chapter I have argued that this exclusion is based on a powerful set of ideas imposed on children by adults rather than any intrinsic weakness on the part of children. By emphasising meaning I examine the different ways that childhood is constructed. I illustrated the importance of social and cultural contexts to the meaning of childhood through our example of the 'playing child'. We are familiar with this image of childhood. It embodies other key features of childhood such as innocence and vulnerability. Moreover, these ideas seem to converge on biological causes. Our common sense tells us that children's smallness, their 'physiological immaturity', effortlessly underwrites our understanding of these key features of childhood. Through a range of analytical techniques, and from a variety of disciplinary vantage points, I have questioned the 'natural' and universal application of this model or construct.

The social-constructionist approach to childhood started off as a critique of what was termed the dominant framework, a set of social-scientific assumptions that conflated the biological and cultural bases of childhood (James and Prout 1997). Arguably now social constructionism has become the dominant paradigm, at least within sociology, and has in turn been subject to critical examination. In emphasising the cultural elements of childhood we are left asking whether there is any solid material basis to childhood. Radical social constructionism takes the meaning of childhood further, for it proposes that we rid childhood of any essence. Childhood is basically an elaborate and very powerful adult myth, a series of stories and accounts that locates children as subordinate figures in society. Within a social-constructionist framework childhood is irrevocably tied to what adults do and think. Whether we are talking about the 'abused child', the 'street child' or the 'child soldier', through discourse and practice adults produce children as social and cultural subjects. Accordingly, there is little sense in which we are able to see children and adults as occupying separate social or cultural positions. We cannot assume childhood; we can only bring it into being. In the following chapter I address a different and to some extent competing theoretical approach that assumes 'child' and 'adult' are equivalent conceptual categories inhabiting opposing social-structural spaces.

2

Childhood and Social Structure

Introduction

In the previous chapter I stressed the importance of the social meaning of childhood. I argued that childhood is a social conception or construction made up of cultural elements found within specific societies. Adults are the key agents here, in that childhood is fundamentally a product of the way adults think about and talk about children. In this chapter I view children and adults as embodied representatives of pre-existing and separate categories, 'child' and 'adult', respectively. Rather then arising out of a discourse on childhood, 'childhood' and 'adulthood' are constituent parts of the social structure. As Mayall (2000, p. 22) argues, childhood is 'an essential component of a social order where the general understanding is that childhood is a first and separate condition of the lifespan whose characteristics are different from later ones'.

I move away from a constructionist perspective in a second way. We have seen how constructionists analyse dominant and pervasive ways of thinking about children through the deconstruction of developmentalism as a dominant account of childhood. However, the emphasis on context and social diversity, has also drawn constructionists towards more localised meanings of childhood (James, Jenks and Prout 1998, p. 214). In turning to structuralist approaches we are examining adult/child relations within a broader framework. Children are located at a macrosocietal level. They make up a particular sector of the population. Thus children and, by implication, childhood are more likely to be located at national and global levels of analysis. A third and associated focus rests on comparative analyses. In a methodological sense, structuralism allows us to compare the conditions, positions and experiences of children within a range of different social, geographical and historical contexts. A fourth focus links a comparative approach more specifically to the structural positions of children and adults by highlighting the role of 'generation' as a key mode of analysis. The oppositional relationship between 'child' and 'adult ' becomes a key focus for comparison. In the first part of this chapter I address key aspects of child-hood and structure with these four points in mind.[1]

In the second part of the chapter the structural analysis will concentrate on the conflictual relationship between children and adults. In setting up a framework which positions children and adults in different categories, we inevitably think in terms of real or underlying tensions between children and adults. In Part One we allude to this when discussing the importance of generation as an analytical frame of reference. Children's structural posi-tion is an antagonistic one, whereby the interests of children collide with the interests of adults. In the second section of the chapter I deal with this, first of all, in our discussions of more familiar sociological approaches: feminism and Marxism. I tease out the possibilities of a sociology of child-hood based on the concepts of feminism and then apply a similar analysis drawing on the Marxist focal points of economic structure and exploitation. I contend that whilst Marxism and feminism emphasise structural conflict, they are both preoccupied with the interests of particular groups of adults rather than the specific positions of children. As a consequence, children's interests are marginalised, hidden within other cultural and economic structures. The concluding comments shift the focus back to the adult/child relationship where I address more directly the idea of children's interests.

Positioning Children and Childhood

The Permanence of Childhood

The European project undertaken in the late 1980s and early 1990s, *Childhood as a Social Phenomenon*, had as its focus the category of childhood as a perma-nent feature of social structures. In particular, it positions children and child-hood as fixed sociological categories in the light of the relativism of the social-constructionist approach discussed in the previous chapter. The assumption here is that children are an ever-present and universal feature of societies. Permanence here refers to the categorical status of 'child' in rela-tion to other sociological variables such as 'adult', 'social class' and 'gender'. Children may pass through childhood – in an embodied sense they are only children for a limited period of time – but this needs to be differentiated from the structural category of 'child' that will always be occupied by differ-ent children at any one time. Permanence can be viewed in a second way, as a corrective to the child's lack of ontology. What I mean here is that ground-ing 'child' as a social structural category is a way of establishing children's social position and status. One of the key themes to emerge out of recent work within the sociology of childhood is that children are normally taken to be going through childhood as a transitional phase, which effectively excludes them from a status or position within society. This cannot be justified simply in terms of age differences. As Qvortrup (1994, p. 4) argues, citing Turner, there are no 'facts about being' that differentiate children from adults and effectively exclude children from being recognised as social. Children's personhood is at best ambiguous in that they inhabit a temporary social space as social apprentices or adults-in-the-making. Children's very being is provisional in that they are expected to acquire a range of appropriate skills and abilities as they develop towards adulthood. To position children within the social structure is thus to challenge their marginal and provisional social status.

Bringing Children into View

The structural approach brings conceptual solidity to the study of childhood in a second way, which dovetails with the permanence/transitional dichotomy. By locating children within the social structure we are, quite simply, bringing children into view. Oldman (1994) refers to children as an 'invisible' social group, an ever-present but unseen social minority. Structuralism explores the possibilities for seeing children as an established if subordinate group within society; children are a *visible* social category. Conventional theories fail to locate children within economic and political arrangements. In most instances children are hidden within larger groups and categories, such as households, families and schools. Children are difficult to apprehend as a separate category or group, first of all because they are not ordinarily counted in this way (Scott 2000). To take one example, *Social Trends,* a UK government statistical source widely used by social scientists, refers to 'adults with one to two dependent children' and 'adults with three or more dependent children' when differentiating household types across the UK. Statistics have tended to subsume children within families and households as 'dependants'. Children thus become subsumed within these broader categories where the key reference point is the adult with or without 'dependants'. The child is thus hidden away as one among several dependants. In a literal sense, children do not count.

One of the key aims of the Childhood as Social Phenomenon project is to bring children into view by establishing children as categories in their own right rather than marginal adjuncts to other individuals and groups within the broader society. Qvortrup (1997) offers us a simple example. He argues that we tend to read information about children's lives from statistics, which often concentrate on 'family' as the unit of analysis. So in Denmark, for example, there was an increase in the numbers of families with one child from 43 per cent in 1974 to 49 per cent in 1985. This is often taken to mean that almost half of all Danish children have no siblings. If we take the child as the unit of analysis, then this statistic is inaccurate, seriously underestimating the numbers of children with siblings. Counting all children rather than all families with dependent children gives us a quite different picture of family life in Denmark The equivalent figures for the same period are 24 per cent and 30 per cent, respectively, meaning that well over two-thirds of Danish children in the mid-1980s had at least one sibling.[2]

We might use this information as part of an analysis of problems children have in making the transition from dependence on parents within the family to a more independent status in the wider society. Corsaro (1997), for example, argues that singledom among children gives us cause for concern in that children without the support of older siblings find it more difficult to negotiate the process of growing up. The family-based statistics on single children, such as those in our example, might be used to support this analysis. Whilst the birth rate has decreased quite significantly in North America and Europe throughout the twentieth century, and assuming that the Danish statistics reflect broader international patterns, the trend can easily be overstated if we do not take account of the numbers of children affected. Statistically, then, if we draw on 'child' as the unit of analysis then we can start to build up a quite different picture of children's lives and relations. Taking account of children in the statistical sense can give us a different perspective on a range of social indicators.

Generational Differences

In asserting the child/adult dichotomy we are assuming that these categories are sufficiently distinct in terms of criteria, what I discussed in the previous chapter as 'dimensions' (Archard 1993). Here we bring children into view by establishing 'child' as a structural category. Qvortrup (2000) refers to three dimensions of difference, three sets of criteria that separate 'dependent' children from 'independent' adults: political, cultural and economic. By locating them along these three dimensions of difference or stratification, we are incorporating children within the social structure.

Political Realm

Children have a different relationship to the political and legal systems with respect to notions of inclusion and degrees of regulation. Adulthood is partly dependent on individuals enjoying full access to legal redress and political rights. Children have limited access and rights here. Children are also subject to more legal controls. There is little logic to the age-graded legal controls on what children can and cannot do. For example, the two-year difference in the UK between the age of heterosexual consent (16) and the age of majority (18) is difficult to justify in developmental terms. Nevertheless, children are regulated in terms of their age in ways that adults are not.

Regulation takes a second form for children through mass compulsory schooling. In a global sense this has become a benchmark for measuring children's social inclusion, with international agencies such as UNESCO aiming to introduce mass compulsory primary schooling to all children.[3] The adult equivalent to schooling, paid employment in most countries, has a voluntary character. Liberal democracies have tightened up the extent to which the unemployed are able to claim an income from the state. However, adults can still choose not to work. It does not make any sense to think in terms of 'mass compulsory employment'. In an important sense, adults have more freedom than children in terms of how they spend their time.

Cultural Realm

Here we are dealing with informal rules or norms that distinguish children from adults. Social dependence is one powerful cultural means of differentiating the former from the latter. In all sorts of ways children are expected to behave according to codes and frames laid down by adults, usually parents or teachers. As I shall argue in future chapters, adults are expected to take responsibility for children's behaviour. These expectations are both formally and informally defined, both extending and limiting what adults can and cannot do with children. Norms relating to behaviour position adults and children differently within the social structure and are grounded in children's imputed dependence, a need to be cared for and controlled. Adults, on the other hand, because of their imputed independence, rationality and competence are positioned as the carers and controllers.

Cultural differences between children and adults can take other subtler forms. We might refer to the way that children's use of space and time are restricted by adults through curfews, homework regimes and chaperonage (Wyness 1994). We can also think in terms of very routine aspects of adult child/relations such as touching, caressing or cuddling. Hood-Williams (1990) talks about adults having authority over children through the exercise of corporal power, the physical access that adults have to children that is taken for granted and largely non-reciprocal. Epstein (1993, p. 321), citing Stevie Jackson's work on childhood and sexuality, nicely brings out the different cultural positions in relation to corporal power:

> Childhood is not just a psychological state, but also a social status – and a very lowly one at that. Take one example: the frequency with which children are touched by adults. The amount of unsolicited physical contact people receive is

a good indication of relative social positions. It has been observed that bosses touch workers, men touch women and adults touch children much more than the other way round. To touch one's social superior without good reason is an act of subordination. Think how frequently children are shaken off when they use touch to attract an adult's attention, and how that same adult can freely take hold of the child, adjust his or her hair, cut short his or her activities.

Economic Realm

I will say more about the economic aspects of childhood later in the chapter when I discuss Marxism. But bringing children into view in economic terms means addressing several concerns. For the moment I will concentrate on just one, poverty. Conventionally, categorising groups in poverty has meant drawing on variables such as income, education and degrees of financial dependence on the state. Analysts have addressed the economic conditions of groups such as lone parents, the unemployed, the elderly and low-income earners.[4] Until recently children have not figured in this analysis as a separate category. Children's 'invisibility' is reflected in the way that different categories of adults are assessed and compared in terms of their relative economic positions, with children, as I noted earlier, relegated to the status of 'dependants'. We know that the unemployed, for example, are likely to be poorer if they have dependent children than if they have no children (Wintersberger 1994). We are less likely to know how poor dependent children are in relation to their adult counterparts. We need to separate children from their households and parents and examine their economic positions.

A report commissioned by the National Centre for Children in Poverty (NCCP) in the United States views age among a number of other variables as significant in measuring poverty (Song and Lu 2002). The authors refer to several key trends. First there has been a substantial decrease in the proportion of children under the age of three ('young children') living in poverty since the early 1980s, from 27 per cent of the population in 1980 to 18 per cent in 2000. Secondly, despite this trend, young children are still the most vulnerable group in terms of age.

As we can see from Table 2.1, a comparison is made across several age ranges, with both categories of children likely to be poorer than their adult counterparts. Other variables are brought into the analysis, such as family structure, ethnicity and employment status. Whilst being black or Hispanic and having one instead of two parents increases a young child's chances of being in poverty, the employment status of either parent is less significant, with 75 per cent of children under the age of 3 in poverty with at least one parent in employment.

For our purposes, two points are significant: we have an example of children being counted in their own terms rather than being subsumed within

Table 2.1

Age as a variable in measuring poverty

Age cohort of population	Poverty rate in 2000 (%)
Younger children (0–2)	18
'Older children' (3–17)	15
Adults (18–64)	9
The elderly (65+)	10

Source: Song and Lu (2002).

statistics on households. The category of 'child' is disaggregated from 'household' to demonstrate the importance of age as a variable. Secondly, the evidence here suggests that children are in a much poorer and more economically vulnerable position than older-generational cohorts.

To sum up the child/adult comparison: the three structural dimensions are clearly interrelated, confirming children's subordinate social positions. Children's economic position vis-à-vis adults is reinforced owing to their invisible political and social status. Children as a social group have little access to the state in making claims on any distribution of resources (Qvortrup 2000, p. 91) At the same time, the various formal and informal rules restrict children's access to the political realm. Finally, children's dependent status and subsumption within families and households makes it difficult to view children as an especially disadvantaged minority group.

Generationing

Leena Alanen (2001b) has been developing Qvortrup's work by more explicitly referring to generation as an independent variable, as well as trying to incorporating a 'microlevel' analysis with an emphasis on structure. Along with Berry Mayall (2002), Alanen has been promoting childhood in more foundational terms by positioning 'generation' alongside social class, race and gender as an explanatory social category. There has been a tendency to use generation in more descriptive terms to denote a category of actors with similar nameable social characteristics. Interestingly, whilst generation has been used to describe the social position of cohorts of people of a certain historical age, beyond talking about the 'younger generation' it is rarely referred to in any analytic way to denote the common situation of children. In part this is because children have no agency. They therefore cannot be considered to be fully formed members of a social group, with their own independent social generational characteristics. Children are at best referred to as the 'next generation', which merely reinforces their status as future social actors and agents.

The importance of the notion of generationing is that it presupposes a relational approach and, by implication, a power dimension between two sets of actors. Thus just as capital and labour presuppose each other within Marxist theory, so 'child' and 'adult' are inextricably linked within an analysis that focuses on generational relations (Alanen 2001b). Moreover, a generational analysis according to Alanen (2001b) goes beyond simply positing the two generational dimensions as pre-existing social categories. A relational focus addresses the processes through which people are positioned as both children and adults; it examines the different ways in which children are denied and subsequently contest any agency. For Mayall (2002), these relations take place at a number of levels: (a) individually between children and adults; (b) between groups associated with the different generations such as parents and their offspring – parents and children as members of different social groups, (c) in relation to broader social norms governing ideas such as parental responsibility, and (d) in terms of policies usually imposed on the child population by the adult population. Thus there is a more complex interplay between all four levels producing the categories of childhood and adulthood partly as a product of individual experience and partly as a result of social forces imposed on adults and children.

Comparing Childhoods

So far I have been trying to establish a separate social status for children by drawing a conceptual boundary between the categories of 'child' and 'adult'. This has necessitated our first comparison between 'child' and adult' categories. The structural approach assumes a degree of methodological equivalence when researching childhood (Qvortrup 2000). To establish the permanence of children and childhood is to assume that we can capture the variability of childhood cross-culturally, nationally and historically. As we saw in the previous chapter, the logic of social constructionism makes empirical comparisons more difficult, for we cannot be sure that we mean the same thing when we talk about childhood in different contexts. If we take the historical constructionist line we cannot even be sure that there is anything to compare. As Ariès (1961) has taught us, in historical terms childhood does not necessarily have to exist. In effect, structuralism means that there is something worth comparing, that its structural form in terms of, say, children's social dependence allows us to make comparisons between different groups of children over and across time. Two examples will suffice here.

As we have seen, statistical evidence places children in the most vulnerable economic categories. This kind of evidence also allows us to compare the relative economic positions of children across a range of geographical areas. A recent comparative study of Children at Risk in Central and Eastern European Countries commissioned by UNICEF (1997) confirms that 'age' is a significant variable in making sense of poverty. Figure 2.1 demonstrates this.

What it also does is to provide data across a broad geographical area; it helps us to identify areas where there is the greatest discrepancy in conditions between children and adults. During the post-Soviet period from around the early 1990s, in five of the six European countries a worsening economic situation in each of these countries has had disproportionate effects on children. The report refers to the fact that children are at greater risk than other groups in several of these countries, with the child poverty rate one and a half times greater than the poverty rate in general (UNICEF 1997). More specifically, we can see that Bulgarian children are more

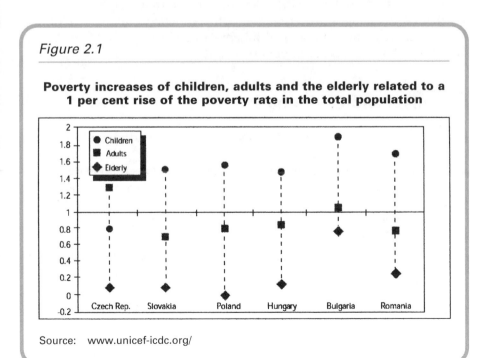

Figure 2.1

Poverty increases of children, adults and the elderly related to a 1 per cent rise of the poverty rate in the total population

Source: www.unicef-icdc.org/

vulnerable than their counterparts in other European countries, with the Czech Republic being the only country where children are less vulnerable than the population in general. The report provides more detail: among other things it suggests that the difference between Czech and Bulgarian children is linked to the higher rates of 'diseases of poverty', such as tuberculosis in the latter case and the much more significant drop in infant mortality rates in relation to the former.

A second comparison deals more with changes in child/adult relations over time. Qvortrup (2000) draws on a comparison of 'East German' childhood in the pre- and post-unification era. Interviews were conducted with a sample of 10–14-year-old children in East Berlin in 1990 and 1994, during the transitional period of unification. Children in the earlier period had a much weaker sense of privacy, with more co-operative relations between family, school and local government. Children during this period were more likely to be exposed to public events and demonstrations. Childhood we might say during this period was less privatised. In the later post-transitional period, children accounted for more individualised experiences, with the social bonds between home, school and local state much weaker. Parents had a more proprietorial relationship with their children and the home was a much more enclosed space. What Qvortrup is demonstrating here is that adult/child relations were altering as a consequence of broader macropolitical and social forces. Referring back to Archard (1993), we might say that macrochanges have generated different conceptions of childhood. German children and adults still inhabit different conceptual spaces but they now inhabit them in different ways.

Feminism and Childhood

Feminism has been crucial to the development of childhood studies. The recent historical and cultural context is one of small groups of women actively bringing to public attention a range of problems that many women face, particularly within families. In the early 1970s the women's movement forced problems such as wife-battering and the emotional abuse of women by their partners on to the political agenda in the UK and the USA. They also eventually forced a variety of state institutions such as the police and the courts to re-evaluate their policies and practices in relation to the treatment of women. It was also through the active resistance of many women to their treatment in these public and private institutions that children's positions were re-evaluated. Women drew attention to a darker side of family life and, in the process, broadened the concept of domestic violence to incorporate the abuse of children as well as women within the home.

In an academic and theoretical sense there has been a similar broadening of focus, with children and women being located together and latterly separately within the social structure. A feminist examination of the social structure in terms of the concept of patriarchy has illuminated the macroprocesses that position women as a subordinate social category. Men dominate in all spheres of social life and either directly or indirectly create the conditions within which women are seen as inferior, less valuable members of society. More recent versions of this have concentrated on a male or a masculine hegemony whereby women are positioned in relation to dominant sets of ideas (Connell 1987). Some feminists have added an 'age' dimension to the domination of women. Hood-Williams (1990) has added a complication to this schema by distinguishing between marital patriarchy, the rule of the husband over the wife, and age patriarchy, the dominance of parents over children. Thus we have two axes of power and authority commonly found within the nuclear family that interact and strengthen the position of the adult male breadwinner. Children, like women, are a subordinate group within the social structure, with the nuclear family the clearest expression of patriarchal relations.

In the past, feminism has sometimes treated children as adjuncts of women, often viewed as a burden or obstacle to the realisation of women's interests (Mayall 2002). There has also been a tendency to ignore the interests of children within the family, with women's status and rights being the sole focus (Delphy 1984). Thorne, in her classic essay 'Re-visioning children' (1987), argues that feminists have been concerned to do two things: to render women visible in historical and cultural terms as social agents and to theorise the effects of motherhood on women's lives. Given the relational nature of concepts such as patriarchy and motherhood, very little work has been done on the material and ideological effects of these ideas on children. Nonetheless, more recent feminist approaches have positioned children *alongside* women; parallel lines are drawn between the position of women and the position of children in historical, political and cultural terms. The paper by Oakley in Berry Mayall's (1994) edited collection, *Children's Childhoods Observed and Experienced*, is useful here. I will go on in Chapter 4 to outline the extent to which childhood can be seen as a social problem in the UK in the early twenty-first century. What is significant for our purposes here is the historical parallel being drawn by Oakley between the contemporary problem of childhood and the 'woman problem' of the late nineteenth and early twentieth centuries. In the latter case there was a discourse around a range of deviant cases of women from the unmarried through to the sexually active that, brought together, constituted women in general as a problem social category. Similarly, a range of contemporary 'deviant' categories of childhood from the truant through to the abused child taken together suggest that the institution of childhood is under threat. Another manifestation of this historical parallel is the way that women in the past were felt not to be capable of acting in their own best interests and were dependent on men to take key decisions on various aspects of their public and private lives. Throughout the twentieth century 'best interests' was a familiar refrain when judgements were made about children by adults. According to Oakley (1994, p. 16), it has become a 'philosophy of exclusion and control dressed up as protection, and dependent on the notion that those who are protected must be so because they are deemed incapable of looking after themselves'. Thus children, like women in the past, are viewed as being incompetent, with 'responsible others' making decisions for them.

A second parallel runs along economic lines. Feminists in the 1980s were active in challenging the gender-blind nature of much class analysis (Hartmann, 1980). Research into poverty and inequality tended to take for granted the male head of household as the primary income provider, neglecting the paid work that many women did and their economic roles. Moreover, the recent increase in the numbers of lone parents in British and American societies has forced academics and policy-makers to take more notice of the economic position of women. Feminists identified what they call the 'feminisation of poverty' (Pascall 1997): women more than men tend to find themselves in poverty owing to a series of structural economic and political factors. The disaggregation of women from men here is starting to be paralleled by a growing awareness that children are more likely than adults to be in poverty. As I set out earlier in the chapter, children's lack of social value as people, their structural invisibility, not only makes them more vulnerable to economic exploitation, it also makes it much more difficult to identify this exploitation.

Feminists have also been instrumental in redefining the concept of work. The informal 'labour' that takes place within the home is mainly the responsibility of women. Marxist feminists have drawn attention to the economic value of domestic work, bringing into the public realm the idea that capitalism is partly maintained through the invisible work of caring, cleaning and cooking carried out by women (Harris 1983). More recently, children have become more visible through research that identifies the domestic work carried out by children (Morrow 1996). There is little mileage in pushing the idea that children's domestic contributions are as economically crucial as women's domestic work. Nonetheless, the concept of domestic labour has allowed researchers to examine the competence of children within the home and thus challenge the stereotype of the dependent child.

In cultural terms a number of characteristics can be attributed to both children and women that position them as inferior and incompetent. Thus women and children are said to be less rational, less independent and less confident than men. Whilst these attributes have been seen as essential characteristics of being a woman and being a child (Gittins 1998), feminists point to the power of culture rather than nature, in particular the influence of a masculine hegemony that focuses on these essential features, in the process circumscribing alternative ways of viewing things. Women and children are also said to respond to male dominance here in similar ways (Oakley 1994): women sometimes react by displaying hostility and bitchiness towards other women; children implode in the playground through bullying. Women's and children's lack of full social status results in individualised attempts to regain control at the expense of other members of their minority group.

Oakley (1994) goes as far as to argue that these parallel historical and structural lines converge in terms of 'mutual dependence' and 'mutual oppression'. Yet there are two key limits to this convergence. First, there are problems in trying to locate children's oppression within a patriarchal system. Children's oppression, whether it takes the form of parental authority or domestic violence, rests on the ability of adults, including women, to legitimate and normalise their relationship with children. Feminism has directed us towards structures that limit the movement and opportunities for subordinate groups within the family. Yet we are still left with questions about the power that women have over children and the extent to which the theory and research underpinning the category of domestic violence can make sense of the abuse of children by women. Hood-Williams (1990, p. 166), in his analysis of patriarchal relations, refers to the 'contradictory location of wives in family patriarchy where wives have authority in age relations but are dependent in marital relations'. Ultimately, patriarchy is a system governed by gendered not age-related structures. Secondly, parallels have been made between the current political position of children and the status of women in the first half of the twentieth century in Western societies. Nevertheless, there are limits to the extent to which children are able to make the same rights claims as women. Oakley refers to the political necessity of establishing an ontology through minority-group action. Again I will refer to this in more detail in future chapters. Here the parallel breaks down. Women throughout the 1970s and 1980s mobilised support for equal rights and equal treatment through the women's movement. Women established themselves as a disadvantaged minority group. Feminist thinkers provided the intellectual basis of this. Children, on the other hand, are not in the same position to establish themselves as a disadvantaged minority group in their own terms. There have been a few exceptions, but the general trend has been for adults to be at the forefront of movements and organisations that seek to alter the position of children. (See, for example, Franklin and Franklin 1996). As I will go on to argue in Chapter 10, children have few rights to self-determination and are still reliant on adults to advocate changes to this state of affairs.

Clearly there are significant differences between the positions of women and children in cultural and political terms. Yet it is evident that theorists of childhood have been able to advance the categorical status of children by both inheriting and adapting key conceptual characteristics of feminism. The 'standpoint' approach is one final example of this. The idea of a standpoint is an attempt to create a dual methodological approach for feminists. The first approach is to be able to analyse the social world from a female vantage point and thus reclaim conceptual territory from what has been seen as a predominantly 'malestream' frame of reference (Alanen 1998). The second vantage point comes more from within or below. A feminist standpoint allows the researcher to identify the complex and lived experiences from their own perspectives. There is an attempt here to integrate macro- and micro-approaches: as Alanen proposes, a standpoint for 'looking down' and a standpoint for 'looking up'. With respect to children and childhood, Alanen's work has been crucial. She makes the assumption that childhood is an inherently structural category. Following the position of Qvortrup in 'looking down', children are an integrated feature of social and cultural systems. In 'looking up', 'a new sociology of childhood would begin from the actual everyday locations and activities of its subjects, and from there turn 'upwards' to account for social relations that over-determine childhoods as they come into view' (1998, p. 33). There is here recognition of children as socially productive actors in the same way that feminism grounded the idea that women are not simply passive recipients of patriarchal forces.

Marxism and Childhood

Feminism identifies home and family as realms of exploitation and subordination. It thus goes some way towards positioning children and childhood in social structural terms. In turning to Marxism we have to move much further in reconciling concepts of economic exploitation with the ordinary lives of children. Despite the fact that working children are a majority sector of the child population in global terms, Marx and Marxists have never recognised children as members of the proletariat. Children as economically productive units effectively disappeared by the time of the development of modern industrial capitalism. Nonetheless, in the nineteenth century Marx and Engels documented the role children played in the early part of industrialisation in two ways (Engels 1958). First, they wrote about children's exploitation in the English factory system, with children as young as seven working in the worst conditions for up to ten hours per day. Secondly, they viewed child labourers as part of the lumpen proletariat, an intermittent and cheap source of labour periodically drawn on by the bourgeoisie as a means of diluting the political power of the proletariat. More recently, Marxists have located children and childhood in relation to three themes: children as protomembers of economic classes, child labour and global capitalism, and children and child workers.

Children as Protomembers of Economic Classes

Children, as we saw in Chapter 1, no longer inhabit the public realm of paid employment. In Marxist terms they became protomembers of economic classes, part of a process through which the economic classes reproduce themselves. Much of the Marxist work on children's social relationships has taken for granted their provisional social status. If we take the work of Bowles and Gintis (1976), their critique of schooling revolves around the different ways that children come to grips with the ideological and material elements of capitalism. Children are positioned within the school primarily as future members of the class system. Reference is made to the correspondence principle that links the conditions of the proletariat and the relations within the workplace to the school experiences of the majority of children in capitalist societies. Thus, rather than talking about subordinate relations between adults and children, the introduction of social class and the economic relationship between the school and the broader society differentiates the positions of children in school. Children from different class backgrounds have different degrees of control and autonomy in school, which reflects the class positions of their parents in the workplace.

The lack of worker control corresponds to working-class children's lack of control over the curriculum and timetable, and the fragmenting of workers as a consequence of technological innovation corresponds to the individualised treatment of children who compete for the scarce rewards of success in education. Finally, the workers' reliance on extrinsic rewards rather than job satisfaction mirrors the way that children are oriented towards seeing education as a means to an end rather than an end in itself. Thus children's economic backgrounds – their families of origin – determine their experiences as children and future members of the workforce, rather than their status as children per se.

While Bowles and Gintis concentrate on the way that the 'hidden curriculum' prepares children for their future class positions, others have looked at the formal curriculum and the ways that knowledge in school is organised and distributed. Richard Hatcher (2000) argues that the school curriculum has to be viewed as a social relationship in terms of the way that individual pupils engage with the learning process. Those from poorer backgrounds are likely to have an instrumental and task-oriented view of their school work. Middle-class pupils, on the other hand, are more fully integrated into the knowledge world, are more prepared to interpret knowledge and see it as an end in itself. There is a form of correspondence here as working-class children are alienated from curricular objectives and, by implication, unable to follow a specialised and high-status career path. Middle-class children, on the other hand, are more likely to negotiate the transition to adulthood through the university sector because of the way that the school has tuned them into a dominant knowledge culture.

If we follow through the logic of Marx and Marxism, the working class are in an irrevocably contradictory situation with respect to capital. This contradiction becomes more apparent as the working class realise their interests. Dominant and dominated classes cancel each other out, leading to a classless society. Interestingly it is a non-Marxist, Ivan Illich (1971), who comes closest to running a parallel argument on childhood. Put briefly, he argues that childhood primarily through mass compulsory schooling is the means by which children are alienated from their 'natural' social environment:

> If there were no age-specific and obligatory learning institution, 'childhood' would go out of production. The youth of rich nations would be liberated from its destructiveness, and poor nations would cease attempting to rival the childishness of the rich. If society were to outgrow its age of childhood, it would have to become livable for the young. The present disjunction between adult society, which pretends to be humane and a school environment, which mocks reality could no longer be maintained. (1971, pp. 34–5)

Illich takes a libertarian stance here, with industrialisation rather than capitalism the source of the problem. Nevertheless it is a rather crude class analysis, with Illich drawing distinctions between three groups of children, only one of which exhibits the hallmarks of 'childhood'. Children in middle-class, industrialised cities can be said to embody childhood because their lives revolve around adult-regulated notions of compulsory schooling, development and what was referred to earlier as 'becoming'. Children of the 'New York slums', on the other hand, aspire to having a childhood but, because of their poverty, are denied the material and cultural resources to bring them in line with the dominant mores of childhood. A third group of children inhabit a different geographical and cultural space. Children from the developing world are, according to Illich (1971, p. 34), outside of the 'childhood' frame of reference and do not want childhood or are insufficiently aware of what childhood means. For Illich the third group, despite powerful Western attempts to export 'childhood', comes closest to a 'state of nature'. Children here live through a more authentic set of child experiences.

Child Labour and Global Capitalism

Global perspectives on childhood have led to much broader understandings of children's roles and identities. From a Western perspective, children's activities remain outside of the economic realm. As we saw in the previous chapter, a work/play division is deployed to accentuate differences between the activities of adults and children. The former have economic responsibilities, the latter have an 'obligation to be happy' through play. From a Western perspective, then, when addressing children's work outside we are usually referring to exceptional or deviant circumstances within which children are forced to take on adult-type responsibilities (see, for example, the discussion of child carers in Chapter 4). One way round this exceptionalism is to concentrate on the forced and exploitative nature of children's 'work' by distinguishing between 'work' and labour'. The latter is exploitative, inviting moral condemnation and typifying the economic positions of children in developing countries; child 'work', on the other hand, refers to the normal developmental processes such as socialisation and schooling attributed to Western children. Yet, there are difficulties with this distinction. It tends to underplay the differences between children's economic activities within both developing and developed countries (James, Jenks and Prout 1998, p. 110). The work of Hobbs, Lavalette and McKechnie (1992), for example, uncovers the extent to which child labour exists in the UK. Children's labour or work is heavily regulated in Western societies, but Lavalette (1996, p. 177) makes the pertinent point that, irrespective of legal and cultural factors shaping the nature of this work, the paid work done by children is always 'poor work', work unlikely to be undertaken by adults.

Lavalette (1996) starts from the premise that children, like adults, in both developing and developed countries sell their labour power. Recent developments in global capitalism have led to a perceived increase in child labour. The internationalisation of capital has brought Newly Industrialised Countries (NICs) into the global economic arena as developed countries look for sources of cheap labour and new markets. Within this broader context, industrialisation has had uneven effects on countries, with developing countries less able to insulate themselves against intermittent economic crises. Countries in Latin America, North Africa and Asia have weaker welfare structures. Any attempts to protect families from economic crises have been offset by deflationary policies imposed by global agencies such as the International Monetary Fund (IMF) and the World Bank. These supranational 'lending' agencies put more pressure on recipient countries through 'structural adjustment programmes', thus restricting their ability to implement social welfare initiatives (Stephens 1995). This has forced many families from the poorest countries into the unregulated sector where

child labour thrives. Lavalette uses the example of India. The carpet industry in India employs a significant proportion of children as it competes on
the global market. In the early 1990s the Indian economy was badly hit by
the world recession, forcing the Indian government to cut back quite dras-
tically on measures to deal with poverty. The net effect of this was to force
more families into drawing on their children as a source of labour, pushing
many of them into the carpet factories where wages and conditions were
poor. Children here are subject to the demands of global capitalism just like
their adult counterparts.

In turning to Western childhoods, the same arguments can be made with
reference to their exploitation. The conventional view on child labour in
advanced countries is that the paid work that children do is harmless and
trivial; it does not interfere with their schooling and supplements their
'pocket money'. A number of surveys of British schoolchildren have been
undertaken since the mid-1980s, which identify children's paid work as
exploitative, in many cases illegal and much more widespread than is
commonly thought (Hobbs, Lavalette and McKechnie 1992; Lavalette 1996;
Moorehead 1987).

From Lavalette's (1996) review of this research, between 35 and 50 per
cent of all secondary-school-aged children are involved in paid work. While
most of the pupils were involved in delivery work, a minority were working in shops and restaurants or looking after younger children. Lavalette
(1996) refers to a number of complex rules governing working children in
the UK. However, employers break many of these rules with impunity.
Children as young as 10 are working, despite the age restriction being 13.
Children often start and finish work before and after the legally laid-down
times of 7 a.m. and 7 p.m., respectively. Children also get paid far less than
their adult counterparts for sometimes heavy and dangerous tasks in all
weather conditions. On the surface, children working in factories in
Pakistan sewing footballs have little in common with teenage boys deliver-
ing newspapers in English towns and cities. A Marxist analysis links the
two together in the way that their work is poorly paid, often dangerous and
rarely recognised as labour.

Children and Child Workers

In connecting economic exploitation with childhood, I have discussed the
dominant image of corporate capitalism exploiting child workers in developing countries. Outside a Western context there is clearly some mileage in
positioning children as economically productive actors in the same way
that we might view their mothers and fathers. Oldman (1994), in an intrigu-
ing article, takes Marxism and childhood in a different direction. Oldman

concentrates more on how economic structures position children and adults differently in terms of what he calls 'child work'. Child work is significant here for it differentiates children from adults rather than the more conventional Marxist approach illustrated by Bowles and Gintis of differentiating from within the child population according to economic factors. Oldman's argument is that family in recent years has become a less significant frame of reference for children because of the increase in the amount of 'child work' done by adults outside of the family. A Marxist analysis of adult/child relations is possible here because of the widening range of activities undertaken by adults for children outside of the family, what he refers to as a process of 'defamilialisation'. Child work thus refers to the kinds of commodified activities carried out by professionals, including non-family forms of care and a plethora of leisure and educational activities open to children, provided by non-family members.

Defamilialisation links fairly disparate trends in terms of the professional and economic interests of adults. To take two examples: the development of the American paediatric profession in the 1950s was partly a response to a perceived increase in the incidence of child abuse, resulting in a more intensive network of state surveillance of families. While in the UK in the 1990s, the increase of working mothers has led to a boom in childminders and a demand for more state regulation of commercial child care. The development of child professions in these different contexts is commonly articulated in terms of the support and enrichment of children's lives. The 'best interests of the child' is by now a familiar refrain in Western professional circles as social workers, judges and teachers legitimate their practices with respect to what they think children need. Oldman's analysis takes us in the opposite direction in that the expansion of modern professional child work furthers the interests of adults at the expense of children. Oldman stresses that the whole process of 'growing up', which presupposes a degree of child 'action', has to be viewed in terms of the material advantages this accrues to adults. Education thus bears little resemblance to the interests of children in that expenditure on schooling is taken up with 'making manageable working conditions for teachers [rather than providing] the optimal conditions for the self-capitalisation of each child' (1994, p. 160). If we refer to child care, the complex network of child protection agencies has only an incidental relationship to children's needs.

Children's Needs and Interests

I have tried to demonstrate the significance of feminism and Marxism to childhood studies in terms of antagonistic social relations. However, with the exception of Oldman's 'economic' analysis of adult/child relations, these approaches draw on different categories in trying to explain the bases of adult/child relations. Childhood is ultimately either a product of patriarchy or capitalism, or possibly a combination of the two. Moreover, if we think of these categories in political terms, we inevitably come to think of the interests of either women or the working class, with children's voices subsumed. In the first part of the chapter I explored the significance of age/generation as a dimension of stratification. Here I want to briefly return to this idea by examining the possibility of children having collective interests as children, rather than simply projecting their structural positions into the future as either class-based or gendered adults.

In many ways, when discussing children's and young people's position within the social structure we are confronted with two sets of ideas, which take children in quite different directions: children's 'needs' and children's 'interests' (Qvortrup 1994). To do this I will borrow a key concept of social constructionism, discourse. The needs discourse dominates our thinking about how to relate to children and young people. It assumes that childhood is a deficit model of personhood and that children's needs have to be met by adults in order for them to attain personhood. There are three versions of this. First, there are comparisons being made within the child population between children 'in need' and those assumed to be enjoying a normal childhood. Thus there are children suffering from abuse, from labour, from poverty and from a range of learning difficulties in school. As I shall go on and argue in future chapters, money, time and energy are currently being invested at national and global levels to bring children 'in need' in quite disparate settings up to a 'normal' standard (Woodhead 1997).

A second and associated 'needs' model is drawn from the work of the Bernard van Leer Foundation, a Dutch-based non-governmental organisation that promotes opportunities for socially and economically disadvantaged young children (Bernard van Leer Foundation 2001). The foundation takes the view that children are entitled to full human rights as set out in the United Nations Convention on the Rights of the Child. I will discuss this in more detail in the final chapter. The foundation's rights agenda is counterposed with a needs discourse. They characterise the needs discourse in terms of several criteria. First of all, children in developing countries are viewed as passive recipients of Western state and charitable donors. Secondly, children's needs are ranked according to the political interests of these donor countries and organisations, with some groups of children being more in need than others. Thirdly, there is little legal compulsion on the part of states to meet the needs of children: political will and charitable benevolence dictate the quantity and quality of support.

A third deficit model of childhood is more pervasive, arguably a central component of Western societies. Here the comparison is not between different types of children, but between the child and the ontologically established adult. As I argued earlier, during the period of childhood children's needs are progressively met by adults until they become fully constituted members of the social world. It is this third model of childhood that I have been concerned with in this chapter. For, as I have stated, children's lack of personhood excludes them from certain common economic and political goods. The needs discourse positions adults as mediators between children and the rest of society. In political terms 'children's needs' becomes a discursive means through which various adult groups struggle for resources and professional expansion (see Parton 1985, 1996 for accounts of this). Political actors within this arena trade on the features of childhood discussed in the previous chapter, such as incompetence and innocence, in staking a claim to meet children's needs more effectively. Children's sense of self, their commitments and expectations are regulated by adults. It is therefore difficult to think of children having an independent status.

In turning to the alternative discourse on children's interests, I am referring to a much less well-established set of ideas which assume that children have a degree of agency. The idea of interests takes children as the primary reference point. Children mediate themselves in that there are channels through which children can make claims, hold others accountable and, more mundanely, express an opinion. I refer again to 'best interests'. The idea of adults acting in children's 'best interests' becomes difficult to reconcile with children having a voice or any means of expressing their interests. Here I want to locate notions of 'self-mediation' and children's interests in terms of children having a degree of separateness from 'non-child' groups in society and the construction of channels through which this separateness can be articulated. Unlike a politics based around children's 'needs' where children are ironically absent, 'interests' suggests that children are viewed as active and involved, a group or body in a position to make claims on the state at various levels. The idea of children's 'interests' is thus fundamentally political, defining the aims of a specific minority group in society. In the earlier discussion of feminism, one of the problems with linking the position of women to the position of children was the inability of children to articulate their interests, move themselves on in such a way that children effectively challenge their inferior status. I can really only speculate here and suggest one approach to children's interests. But theoretically speaking, if we can imagine children as a minority group with their own commitments and interests, we are able to move beyond feminism and Marxism and think of children as a separate social group and category.

Conclusion

As I have argued, the categorical status of 'child' is relatively new and reflects the burgeoning field of childhood studies within sociology. Theoretically things have moved on since the early stages of an 'emerging paradigm' which proposed social constructionism as a challenge to old, some would say now outdated, models of childhood. James, Jenks and Prout (1998) refer to a fourfold theoretical challenge, social constructionism, the tribal-child approach, structuralism and the minority-child approach. All four presuppose that childhood is a quintessentially social phenomenon, and in varying degrees all are concerned to draw out the possibilities of seeing children as full and competent members of society. In this chapter our concern has been to outline the key features of structuralism, but I have also drawn on the minority child as 'an embodiment of the empirical and politicised version of the "social structural childhood" ' (James, Jenks and Prout 1998, p. 210). I have brought both the structural and minority child together because they both emphasise the categorical status of children vis-a-vis adults in social and sociological terms.

In sociological terms children have been brought into view. In the process they have acquired full social status, occupying subordinate positions within the social structure, as 'dependent beings' rather than 'dependent becomings' (Lee 2001). Childhood thus becomes a fixed rather than transient category. The attempts of Qvortrup and his colleagues (1994) to bring children into view in the macro sense is not just a theoretical exercise, it has real political and policy consequences. If we take the problem of poverty, the general concern has been to increase the opportunities for men and women to get back into the labour market. Various Western governments have done this by making it easier for parents to take up private and public child care. Bringing children into view would mean having to take account of the effects of this on children. Rather than simply counting the numbers of men and women off the unemployment registers, and assessing the quality of public child care available, we would have to try and measure the effects of child-care arrangements on the children themselves (Lee 2001, p. 50). Whilst we do not want to pursue this example here, we would need to ensure that we had methods for measuring the quality of child-care arrangements from the recipients' perspectives, predominantly for those children under the age of 6.

In the second half of the chapter I examined two dominant structural approaches that concentrate on the categories of 'gender' and 'class'. Whilst feminism and Marxism are well-established approaches, conceptualising childhood within these frameworks has proved difficult. Marxists tend to locate children within an economic structure as provisional members of social classes. There are thus similarities with less conflict-based approaches such as structural functionalism. Socialisation is not a key concept within Marxist thinking, but it is implicit in much of the theorising on social and cultural reproduction of capitalism. Children grow up into social classes through a range of formal and informal structures. Children become bearers or members of economic classes. Feminism, on the other hand, draws attention to the contexts within which women are positioned as subaltern members of society. In this sense we can draw parallels between the position of women and the position of children. However, as I have argued, patriarchy cannot fully explain the structural positions of children, especially where regulative strategies are often imposed on children by women.

Feminist and Marxist formulations of childhood rely too heavily on the pre-existing categories of social class and gender and thus fall into the trap of treating children as transitional beings. The notion of generation, on the other hand, acts as a corrective in identifying processes whereby children as children are established from the outset in contradistinction to adults. As Alanen puts it, 'everyday knowledge and the evidence accumulated in social scientific studies on childhood demonstrate that being a child (or an adult) does make a difference (or differences) in terms of one's activities, opportunities, experiences and identities' (2001a, p. 130).

However, whilst age/generation can be seen as part of a strategy for promoting age or generation as a sociological variable alongside class, gender and ethnicity, it sits uneasily next to any approach that affirms the diversity of childhoods. The question remains as to whether there are sufficient grounds for treating children as a social minority group. By affirming the category of childhood, significant aspects of children's lives – their gender, ethnicity and geographical location – become far less significant than their generational membership. As I shall discuss in the following chapter, childhood has grown up at a point in time where 'metanarratives' such as class and gender inequality have become far less potent frames of reference.

3

Children and Childhood in Late Modernity

Introduction

In the previous chapter we had difficulty locating children within Marxist and feminist theories. I tried to accommodate children's invisibility with reference to the categorical status of generation, an alternative means of explaining inequality that takes children and childhood as the starting point. Whilst we are not simply trying to replace one 'grand theory' with another – 'generationing' is hardly an established theoretical perspective – there is clearly an attempt to argue that the adult–child relationship takes precedence when trying to understand the social position of children. However, if we see generationing as an attempt to render the sociology of childhood as a mature and established sub-discipline within sociology, then arguably the categorical status of generation suffers from the same limitations as 'grand theories' as do Marxism and feminism; it cannot accommodate political, social and cultural changes that emphasise diversity, plurality and scientific uncertainty.

In this chapter I try to locate children and childhood within recent sociological theories that incorporate these three contemporary themes. The recent sociological emphasis on late or reflexive modernity challenges the universalising impetus within grand theories or 'meta-narratives' (Lyotard 1984). The search for truth and final causes, and the deployment of the social sciences to these ends, which characterised modern societies throughout most of the twentieth century, is replaced by a more internally sceptical or reflexive set of ideas and practices. In the first section I look at one dominant variant of late-modern thinking: the idea that modern societies have been individualised. Ulrich Beck's (1992) argument about the shift from collectivist to more individualised frames of reference opens up possibilities for repositioning children within the social structure. Whilst Beck himself has little to say about children as individuals, I examine the logic of his argument with reference to children as both individual social agents and members of a social minority group.

In the second section I go on to examine recent theorising of family life, which offers more possibilities for viewing children as individuals and social agents. Morgan's (1996) notion of 'doing' family rather than simply 'being in' a family provides us with the conceptual tools for viewing children as co-constructors of their social environments. Dominant political and social scientific discourses tend to view children as victims of changes that take place within families, particularly in relation to separation and divorce. Drawing on recent illustrative research, I assess the extent to which the widespread practice of divorce illustrates what we might mean by the child of late modernity. In the third section I draw on another powerful sociological framing device: globalisation. I look at this in a number of associated ways. In one sense a global dimension to social analysis brings us in line with Beck's processes of individualisation, in the marginalising of conventional sociological metanarratives. I assess the different ways in which children and young people draw on the global and the individual as framing devices in both constructing and managing their nascent social identities. I also examine the increasing power and influence of consumerism and the mass media as ways in which children and young people mediate these processes.

In the final section I examine the effects of late modernity and globalisation on children in terms both of reinforcing more long-standing social divisions and of generating new forms of social inequality and social exclusion. In this section I also go on and assess the paradoxical effects of individualisation: not only does it create forms of social exclusion, it also generates more awareness of these processes of exclusion, offering new ways of tackling these problems that converge with the commitments that young people have to social justice and fairness.

Childhood and Individualisation

There has been fierce debate about the extent to which we can characterise contemporary social life as a new historical phase called postmodernity or simply an extension of modernity (Moss and Petrie 2002, p. 26). But whether we are talking about a rupture with the past or a degree of continuity, there have clearly been important economic, political and social changes from the late twentieth century onwards that have altered the way we see ourselves and our ability to develop a social identity. Beck (1992) refers to the expansion of corporate capitalism across national boundaries in the second half of the twentieth century in the pursuit of profit and material growth and the concomitant rise in scientific knowledge. Capitalism makes more demands on state welfare systems to produce a more educated workforce. At the same time it produces a reaction or critique to this use of knowledge in the pursuit of profit, in particular a greater awareness of the environmental costs of economic growth. Whilst the pursuit of economic growth has largely alleviated the worst effects of material scarcity in Western societies, it has also generated powerful, but often invisible, risks to health and the quality of life. As a consequence, individuals within Western cultures have become both more knowledgeable and more critical about their social worlds. Beck refers to this process as reflexive modernisation: '[Modernization] is becoming its own theme. Questions of the development and employment of technologies (in the realms of nature, society and the personality) are being eclipsed by questions of the political and "economic" management of the risks of actually or potentially utilised technologies' (Beck 1992, p. 19).

For Beck as for Giddens (1991), this reflexivity reaches down into the consciousness of the individual, providing broader, more flexible contexts within which the self can be monitored and refashioned. This 'globalising' of our consciousness has important consequences for identity-formation. Conventional (modernist) social frames of reference are weakened, producing levels of social fragmentation and flux. Beck refers to the declining significance of a range of external collective influences: the nation/state, social class, gender, community and the nuclear family no longer provide unambiguous building blocks and life trajectories in the structuring of who we are. Individuals are thus relatively free to pursue a range of moral, professional and social careers.

The emphasis here is on notions of choice and opportunity. There may be elements of neoliberal thinking, in that the weakening of these relatively fixed collective reference points creates space for more individual projects. And there is a sense in which the absence of certainty can force people to take more personal responsibility for their mistakes. At the same time, individualisation does not imply a return to an idealised natural state where the rational individual is freed from the shackles of 'external' collective constraints. Prout (2000a), puts this point well: 'the phenomenon of "individualisation" is the product of new social processes rather than a recrudescence of an essential, autonomous individual who exists prior to social relations' (2000a, p. 307). These new social processes allow people to pursue new careers and form new social groupings.

Women in particular are affected by these processes. Beck refers to their 'liberation' from gendered structures and futures. Technological, demographic and economic changes have altered their status: child-rearing, work and lifestyle choices now dominate. Yet, this liberation is conditional;

women are now in a position to weigh up the risks with the opportunities. Consequently, women find it easier now to free themselves from an unhappy family situation. Yet separation and divorce for many spells a drop in income and an adjustment to child-rearing on their own. In these terms Beck applies reflexive modernisation to family relations: the conventional division of labour between spouses becomes more fluid as men and women try to reconcile the demands of child care with the need and desire to maintain a career. Thus one of the key axes of power within the conventional nuclear family modelled by an earlier generation of functionalist sociologists is rejected. However, the other axis of power, the generational boundary between parent and child, is held firm, if not strengthened, by the shift towards greater adult choice. Whereas women as well as men can choose to take on the mantle of 'economic man', there is no new conceptual space for children.

The calculation of risk for Beck starts at the macroglobal level as supra-national organisations and governments assess social and environmental effects. It works its way down as far as the generational boundaries of the nuclear family. Choice and, by implication, risk-assessment is envisioned for adults; children remain, in Beck's words, 'the last remaining irrevocable unexchangeable primary relationship' (1992, p. 118). Children become the projects of adults, to be shaped and moulded; children's dependence, obedience and their subaltern status become central to adults as they seek to recentre themselves within a context of moral and social flux. Thus theories of late modernity tend to follow classical and modern sociological thinking. Children are the projects and responsibilities of adult others, confirming what was argued in the previous chapter, that children are becomings rather than beings and therefore unworthy of comment in terms of meaningful social action. Despite the logic of individualisation that opens up space for individual action, contemporary sociological theory ignores the position of children. We might speculate that this is due to children's lack of social ontology, their assumed lack of rationality and social competence.

There is little understanding of children's positions within a new social order. By implication, late-modern constructions of childhood become a form of moral rescue, a means by which adults try and recapture a sense of purpose and belonging. Whilst there has always been a tendency for adults to romanticise childhood by harking back to their own halcyon childhood experiences, our understandings of childhood usually bore some resemblance to the contemporary lives of children. The search for certainty within postmodern thinking, and the centrality of childhood as a response to this search, creates a massive gap between 'children' and 'childhood'. 'Childhood' as an adult construction is now more remote from the flesh-and-blood actions of children. In many ways this is what commentators and theorists are saying when they identify the rise in childhood deviance. I will come back to this point when reviewing the 'crisis of childhood' in the following chapter.

In a more recent text, Beck (1998) refers cursorily to processes of 'self-socialisation' and negotiation within families in the period of reflexive modernisation. However, for satisfactory answers as to who children are in late-modern society, we need to turn to researchers who have worked extensively within the sociology of the childhood. Jenks (1996) more fully develops the gap between children and childhood through the idea of nostalgia: 'the child becomes a longing for times past . . . The trust that was previously anticipated from marriage, partnership, friendship, class solidarity and so on, is now invested more generally in the child' (1996, p. 19). Concessions are made to children in order to maintain this attachment to children. Thus children are granted rights, and much more time is invested by parents in finding the right carers in situations when they cannot look after their children themselves. More significantly, adults' feelings of insecurity are projected on to their children through the tightening-up of mechanisms for controlling them. Seabrook (1982), in his analysis of working-class childhood, refers to the exaggerated responses of parents to any hint that their children were at risk from abuse:

> I can remember many parents who felt very insecure and inadequate as parents, and who would whip themselves into a frenzy about imaginary assaults on their children. 'I'd swing for anybody who touched my kids'; 'If anybody laid a finger on any kid of mine I'd slit him from his crotch to his throat' were extreme versions of this reaction. The fear of children being molested in some way has such resonance because it is not only a real fear, but also a metaphor for parents' sense of their dwindling control. (Seabrook, 1982, pp. 13–14)

The public reactions after the James Bulger case was tried in Liverpool, England in 1993 (for more detail, see Chapters 4 and 5) were similar, with parents going to obsessive lengths to keep their young children safe in public places (Wyness 2000, p. 21). More routine, everyday actions, such as the marked increase in transporting of children to school, have been partially attributed to what Scott, Jackson and Backett-Milburn (1998) refer to as 'parental risk anxiety', the fear that children are no longer safe walking to school on their own.

Jenks (1996) contrasts this 'post-modern' childhood with an earlier modernist construct where the child was more a purposeful project through which adults invested in the future. Control was proactive rather than reactive: children were carefully regulated in terms of their futures as adults. Jenks refers to this as a more optimistic period within which children were carefully nurtured as future citizens and productive members of the workforce. The control of children within the later period, on the other hand, is seen as a means by which adults attempt to 'recentre' themselves.

While Jenks (1996) differentiates between early and later forms of childhood, others emphasise continuity between the past and present (Prout 2000a; Moss and Petrie 2002). Contemporary relations between adults and children can be viewed as reflecting elements of nostalgia, futurity and self-realisation. For Moss and Petrie (2002) the modernity project of control and regulation still dominates policy and professional practice with regard to children and childhood. Education is a good example here: children are increasingly caught within a complex network of demands placed on teachers and administrators to produce a quality product for future consumption. Policies on homework, curriculum guidance and child care within early-years education emphasise work done on children from an early age framed in terms of their 'needs'. As I set out in the previous chapter, children are invisible in the dual sense of being measured against a normal childhood and a future adulthood. Moreover, children become objects or projects in the sense that the work done on them by professionals is judged against the balance of inputs and outputs, what is referred to as a 'new technology of control' (Moss and Petrie 2002, p. 79). Here the *performances* of both child professionals and children are being measured. Thus adults need to be seen to be taking control and responsibility, erring on the side of keeping children close and restricting their access to 'risky' public and private spaces.

Prout (2000a) concentrates on the tension between control and self-realisation. Drawing on a public/private distinction, this tension plays itself out in a number of complex ways. Adults still dominate children's lives, with residual effects on children as agents. Thus, despite concerns for children's safety, development and welfare, there is some evidence that children are more assertive within the private sphere of family where there are some expectations among the young that parents now need to earn their children's respect. By implication, this gives children more space within the home to negotiate through an 'ethic of reciprocity' (Holland and Thomson cited in Prout 2000a, p. 308). Langford et al. (2001) reinforce the notion of more open and democratic relations between parents and children, at the same time noting more complex motives behind these trends. From their sample of children aged between 11 and 16 and their parents, they argue that both parents and children sought a more open and communicative atmosphere within the home. However, there were more complex reasons for this. While companionship was a shared goal, openness was often part of a broader power struggle, with parents using these more fluid channels of communication to gain control of their children's lives, and children simultaneously withdrawing information as a way of maintaining a degree of autonomy.

If we briefly turn to the public sphere, this space is still very limited. As we shall see in the final chapter, there is an interplay between control and self-realisation within the civic and political realms. But, as Prout makes clear, this is much more evident in the Nordic countries. The European origins of 'individualisation' are evident here in the way that an agenda for children's choices and voices is much more developed in countries such as Denmark and Norway, with children's 'interests' having far more legitimacy than in neoliberal countries such as the UK and USA.

Children and the Family in Late Modernity

In searching for approaches that take a more inclusive view of children and childhood, we might also turn to the recent work of theorists of family life. First of all, recent theorising of the family introduces us to the idea of family diversity. 'The family' (with its specific use of the definite article) is eschewed in favour of 'families' or 'family life', as sociologists try and grapple with a shifting moral and social landscape that incorporates a diversity of family types (Bernardes 1985). Whilst there is some ambiguity as to the status of the nuclear family, the decrease in marriage rates and the rise in divorce from the 1970s onwards and the increase in the numbers of children being brought up by one parent attest to a range of family arrangements now on offer. This suggests a possible diversity of positions that children might occupy within the domestic sphere.

Secondly, Morgan's (1996) distinction between 'being in' and 'doing' family life is useful in relation to debates about agency within family. He associates 'being' with a more passive notion of family life. Families are thus things that we inherit, drift into or conform to in terms of pregiven roles and responsibilities. 'Doing', on the other hand, implies a more active involvement in choosing, creating and changing the individual's family situation. We might adapt this distinction to the present and future family situations of children. Being in families is consonant with the conventional status of children as dependants, with their silent, invisible and subordinate membership. Doing family life challenges this by incorporating the different ways in which children are active within families, as recipients of care, as helpers and as individuals who negotiate family routines, what Morgan refers to as family 'practices'. Thus whilst convention would tend to take for granted a range of arrangements found within the family home, closer inspection is likely to reveal a repetoire of relations, situations and contexts that have been built up over time between a range of family members, including children.

Thirdly, David Cheal (2003), in his attempt at making sense of the range of family practices at a more global level, discusses two forms of diversity.

Cultural diversity refers to different family types based on cultural, national or ethnic differences. They can be found between and within different societies but are commonly differentiated into traditional or modern family forms. Situational diversity, on the other hand, refers to 'people with the same cultural ideals of family life [who] may live in different ways because practical circumstances affect the choices they make' (Cheal 2003, p. 27). Thus the trend towards more single-parent households is not, as some commentators contend, simply a consequence of the choices that young women make with respect to bringing up their children, but the outcome of marital break-up.

Similarly, a framework of cultural and situational diversity positions children differently. Situationally, children are likely to become more proactive when their circumstances change, for example where parents separate and decisions need to be made about residence and care arrangements. Thus, if we refer to the situation in England and Wales, the 1989 Children Act makes it easier for children to have some involvement in deliberations over custody. The cultural diversity of families connects directly with the cultural diversity of childhoods. As I argued in Chapter 1, the logic of social constuctionism, which is often taken as a concomitant of late-modern thinking (Moss and Petrie 2002), is the existence of a range of ways of thinking about children. If we take this with reflexive modernisation and our growing awareness of others beyond the limits of modernity, then we have the potential to think about children's lives in quite different cultural settings that cannot be simply measured against a white, middle-class ideal. Thus if we take cultural variation in the UK, for example, children are economically more productive in Chinese take-away food businesses (Song 1996). This is the result of a combination of factors such as the influence of Confucian principles in relation to filial loyalty, and the response of families to their ethnic migrant status. Children in indigenous white families, on the other hand, are probably less likely to contribute significantly to the household income.

Fourthly, I referred earlier to the ambiguous status of nuclear family. By this I mean that current living arrangements both depart from and are constructed out of the nuclear family. Statistical pictures of family life tend to focus on diversity across time: if we refer to a key statistical source in the UK, discussed in the previous chapter, *Social Trends*, we get snapshots of family membership that tell us little about the movements in and out of families over time. If we refer to the family life-cycle, there is a more complex moving in and out of the nuclear family form. Thus families made up of same-sex adults and lone-parent families, often taken as an indicator of social and moral breakdown, tend to come out of nuclear forms, a case of the aforementioned situational diversity (Dallos and Sapsford 1995). Thus, although across time we can talk of a diversity of a family types, many of these families can be seen as variations on a nuclear theme over time. Moreover, there is the growing popularity of the reconstituted family, or stepfamily, where parents bring children from previous relationships into a new family situation which contains members who have changed their circumstances several times.

If we apply this to the position of children, it is estimated that 28 per cent of children in the UK will have experienced divorce by the time they reach 16 (Allan and Crow 2001). Some will find themselves back in a two-parent family having to renegotiate sibling- and parent-type relations with stepchildren and parents; the majority will experience a period with just one parent looking after them. What we are saying here is that children are now more likely to move in and out of the nuclear family as they grow up.

I have so far concentrated on trends that open up more possibilities for seeing children differently. I now want to examine in a little more detail one contemporary trend that illustrates quite nicely children's changing social worlds within late-modern society, that of divorce. Recent research on children and their experiences of divorce has focused on three key inter-related concepts. First, there is a *diversity of experience* as separation and divorce generates quite different and distinct situations for children both across and over time. Secondly, and following Beck, there is the exposure of children to a number of *risks* as divorce rates continue to rise. And thirdly, there is a degree of *resilience* among children as they come to terms with their parents breaking up (Hetherington 2003; Pike 2003; Flowerdew and Neale 2003).

Diversity of Experience

Youngsters are confronted with a bewildering array of changes to their lives when parents break up and form new partnerships. Step-parents and siblings appear in their lives, there is greater fluidity of movement between households within relatively short periods of time owing to changing custody arrangements and problems with newly acquired family members. Flowerdew and Neale (2003), in their British study of 'multiple transitions', report that their sample of 11–17-year-olds have had to adapt to quite different situations when their parents break up and over fairly short periods of time their experiences can change quite dramatically. Custody arrangements can change quite quickly, with children having to adapt to new households and new 'family' relations.

Flowerdew and Neale (2003, pp. 154–5) refer to two cases. One, Percy Drew, a 14-year-old boy, had a fairly positive experience of 'adaptation':

My dad's girlfriend is really nice and helpful and stuff. She sort of gets into things that we like . . . And Mum's just married Steve. He got me into cricket and stuff like that . . . And he's good 'cos like he'll come home and I've got to go out somewhere in half an hour and I haven't told him and he's fine about it.

The second case of Becky, aged 16, was more problematic:

Mum and dad have both gone their separate ways and they seem happier, so let them be . . . I used to get on really well with my stepmum but soon as she got the ring on her finger that were it, she changed . . . And I didn't use to get on with my stepdad when he arrived, when we moved in with him. I'd say it's got better but I don't see that much of him 'cos he worked through the day and works at the club at night. But there were like four kids all of a sudden in the house. If we'd more space, like somewhere to go when you wanted to be on your own, that'd make it easier.

Risks

Diversity of experience brings with it a range of risks to which children are exposed. A series of large-scale surveys in the USA reveal a range of problems that children encounter (Hetherington 2003). In the immediate post-separation period, children are likely to be emotionally distressed. Sometimes this distress is delayed, affecting their schoolwork and levels of self-esteem. Age and gender were significant in offsetting these effects. Thus pre-adolescent boys were more at risk than their female counterparts in the post-divorce period, with pre-adolescent girls less able to cope than their male counterparts when their parents remarried. Children are also likely to suffer economically, with lone mothers having far fewer resources, becoming more dependent on welfare and being more susceptible to health problems as a result of marital break-up.

The 'divorce' risks to children were easier to manage where separated parents had strong lines of communication between each other. This was confirmed by Flowerdew and Neale's (2003) sample of children: they were better able to cope with parents breaking up where both parents still communicated well with each other in the post-divorce period. Other members of the family were significant, acting as a support network for children. Ongoing positive contact between various members of this network provided more insurance against children being adversely affected. In some sense the continuity of relations with both parents means that children 'get to keep their famil(ies)', reducing the possible stress that results from the movement of one parent into another household (Moxnes 2003).

Resilience

As with a diversity of situations and variable levels of risk to children, divorce is also an occasion for children to demonstrate a range of coping strategies. Children are more likely to be viewed as competent, developing strength of character and resilience as they negotiate rapid changes to their circumstances. This is at variance with the discourse on risk, which tends to emphasise children's vulnerability to external forces. Recent studies challenge the 'victim' status usually attributed to children when their parents separate. Children are often forced to adapt to their parents' divorce, but sometimes do so in ways that demonstrate a degree of social competence and maturity. The implications of competence are that children develop more resilient characters at a much earlier age. We will see later on in the book that the rise in the numbers of children being brought up within one-parent families may have a significant impact on the character of parent/child relations in the early twenty-first century.

Hetherington (2003, p. 223), for example, refers to small clusters of 'competent' children in her study: 'It has been remarked that children in single-parent families grow up faster and this certainly seemed to be the case in our "competence at a cost" and "competence caring" children'. This resilience and ability to cope can sometimes work against the formation of new family relationships. Step-parents are more likely to have difficulties forming relationships with their stepchildren if the latter have 'precocious independence and power' (Hetherington 2003, p. 230). Thus children can become quite protective towards their lone parents over a period of time as well as becoming more domestically adept and emotionally self-sufficient. With the advent of a new step-parent, the child has a more powerful bargaining position in this new family situation, with new rules and boundaries having to be carefully broached by an incoming step-parent.

As we saw earlier, some children have difficulties getting on with step-parents. Some of this can be put down to a degree of precocity among children who have been instrumental in re-establishing new family relations with a lone parent and siblings. Yet children, along with their lone parents, are able to move on and renew normal family relations after a period of transition. Processes of normalisation can take place: 'what was an "extraordinary" period of transition in their lives had become wholly "ordinary"' (Flowerdew and Neale 2003, p. 151). In these situations children can have difficulty reforming nuclear household bonds.

Up to now I have discussed post/late-modern theory as a dominant strand of contemporary sociology thinking. Whilst this approach seems to embrace the possibilities for choice and self-realisation in society, there is little or no discussion of how this plays out in the lives of children. As was discussed in the previous chapter, children are invisible. Late-modern constructions of childhood tell us very little about children's lives; childhood is largely understood in terms of the needs and interests of parents. I have had to draw on the work of childhood and family theorists in locating children within contemporary society.

The Global Child

In this section I want to pick up on one of Beck's themes discussed in the previous section, the idea of globalisation. This refers to a series of objective processes that bring political, cultural and economic systems together. Technological developments have brought communities, nations and cultures together, creating a range of interconnected ties and interests as well as increasingly shared environmental problems. For some this has led to a breakdown of conventional hierarchies. Returning briefly to Beck (1992, p. 36), his claim that 'poverty is hierarchic, smog is democratic' refers to a paradoxical situation that the industrialisation of the nineteenth and twentieth centuries created both social and economic inequalities and environmental threats that affect rich and poor equally. Others are more critical of globalisation, seeing it as the speeding-up of processes that widen the gap between the rich and the poor. Economic and social differences that exist within one country are now more apparent across larger geographical areas (Townsend 1996). This structural global inequality is accompanied by forms of cultural imperialism, with Western ideas taking hold in developing countries (Barber 1995).

At the same time, there is a greater social awareness of what Harvey (1989) calls the 'compression of time and space': pollution affects future as well as present generations and its effects cut across national boundaries. The expansion and increase in power of the mass media further compresses time and space through the presentation of world events in real time and in the way that the television and the internet alter our sense of distance from places on the other side of the globe. Thus local and national environmental problems are experienced concurrently in different geographical locations, generating more global ways of seeing things.

As with post/late-modernity, globalisation theorists have had very little to say about children and childhood and their significance within a global context. There are important continuities with theories of industrialisation and capitalism, in particular the implicit binary divide between public and private realms, privileging the former as the site of social action and change. The private realm of family and children is a marginal institution, responding to and reflecting broader structural trends. However, for some this divide is breaking down, with globalising processes dissolving boundaries between 'inside' and 'outside' worlds. According to Sharon Stephens

(1995), children are associated with other 'domains of nature' such as the animal world and the physical environment that have now been colonised as protective social spaces and brought within the vocabulary of 'risk' and rights. Paradoxically, children have been brought within these social spaces as a way of protecting their status as 'natural' biological entities in need of nurturing and protection. Problems such as child abuse and school disaffection are being tackled through more concerted state action: formerly private arrangements between children and adult authority figures are now under more public scrutiny. These processes have had global implications. Not only are Western children and families being exposed to more 'internal' regulatory demands, children in quite different cultural settings are subject to similar demands, with economically active children on the streets and in factories becoming 'colonial projects' for international organisations (Stephens 1995, p. 16). According to this view, a form of cultural imperialism is taking place, with constructions of childhood in developing countries being subsumed within more dominant models of the welfare child.

Globalisation Consumerism and Mass Media

In examining globalisation from a Western vantage point, much has been made of the way that growing up has become a process incorporating a much wider range of global reference points. One of the most significant reference points is the mass media, through which children and young people become a more integral part of a globalised consumer culture. In Chapter 8 I discuss the way that young children generate their own meaning system through 'children's cultures', which are largely disconnected from the adult world. When referring to older children and the process of identity-formation, there is a much stronger sense in which children and young people are part of a 'grown-up' environment of consumer choice. Thus children are encouraged to appropriate designer labels and branded goods mass-produced by multinational corporations as a means of buying into a particular life-style.

As I argued earlier, the emphasis on late modernity heightens the role of the individual over and above 'external' social factors. In referring to a globalised consumer culture, there is a much stronger sense of children as individuals. Hence children are like adults, part of an ever-broadening, age-segmented market, made up of consumers, the significant difference being that children are now growing up as a generation whose identities are now more heavily influenced by consumerism than those of their parents. Some have argued that this foregrounds a stronger image of children as social agents: the emphasis is on children creating their own identities, rather than assuming one as a consequence of class, gender, ethnic or 'family' origins.

Thus, as with theorists of the contemporary family, children primarily with peers and the media are 'doing' rather than having or assuming an identity (Miles 2000).

In one sense, children and young people are the quintessential consumers, using the most up-to-date technological means to scan, exploit and extract the maximum from the images, sounds and objects on offer. Young people are more receptive to images and messages, which are nowadays transmitted via a global mass media because they are seen as 'gatherers of sensations' (Miles 2000, p. 65). Television, video and, probably most importantly now, the internet provide children and young people with a wide-ranging choice of material and cultural artefacts that become part of a repertoire of resources for identity-formation.

Hybridisation, Consumerism and Identity

One effect of a globalised consumer culture is the mixing-up of a range of practices and ideas with different cultural origins through a process of hybridisation (Kenway and Bullen 2001, pp. 58–9). Thus, rather than a simple process of assimilation or, for that matter, the imposition of a dominant set of ideas, at a local level children and young people in their peer groups play around with musical, televisual and filmic reference points and create their own cultures. In developing countries, for example, children may draw on designer clothes and objects in order to improve their social status locally (Miles 2000, p. 64). In Western cultures, the idea of 'culture trading' is more likely to be practised among the Y generation, those born between 1980 and 1995, because they were born into an established late-modern culture: '[W]ith no alternative but to accommodate change, this generation is patient and fluid. Its members keep their options open, remaining non-committal for as long as possible ... They do not expect stability and predictability. Neither do they fear change' (Kenway and Bullen 2001, p. 59). There are intra- and intergenerational implications. A global framework both opens up possibilities for cultural expression among the young and offers resources for identity-building. At the same time, forms of cultural exchange are taking place between adults and children, for identity-formation has conventionally been about the parent generation establishing the structures within which young people have made their way within society. As I have argued earlier, children have usually been seen as carriers of their parents' habitus, the embodied dispositions of the parent generation (Bourdieu 1984). In one sense, hybridised cultures have always been integral to the process of identity-formation: there is a constant struggle between the parent and the teenager in establishing the latter's sense of self, with adult and child cultures in creative tension. Now there is a more complex interplay, with young people incorporating parental habitus as modernist conventional reference points with new 'post-modernist' frames such as the global media and the consumer market.

However, there are subtle differences of interpretation here. Conventional reference points for identity-formation tend to revolve around the power and authority of adults. The exchanges that take place between adults and children are now quite likely to produce degrees of personal instability. As was stated earlier, there are far fewer clear-cut trajectories for young people to follow. Thus the reliance on the self from a much earlier age, what Buchner referred to as the 'biographisation of the life course' (Buchner 1990, p. 78), means that young people are now far more reliant on the media, the market and each other in trying to answer who they are and where they are going. In these terms a global consumer culture is drawn on by young people in an attempt to provide answers.

Whether consumerism actually functions in this way is open to debate: various commentators have argued that consumerism is an ideology offering at best short-term solutions, at worst sucking the young into a superficial world of fleeting appearances (Melucci 1992). However, some take a far more positive view and argue that among young people instability and unpredictability become virtues, with consumerism producing an ever-changeable repertoire of resources that young people continually draw on in recreating themselves. Bauman, for example, argues:

> And so the snag is no longer how to discover, invent, construct, assemble (even buy) an identity, but how to prevent it from sticking. Well constructed and durable identity turns from an asset into a liability. The hub of post modern life strategy is not identity building but avoidance of fixation. (cited in Miles 2000, pp. 157–8)

Miles (2000) uses Bauman's argument to argue that consumerism among the young can be seen as a creative response to the difficulties that they have in establishing themselves within contemporary society. Thus the lack of given identity structures becomes a fashion statement, with young people extolling the virtues of an ever-changing cultural landscape.

Childhood, Ethnicity and Hybridisation

Hybridisation can take other forms, particularly in relation to tensions between a dominant indigenous culture and a minority culture and how they are experienced by children from the latter. These tensions are resolved or mitigated in a number of ways by young people from minority cultures who increasingly draw on a range of globalised resources on offer (Hall 1995; Mandel 1995). Kathleen Hall's (1995) essay is illuminating here. Her research focuses on the lives of young Sikhs living in the north of England in the late 1980s. The overarching identity of being a British Sikh is complex, and Hall illustrates the ways that her young respondents manage the demands made on them by their 'home' culture through their family, and the host culture through the school and locale. Borrowing Bourdieu's notion of cultural field, she argues that Sikh teenagers skilfully negotiated expectations of being British and Sikh in a number of different social settings. In Sikh communal gatherings such as worship they acted 'exclusively Indian' within the Sikh temple: their clothes, language and behaviour displayed their home culture and they were carefully watched by the parent generation. Yet, even within the constraints of Sikh communal gatherings, girls were sometimes able to create some space for themselves and at the same time improvise with Sikh symbols. For example, girls' lives were heavily regulated by family and community; they were rarely able to spend their leisure time outside the family. Fashion shows were popular among young Asian women because they allowed them to congregate in their leisure time and they were able to take traditional Sikh outfits, tinker around with shape, colour and style, and borrow from more Westernised fashions. A second cultural field was the home, where the girls 'acted mainly Indian'. Punjabi was the dominant language spoken and Indian 'codes' characterised relations between the girls and their parents. Education was a mediating factor: girls were normally constrained in choosing a partner for marriage. However, gaining qualifications for university allowed them a degree of autonomy in choosing the timing of their marriage and their future partners.

A third dominant field was schooling, where the girls acted 'mainly British'. There are two interrelated features here. First, the dominant norms of schooling are white and middle class; Hall comments on the subtle ways that teachers marginalise anything that departs from these norms. Citing one teacher of those Indian pupils who did well in her English class:

> kids who are in the top set are largely middle class Asian kids and, they've taken on so much of our culture that they think like the rest of the class. . . . And the Asian kid in the top set is exactly like the middle class English kids, it is class rather than ah culture. (Hall 1995, p. 250)

Thus children have to mask part of their identity to achieve academically. The dominant culture marginalises difference. At the same time, a second feature of schooling, peer relations, creates both difficulties and opportunities for female Sikhs. Some girls have difficulties narrowing the gap between the restrictions imposed on them within their families and the individualism expected of them when interacting with 'English' friends in the classroom. Yet for others the school becomes the site for exchanging ideas, symbols and routine practices. Uniforms and hair are carefully rearranged, boys become more accessible as friends, and television and music from a range of global sources become the stuff of conversation. Finally, Hall refers to Sikh children's access to the local city or town. Here there are two cultural fields: the shopping mall and the nightclub. Wary that members of their community may see them, in the former they tend to act 'cautiously English'. The latter, on the other hand, is a forbidden field, particularly for Sikh girls. Here the parental culture dominates, with the girls' heavily circumscribed home life restricting any access they have to the public realm at night.

Individualisation and New Inequalities

In the last section I highlighted the possibilities for seeing children and young people as social agents, utilising the choices that a late-modern society offers them. Whilst there is potential for children to have more control of their lives, some critics argue that the evidence of actual self-realisation and the demonstrable sharing of processes of identity-formation is too slight to radically alter the social structural positions of children. Moreover, individualisation weakens the position of many children in as much as individualisation presupposes equal access to the marketplace as consumers. Prout (2000a), for example, takes a critical line in relation to individualisation, not simply because there is little evidence of children being freed up from conventional constraints, but because individualisation per se reinforces processes of social exclusion. There is an ideology of choice: individualisation generates expectations that all can benefit from the shift towards mass consumption. At the same time, those in poverty are less able fully to benefit from consumption choices and, with identity now more reliant on market choices, large segments of the population are excluded.

As I argued in the previous chapter, children are disproportionately affected by poverty. The UK Labour government's commitment to tackling child poverty is now starting to have some effect. But throughout the 1980s and 1990s, under a neoliberal Conservative government, the number of children in poverty rose quite dramatically (Bradshaw 2003). 'Poor' children are found in households with 'lone parents', where parents are unemployed and/or claiming welfare and where the household contains either a disabled adult or child. There are also considerable ethnic and regional disparities: children of Pakistani and Bangladeshi origin are more at risk than their white counterparts and children in poverty are more likely to be found in large cities such as Glasgow, Liverpool and parts of London. Late modernity has arguably accentuated this situation and at the same time created new forms of social and economic division.

In Chapter 8 I refer to the 'digital divide': the differentiation of children on the basis of their access to the internet. Despite the current Labour government's commitment to equality of opportunity, children have differential access to knowledge. This is an important indicator of the social exclusion of children and one that hints at new forms of social and economic inequality. However, almost all children are exposed to other media such as television. Here we can see that children, like adults, are exposed to a range of role models and lifestyles that many can only really aspire to, making them more likely to feel different from their peers in school. As I argued earlier, the media can expand children's repertoire of resources for identity-building; it can also isolate and marginalise them, creating a sense of detachment from the dominant norms. Children in poverty may be exposed to similar influences from their peers in school and the mass media as more affluent children, but the dominance of individual choice and consumption as framing devices for making sense of the world as they grow up makes it much more difficult for them to connect socially with those around them.

Poverty is one problem; another associated and possibly symptomatic phenomenon is the reported rise in the numbers of children with mental health problems. Children now appear to have problems coping with everyday routines, generating an increase in cases of depression, self-harm and obsessive behaviour among the young. Recent reports attribute around 20 per cent of all young people's deaths to suicide (James and James 2004, p. 163). One commentator referred to these as symptoms of the 'meaninglessness of modern life', a problem that arguably affects all children. This is expressed in terms of the decline of accounts or reasons, 'metanarratives' that help us to make sense of our lives. The evidence for this comes from a recently commissioned survey where over 50 per cent of 4–16-year-olds reported being 'stressed out' (Bunting 2004). Children, like adults, are less likely now to be able to rely on familiar reference points. I discussed one familiar reference point earlier, the nuclear family. I took a fairly sanguine view of the way that children manage family break-ups. At the same time, parental divorce and separation have taken their toll on a number of children. Whether we see divorce as a symptom or a constituent feature of late modernity, individualistic values have had negative effects on the ability of some children to cope with the pace of social change.

One other possible source of discontent among children, creating mental health problems, is the school curriculum. As I discuss in Chapter 7, the demands of the National Curriculum in England and Wales and the rising expectations of teachers and parents have put more pressure on those children least well-equipped to deal with the intensifying of school work. A recent front-page headline in a British Sunday newspaper, the *Observer*, claimed, 'Exam fears driving teenagers to Prozac'. Doctors and mental health groups articulate concerns over the rising numbers of school students taking prescribed drugs in order to cope with the stress of examinations (Townsend 2004). The dominance of target-setting, the intensification of assessment and the pressures of external accountability have created more visible winners and losers among the school population. Wexler's (1992, p. 65) perceptive commentary on middle-class schooling in the USA identifies similar pressures. Parents and teachers direct pupils' energies towards academic success. Schooling here takes an extreme form of individualism, with some pupils exhibiting strain, anxiety and a sense of failure as they move from being 'A' grade students to 'B' grade 'failures'. One of Wexler's teachers referred to 'kids having nervous breakdowns – getting ulcers. Some of them just keep working but they are very depressed. Others give up and become trouble makers. They wind up being sent away' (Wexler 1992, p. 59).

We might see the relations that children have with each other in school mitigating the worst of these pressures. This is more difficult where the social centre has been 'emptied' under the pressure to pursue better grades (Wexler 1992, p. 65). Stress not only manifests itself in concerns over good grades, children also feel stressed by the possibility of failure in forming same- and opposite-sex friendships. One commentator reports from a recent survey of British schoolchildren:

> "It's really hard if people you want to be with don't like you", said one 11-year-old boy. "That really does your head in." One nine-year-old said he suffered after "breaking up" with his girlfriend. "It really freaked me. I was totally stressed out", he said. (Burke 2000)

Interestingly, one indicator of a more reflexive society is the rise in the numbers of surveys involving children. We are therefore more likely to know about children's mental health compared with previous periods. Differentiating between a rise in the numbers of children with mental health problems and a growing awareness of these problems is therefore difficult. Be that as it may, a perceived increase in mental health problems may be an important consequence of a society that provides children with fewer fixed social reference points now.

It is also worth noting that social inequalities are central in the work of researchers who underplay the significance of these new frames of reference. Roberts (1997), for example, argues that individualisation, consumerism and globalisation have less determining power in terms of identity-formation. He contends that social class, ethnicity and gender still shape the way that young people see themselves. Consumerism and individualism are significant in terms of play and leisure: the semi-autonomous realm of the peer culture is retained and, within this, children's activities have undoubtedly been influenced by a global mass media. However, these are secondary and less important influences on a child's identity: gender, race and social class still determine children's trajectories; the family still acts as a powerful force. Roberts cites a large-scale survey of young people aged 16–19 across the UK in support of his argument. Thus, while there are subtle ways in which young people's trajectories can be differentiated, these reference points still tend to converge around social class and gender differences.

Globalism: Understanding Inequality

Globalisation has undoubtedly become a powerful economic, political and cultural frame of reference. The rise of the individual and the emphasis on choice encourage children and young people to have a more active role within adult settings as cultural and economic agents. However, globalisation also offers a broadening of perspective on the way we see the world. At the same time as becoming global consumers, we are also likely to make connections between our own local and national situations and the situations of others in quite different national cultural contexts. This has been referred to as 'globalism', 'the subjective personal awareness that many of us share common tastes and interests' (Cohen and Kennedy 2000, p. 11). In some ways these connections are made through the aforementioned process of hybridisation. The globalising of music, fashion and symbols of 'youth' also allows us to make political and sociological connections; it offers us possibilities for becoming more aware of inequalities within and across national boundaries (Moss and Petrie 2002, p. 44).

Globalisation creates new forms of inequality and, as I have argued previously, they disproportionately affect the young. At the same time, a global sensibility also has the potential to generate new forms of collective responses to these inequalities. Beck's individualisation emphasises notions of individual responsibility and personal biography and the weakening of conventional attachments to family, community and social class. However, whilst some have seen this in terms of anomie, we can still detect trends towards new social and political formations that challenge global inequalities. Thus environmental and peace movements, anti-nuclear groups and the women's movement work largely outside of conventional party political structures with more symbolic goals relating to rights and ethical issues. To some extent, politics has been reconfigured: new social movements have become highly politicised over global and environmental trends. What is interesting here is that enthusiasm for new social movements is more likely to be found among the young. Currently, political commentators are expressing disquiet about the disaffection of the young from politics because of the low turn-out of first-time voters at national elections and the declining membership of youth sections of conventional political parties (Craig and Earl Bennett 1997; National Centre for Social Research 2000). I take this up in more detail in Chapter 10. For the purposes of our present discussion, if we link these new political commitments to young people's more long-standing concerns over fairness and social justice, then what we have potentially is a greater awareness among the young of global inequalities (Roker, Player and Coleman 1999). One recent example of this in the UK was the organisation of city and national demonstrations against the war that recently took place in Iraq involving British and American troops. School students took the day off school to attend rallies protesting against the perceived intrusion of Western forces and the effects of the war on innocent Iraqi civilians (Cunningham and Lavalette 2004).

Conclusion

Whilst the rise of new social and political formations and an enthusiasm for a more globalised political perspective suggests new ways in which young people can express a political voice, the evidence is contradictory on whether or not children and young people have become more politicised. On the one hand, schoolchildren's recent political activism in relation to the Iraq war had significant costs, with youthful political action being interpreted by the authorities in negative terms as truancy (Cunningham and Lavalette 2004). This belied the powerful commitments that young people have towards global justice and fairness (Maitles 2004). On the other hand, the emphasis on control and performance in UK secondary schools may mean that children are simply too preoccupied with their exams and grades to have the energy and commitment to support political causes. Ultimately, the backdrop to any commitment that children may have to political causes is children's and young people's long-standing apolitical status. I discuss a structure and culture that excludes children from the political world in Chapter 10. What is worth mentioning here is that contemporary society both expands and limits children's frames of reference and abilities to construct their own identities. The impetus to protect and control is strengthened as the values of late-modern society disorient adults. Children can be found within the realm of 'nostalgia' and 'futurity': in the first case, adults try to recentre themselves through their children – childhood thus becomes a form of moral rescue, with adults trying to hold on to an out-of-date conception of childhood. In the process, this produces more tension and anxiety as adults try to maintain the upper hand within a context where children expect to be consulted.

In the second case, futurity is one configuration of the late-modern child. Whereas, nostalgia refers to adult constructions of childhood, futurity sees children as an extension of the process of individualisation in a limited, market-oriented way. Control is maintained and children's abilities to contribute are equally attenuated as parents and educationalists try desperately to appropriate children's futures as adults, citizens and workers. In this chapter my reading of recent sociological theory confirms many of the claims made in Chapter 2 about the social positions of children. Despite the breakdown of conventional modernist metanarratives, the concomitant rise of the individual and the opportunities for more diverse life-styles, children play at best a peripheral role within new social formations that theorists of modernity argue have replaced old social structural categories. For theories that locate children within processes of social change, we still have to rely on the work of childhood and 'youth' specialists. It is here that the notion of children's social agency is most potent.

Part Two

Childhood as a Social Problem

4

Childhood in Crisis: Social Disorder and Reconstruction

Introduction

One of the dominant themes in contemporary Western society is the idea that childhood is in crisis. Our understanding of who children are and what childhood means as a phase of the life-cycle are threatened by the weakening of structures that both care for and control children. The family, the school and the welfare state are said to be unable or unwilling to regulate the process commonly known as growing up. In some instances the alleged breakdown of relations between adults and children is linked to broader problems of social disorder. As with 'the family', childhood is seen by some to be a bedrock institution. The problem of childhood is thus intimately connected to broader questions about social change (Lee 2001).

What this crisis means and how it serves to reinforce a powerful set of ideas about where children ought to be within the social structure is the subject of the first part of this chapter. Crisis is subdivided into three themes. The first theme revolves around the association of youth and trouble. I refer briefly to the historical dimensions of this enduring and, for the most part, mythical motif in the UK and USA. I will mainly be concerned with two current versions: the 'demonisation' of childhood and the teenage mother. Both serve to crystallise public commentary that children are conceptually and physically out of place. A second theme draws on a more global frame and locates the street child as a visible and worrying symptom of social disintegration within developing societies. In the first two cases, crisis is viewed in terms of a breakdown in parent/child relations with the generational boundary a key element in the composition of childhood. A third theme, the cyber-child or 'the child trapped in the net', views crisis not so much in terms of breakdown within family or community but as a threat to the residual autonomy provided for children through the world of play. The involvement of technology in the child's world of play is said to compromise the moral integrity of childhood – the idea of innocence – as well as to threaten generational relationships found within the home and the school.

The second part of the chapter casts some new light on the idea of crisis. First of all, I question the way that childhood is viewed from this perspective by returning to the idea that childhood is a social construction. In an attempt to broaden the perspective on children's social positions, I address two forms of childhood that assume crisis proportions in terms of their status as 'deviant' categories of childhood: child soldiers and child carers. I draw on these two cases in reconstructing childhood. That is, I explore the possibilities for viewing children's social activities and relations outside of a narrowly conceived Western or 'welfarist' view of childhood.

The Problem of 'Youth'

Four reference points are significant here: the 'problem of youth', the correlation between truancy and delinquency, the 'demonisation of childhood', and the problem of single teenage mothers. The first two are well documented as recurring historical themes which periodically generate demands for more surveillance of young people within the public sphere (Humphries 1981; Pearson 1983; Carlen, Gleeson and Wardhaugh 1992). Pearson (1983) challenges the contemporary idea that young people are more delinquent now than in the past. He argues that young people have regularly been scapegoated as problems during periods of social dislocation. Since the middle of the nineteenth century there have been recurring fears about young people being out of control, and complaints about binge drinking, criminality and moral degeneration.

The second theme, truancy, is discussed in Chapter 7. Yet it is worth stating here that truancy has regularly been viewed as the first step to criminality for young people. Social scientists have never been able clearly to articulate the relationship between truancy and delinquency. Nevertheless, a common perception is that being out of school during school hours provides children and young people with more opportunities to commit crime. The third theme, whilst overlapping with the first two, is more recent, developing in the immediate post-Bulger era. The details of the Bulger murder are by now well known, but to recap briefly: James Bulger, a 2-year-old boy, was murdered by two 10-year-old boys in 1993 in Liverpool, England. The public furore after the trial of the two boys, a trial that took place in an 'adult' court, generated endless speculation on causes, motives and blame. The Bulger case and its aftermath present us with a harsher and more extreme vision of young people in the public sphere. There is a shift away from the troublesome delinquent teenager towards striking images of much younger children causing widespread disruption in the public sphere. For some, childhood has been 'demonised'. Franklin and Petley (1996, p. 134) argue that the Bulger case offered 'journalists . . . a new definition of childhood; the "innocent angels" were replaced by "little demons".' It also seemingly crystallises ideas on the decline of authority and the breakdown in relations between adults and children, two indications that childhood is in crisis.

I will discuss the implications of this conception of childhood for the criminal justice system in the following chapter. What I want to do here is to address these two indicators in relation to what I call the boundary problem. That is, one of the fundamentals of adult/child relations in Western societies is that adults have authority over children. In the previous chapter I made distinctions between different kinds of adult/child boundaries depending on social class and gender (Bernstein 1971; Newson and Newson 1976). Notwithstanding these differences, the general tendency is towards parents being positioned as authority figures over children. Crisis amounts to the weakening or loosening of the hierarchical boundary between adults and children such that children are now seen to be out of position.

The idea of a generational boundary or hierarchy is part of a dominant train of thought that can be traced back to sociological and psychological theories of socialisation and child development (to be discussed in Chapter 6). Children are socialised by adults, primarily parents, a process of character-building that involves elements of care and control. Various theories from across the ideological and political spectrum converge on the idea that the source of many current social problems is within the family, particularly the nature of child socialisation (Wyness 2000). One current popular theorist of the political right, Charles Murray (1994), asserts that growing numbers of parents are both unable and unwilling to provide their children with the required internal moral structures, what David Riesman (1950) in a much earlier period called 'inner directedness'. Murray concentrates his analysis on a sector of the population, the underclass, allegedly dependent on welfare payments, allegedly more likely to reject the moral bedrocks of work and marriage, thus providing fewer and weaker moral reference points or boundaries for their children. Within this context, children are likely to be exposed to the adult world from a much earlier age, making it more difficult for parents to restrain their precocious appetites.

From a centre-left perspective, the same kinds of claims are made, particularly in relation to families where the father is both physically and morally absent. We are more familiar with the former case in that children brought up solely by mothers are allegedly less likely to be nurtured within the protective environs of the two-parent nuclear family. They are thus more likely to experience the pressures of adult life at a much earlier age. This early exposure to the adult world is said to put children at risk by increasing the opportunities for them to commit crime. In the latter case, Dennis and Erdos (1992) refer to fathers from intact families with little or no involvement in child care, 'uncommitted fathers'. They argue that boys with 'uncommitted fathers' are more likely to become delinquent than boys with what they call 'effective, kind and considerate' fathers. Families with 'absent fathers' are thus part of the broader problem of dysfunctional social relations, which produce what Phillips (1996, pp. 270–87) calls the 'disordered child'.

The disordered child and the demonisation of childhood are brought together through a discourse that generates demands for tighter controls and more adult responsibility for the development of young boys. Another illustration and potent symbol of the disordered child is the single teenage mother.[1] Whilst single teenage mothers make up a small minority of all lone parents, 'single' mothers, that is, never-married mothers, are a growing minority. In 1981, single mothers made up around a fifth of all lone parents; by the turn of the century, this proportion had doubled. The problem is more marked in the UK and USA. The former has one of the highest proportions of single teenage mothers in Europe. This in turn is a far lower figure than in the USA (Corsaro 1997, pp. 232–9). Girls brought up in an environment where there are allegedly weak moral and legal attachments between the father and mother are likely to follow suit and become single parents. Phillips' (1996) argument, based on anecdotal evidence, is that mothers without the binding commitment to one male spouse are likely to have a series of male partners. Young girls are said to be brought up in an environment of 'casualised' sexual relations, producing a state of 'emotional chaos or neglect' (1996, p. 263). Moreover, girls exposed to this from an early age are likely to become sexually active from an early age, producing what Pearce, from a US perspective, calls the phenomenon of 'children having children' (1996). Thus, as with the male delinquent product of the underclass family, we also have the sexually precocious female child, another ambiguous conception of childhood.[2]

Street Children

A second version of childhood in crisis deals with global images of problem children on the street. The image of the street child is the abandoned child left to fend for himself or herself in an alien, dangerous and foreign environment. There are similarities with the disordered child. Street children inhabit adult spaces; they can create the same sense of unease and anxiety as the street gang or the child criminal. As we shall see in the following chapter, the disordered and demonised child generates demands for mechanisms of control. The discourse here emphasises greater public surveillance and more punitive courses of action. At an international level we can see elements of this: street children have been subject to some of the most repressive courses of action by the police and state in some countries (Rizzini 1996). Glauser (1997) in his research found that children on the street were often seen as a physical menace by the authorities because they were seen to be threatening private property and in some cases they were seen as being detrimental to the tourist industry. Yet, at the same time, street children connote more ambiguous images of what Boyden calls 'the most deprived and the most depraved members of society' (1997, p. 196). The street child threatens the adult/child relationship in another way: children lack the required levels of care that pull them within the conception of the carefree child without responsibilities. Street children seem to challenge the idea of adults closely regulating their emotional and physical needs as well as the dominant role that adults play in regulating their behaviour.

I have argued that the demonised child is often linked to inadequate socialisation or some sort of familial deficiency. Yet, rather than pathologise the problem of the street child, the analysis of crisis here rests more on broader structural factors. From a Western vantage point, street children are children in extreme poverty. Our analysis will not be able to unravel the complexities of the concept of poverty here. What I can say briefly with reference to child poverty is that comparisons are made within countries and between developing and developed countries. The general trend is towards child poverty growing in both contexts, with the most serious consequences being felt in less-developed countries. Natural disasters, civil war and an accumulation of foreign debt have affected the poorest countries. In developing South-East Asian economies, financial crashes have left many vulnerable, with a disproportionate effect on children. If we take the case of countries like Brazil, a combination of economic recessions in the 1980s after periods of economic growth reduced the household incomes of the worst off by a third. Along with a rise in the birth-rate, more intensive urbanisation during this period and striking inequalities in the distribution of income, we have situations of severe poverty for children (Corsaro, 1997, p. 209).

This has led in some contexts to children being ejected from their homes and spending periods on the street. Whilst the concept of child poverty is quite complex, the link between child poverty and the street child is normally made quite simply: in cultures with an underdeveloped welfare state, children are forced through economic circumstances to take to the street. For Corsaro (1997, p. 207) 'poverty clearly steals the childhoods and often the very lives of many children in the developing world' (1997, p. 207). What Corsaro means is that poverty propels children into dangerous adult territory, both as inhabitants of the street and as economically productive actors. Street children often have to fend for themselves, developing precocious cognitive and social skills, and in general exhibiting many of the characteristics and responsibilities of adults (Williams 1993).

Street children in developing countries are an ill-defined sector of the child population. Glauser's (1997) paper on the measurement and assessment of street children tries to distinguish between children 'in' and children 'of' the street. The former refers to children working on the street and living at home whilst the latter denotes children both living and working on the street. As Glauser (1997) states, this is only a starting point for identifying and supporting street children. There are still many ambiguous cases of children 'on' the street who, on certain days of week or for periods throughout the year, work and live on the street, and at other times use the street for purely economic purposes. Researchers in the field contend that a clearer definition of the street child and how he or she uses the street is crucial in allowing agencies to make more informed decisions as to the kind of support needed (Williams 1993; Glauser 1997).

Despite these attempts to clarify the problem, the general impetus has been to try and take children off the street, irrespective of the way they use the street. Ironically, it is the children who arguably play a more valuable role on the street, those with economic responsibilities, who are more likely to come into conflict with Western social values. This is because two social norms are being flouted: children are on the street in adult territory and children are involved in the adult world of work. A tendency to take a more inclusive view of the street child – to remove children irrespective of their motives, commitments and levels of responsibility – often leads to intervention, with quite damaging consequences for the children and their families. If we take the example of children 'in' the street: many are chaperoned by their parents on to a relatively safe part of the street where they can ply their trade in relative security. Boyden (1997) refers to the way that these children can be defined by agencies as abandoned children, leading to them being separated from their families and placed in orphanages. Two sets of consequences are possible: the children's families have difficulty keeping things together because of their reliance on the 'street' child's income, and the street children themselves have difficulty coping with the institutional constraints of the orphanage. This can result in them escaping back on to the street and becoming involved in more criminalised activities, what Williams (1993) calls a process of 'degenerative estrangement'. To sum up here: when discussing the street child, we have a more measured, less intemperate analysis of children and their families than the discourse on the demonised child. Nevertheless, from a Western or developed vantage point there is still the sense that the outcomes of global poverty, the street child and child labourer, are thought to be 'out of place'.

I have discussed crisis in terms of children being viewed as out of place in both physical and metaphorical terms. We can take this further by talking about the linguistic incongruity of the 'street child'. Whether we are talking about the 'disordered child', the 'street child' or even the 'precocious child', the need to attach an adjective to 'child' connotes a problem. Thus 'normal children', those located within the perimeters of home, school and playground, are simply known as 'children'. As Glauser (1997, p. 152) pithily states in deconstructing the 'street child':

> children can also be found using fields, lofts and gardens without there being any apparent need to coin terms such as 'field children', 'loft children' or 'garden children'. The need for a name seems to arise therefore when the situation departs from current social norms.

Children and Play: Lost on the Net

I have argued so far in this chapter that conceptions of childhood are shaped by the actions and interests of adults. Any judgements made about the changing nature of children's lives tend to revolve around the way in which adults view the boundaries between themselves and the child population. I identify elements of this in the following analysis of adult fears of technology. Thus the television and internet weaken the dependency and authority-type relationship between adults and children. In the process, technology is also said to challenge an important aspect of childhood, the notion of child's play, which we encountered in the first chapter. When Corsaro (1997, p. 38) comments, '[k]ids seem to have less time to be kids', he is referring to the attenuation of time, space and autonomy for children to play in their own terms. Play illustrates the centrality of childhood in that it locates children close to nature and thus closer to a pure and unmediated world of spontaneity, imagination and creativity. As I argued in Chapter 1, a dominant conception of childhood is the idea that children are 'irresponsible' in the sense that they have limited social responsibilities; play takes place within a world segregated from adults, a temporary period within which children are allowed to demonstrate their 'childish' inclinations.

In the following I address the distorted relationship between technology and play in three ways. First, I address adult fears of technology with reference to children's physical and emotional integrity. In particular, I examine the view that the internet replaces the desultory, collective activity of children playing together with the image of the solitary child in front of a computer screen prey to the predatory influence of on-line strangers. Secondly, I outline the view that technology challenges the moral integrity of childhood by creating images of the 'dangerous' child and the 'knowing' child. Thirdly, I address the notion that technology subverts the authority of parents.

Fears are constructed out of the quite complex and contradictory messages that parents pick up. The 'stranger-danger' theme dominates concerns that adults have about children's safety. Despite greater public prominence attached to 'dangerous families' in relation to child abuse, there is still a tendency towards locating trouble relating to children outside the home and family. I noted this earlier in the chapter when referring to the 'youth as trouble' theme. The stranger-danger theme concentrates on the physical and emotional safety of children outside the home, generating protectionist impulses from within the adult population and drawing children within the secure borders of family.

At the same time, parents are aware that older children require more autonomy and space, making demands on them for more freedom and independence. Whilst social geography and gender are important considerations when trying to meet these demands, parents are juggling the impetus to protect their children and the need to loosen the dependency-type ties as they get older. Existing research suggests that parents invest in computers to improve their children's educational life chances (Livingstone 2003). Yet the introduction of electronic media within the home has other roles to play. The television, video games and the computer become electronic baby-sitters: parents offer them as one way of keeping their children close and occupied, as a means of regulating their leisure time (Wyness 1994). However, Facer et al. (2001, p. 23) argue that electronic baby-sitters, particularly the internet, contain hidden threats to children's integrity. They refer to the way that 'outside dangers (are) brought inside'. The internet brings the child in touch with a vast network of images and knowledge that enhances their understanding of the global world; it also potentially puts them in touch with 'strangers'. This can be illustrated through the increasing popularity of chat rooms, where children can communicate in real time via the internet with those outside and build up 'virtual' friendships.

Around three-quarters of all 7–16-year-olds use the internet, with one survey reporting that around 60 per cent of youngsters who use the internet have had contact with strangers on-line (Livingstone 2003). What is most worrying for adults is the extent to which these strangers have sexual motives. A series of high-profile cases in the UK and the USA have highlighted the way that paedophiles can 'groom' children for sexual purposes, that is, use chat rooms to pose as children in order to befriend and meet up with them. There is as yet little research on the different ways that children make sense of chat rooms and no clear-cut view as to whether children in general share their parents' anxieties (Livingstone 2003). Nevertheless, the political and public significance attached to this connects with parents' fears of a perceived intrusion from the outside, which has the potential to lead to sexual abuse. In the UK a range of initiatives and television campaigns have been set up to warn children and parents of the dangers of unwanted contact from strangers through the internet, and the UK and Scottish parliaments have recently made grooming a criminal offence (MacDonell 2004).

A second fear comes out of concerns about the way that technological advances open up the adult world to children before they are 'developmentally' ready (Postman 1982). Thus, like television, the internet exposes children to a range of adult images and stimuli which threaten the moral and social integrity of the concept of childhood. Here the issues of care and control reappear. Constructions of children as both 'dangerous' and 'knowing' are placed together: children imitate the violence they see from the media they also become more cynical, streetwise and precocious as they assimilate knowledge about the worlds of sex, economics, war and politics (Selwyn 2001).

If we take the 'dangerous' child first of all: in the 1980s there were political fears which firmed up the link between video games and violence; impressionable children were likely to either imitate the violence that they saw on screen or become addicted to the violent characters and fail to differentiate between fact and fantasy in their everyday relations with others (Oswell 1998). The links between on-screen violence and real-life violence are notoriously difficult to establish. Nevertheless, images, theories and commentary assume a causal link between the mass media and real-life violence, particularly in the aftermath of high-profile incidents involving young people and violence. Thus the teenage boys who massacred 13 of their classmates at Columbine High School in Denver in the USA, were allegedly plotting to set off home-made bombs put together from information downloaded from the internet (Giles Whittell 'Police hunt "Trenchcoat" accomplices', *The Times*, 23 April 1999).

Citing Sgroi's analysis of constructions of child sexual abuse, Kitzinger (1997, p. 169) argues that 'the "knowing" child is neither a child nor an adult but a piece of damaged goods, lacking the attributes of both childhood and adulthood'. The dichotomising of the 'knowing child' with childhood innocence can also be usefully applied to children too immersed in the internet. Survey evidence from North America estimates that between 20 per cent and 35 per cent of youngsters have found 'undesirable' sexual material on the internet (Livingstone 2003). A recent nationwide survey of 12–15-year-olds' attitudes to pornography commissioned by Channel 4 (2003) in the UK claimed that 45 per cent of boys who had watched pornography had gained access to it via the internet. Whilst it does not follow that children are damaged as a consequence of this, the dominant perception is that the internet, as with other electronic media, offers children too many choices.

Thirdly, in relation to adult/child relations, Postman's (1982) construction of childhood views technology as a potential threat to adult authority. In both cases the dangerous child and the knowing child are a threat to childhood because they disrupt the boundaries between adulthood and childhood. The dangerous child becomes addicted to or immersed in visual media such that it challenges the constraining influence of the parent or teacher.

With reference to the 'knowing' child, some have gone as far as to suggest a form of role reversal here, with adults becoming more dependent on their children when gaining access to an increasingly powerful economic media. More generally, the 'cyber child' compromises the monopoly that adults have over knowledge, making it more difficult for it to be discreetly and incrementally distributed from adult to child (Postman 1982).

Reconstituting Childhood

In responding to the childhood in crisis discourse, I return to two of the book's key themes: the significance of culture in determining the nature of childhood, and the tension between adult-generated conceptions of childhood and the variable experiences of children. Let us deal with childhood and culture first. The various child-related problems referred to in this chapter are based on a simple underlying principle, that children are physically and morally weak and vulnerable and that unregulated exposure to the adult world of sex, the street and work damages them. If we dig a little deeper we find a fixed and quite static view of childhood based on biological and psychological inferiority. I have discussed this in some detail in Chapter 1. What I want to say here is that the linking of biology to culture produces an incredibly powerful conception of childhood. It is nevertheless just that: a conception of childhood, a set of common understandings that derive from a particular culture. I propose that by separating the biological from the conceptual or, in Archard's (1993) terms, the 'concept' of childhood from 'conceptions' of childhood, we open up the possibility for viewing children differently. In this way we can take account of culture and the different, often conflicting sets of circumstances within which we find 'problem' children. By also prising children from their biological and developmental roots, we can start to understand how childhood has not simply disappeared but has changed over time. In foregrounding the cultural significance of childhood we are saying that children are in and of the social world, part of the broader pattern of social change.

The second related theme is that a Western conception of childhood has been dominant for so long partly because adults have resisted the notion that children themselves are social agents and thus unlikely to play a significant role in conception-building. To assume that childhood is an essential feature of culture based on biological and psychological inferiority is to make it well-nigh impossible for children to be taken seriously in their own terms. Children are locked into a situation that excludes them from making claims to competence or attempting to change this situation. Thus children who demonstrate competence outside of what we might call developmental or educational paradigms (see Chapter 6 for more detail) are precocious or overdeveloped. Children who challenge rules or laws are delinquent and troublesome. Children who assume a different position within the generational hierarchy are a social and moral threat. Children here are deviant and need to be brought back into line through protection, correction or education. There are clearly some interesting changes taking place that provide space and fresh opportunities for children to demonstrate competence. I shall discuss these in later chapters. For the moment I contend that the 'crisis of childhood' is still a potent social and moral reference point for the mobilisation of forces that seek to bring children back into line. What it is does not allow for is the possibility that these 'lines' or boundaries can be legitimately contested as we both move away from the biological basis to childhood and broaden our understanding of the different roles that children play.

I discussed globalisation in Chapter 3. I want to pick up on the way the term has been used here. The 'global' seems to assume a degree of universalism, or at least implies attempts to universalise a Western model of the 'welfare' child. A second usage of 'global' is to take a much broader view of children and childhood that allows us to pick up on more culturally distinct, localised practices of children. It is this second meaning that informs our analysis. Taking a global view here allows us to appreciate the different ways that children contribute to their social environments.

Returning to the constructed nature of childhood, I take the point made by Hendrick (1997, p. 34) that childhood is normally 'composed by adults, usually those of the professional middle class'. At the same time, researchers within the sociology of childhood are starting to talk about children as 'co-constructors', or as having some involvement in the process of conception-building (Christensen and James 2000). At the very least this means taking seriously what children say and do in social settings. What I want to do now is to look at two cases for 'co-construction', child soldiers and child carers. Both can easily be used to strengthen the idea of crisis, as they are both taken as social and, in the former case, growing global problems. But both can also be viewed more positively in terms of children occupying different social spaces with a degree of courage and self-control.

Case Study 1 – Child Soldiers

In a recent paper Hanne Beirens (2001) argues that conceptions of child soldiers reflect the view that children are quintessentially vulnerable and incompetent. It might be useful to explore this argument a little further for here we have a clear example of children being 'out of place', children who do not conform to the dominant Western conception of childhood. The placing of 'child' next to 'soldier' is commonly counter-intuitive, depicting the child in a clearly defined 'adult' role, one that exhibits all the features of the social world that marks adults off from children.

Recent global estimates suggest that around 300,000 children from 41 countries are involved in armed conflict, with between 9 per cent and 22 per cent of the combatants in some conflicts under the age of 18 (Brett and McCallin 1998, p. 30). In one sense, children's 'childish' natures make them an ideal target for recruitment. In some cases, children are recruited because they are seen to be more obedient and easier to exploit than adults. As one young recruit involved in the Mozambican civil war stated, 'RENAMO (resistance force) does not use many adults to fight because they are not good fighters ... kids have more stamina, are better at surviving in the bush, do not complain, follow directions' (cited in Goodwin-Gill and Cohn 1994, p. 26). Some have gone further and asserted that children are far more brutal than adults, more willing to commit atrocities. Boyden (2003) refers to the example of the Cambodian war, where the Khmer Rouge often put young combatants in charge of groups of civilians because they were more likely to follow the orders of military command to the letter and less likely to suffer any remorse for their actions.

However, several factors are cited behind a dramatic increase in the numbers of child soldiers. First, children are more likely now to be drawn on as a 'reserve army' owing to an increase in armed conflict and a shortage of adult recruits (Harvey 2000). This is accentuated in some countries where the majority of the population are under the age of 18. Secondly, in the post-Second-World-War period armed conflict has been internal or civil, that is, between an incumbent government's army and internal opposition force or forces rather than between two sovereign states. The implications for the greater involvement of children is twofold. The development of civil war makes it more difficult clearly to distinguish between the military and civilian populations. Families and communities are more likely to be involved as both victims and perpetrators, and children are more likely to be involved in a number of roles as combatants. Thus children may find themselves on the front line. They may also be used in a number of ancillary military roles as messengers and spies. The increase in civil war also means that children can be more easily recruited, with oppositional forces less likely effectively to regulate recruitment, making it easier for both conscripted and voluntary recruits to be accepted under the age of 18 (Brett and McCallin 1998). Thirdly, access to a wider range of cheaper, smaller hand weapons has made it easier for children to play a role on the front line (Boyden 2003).

Interestingly, there is no clear-cut, unified image of the child soldier. In some cases they are victims, in other cases they are offenders. The conventional Western interpretation is of children being forced to become combatants or at least exploited by powerful adult groups to take up arms. In these terms child soldiers are usually seen as victims of circumstances. However, there is a tendency to demonise child soldiers within many of the combatant countries. Children serving in the Sierra Leone rebel army, for example, are portrayed as 'criminals and bandits with no political purpose' (Beirens 2001, p. 13). Boyden (2003) refers to the way that child soldiers in Uganda were imputed to be 'contaminated' by demonic forces, generating fear of former child soldiers from within their communities.

Rather like the conflicting images of childhood generated by the Bulger crime and the street child, child soldiers induce feelings of condemnation as well as pity. What is striking about this conceptualisation of childhood is its limited 'Euro-American' appeal. Again I come back to a limited model of childhood that locates children in time and space as social, moral and emotional incompetents. This construction of childhood, as I argued earlier, generates, first of all, protectionist impulses and, secondly, ideas that locate children within a constraining developmental frame. The traumatic effects of war on both adults and children are well documented. In the latter case, the effects are foregrounded. The significant additional factor here, children's imputed incompetence, means that the effects of war are more striking, more long-term, more indelible. War and conflict seem to accentuate children's vulnerability in terms of their physical and emotional inability to withstand the pressures. Children's involvement in war also highlights either the temporary withdrawal of normal social relations or the abandonment of moral and social commitment. In both cases there is a presumed lack of socialisation, with the adult/child boundary subsiding, producing children with a limited grasp of social values leading to later aggression and criminality.

It is difficult to think in terms of agency here. Many children are press-ganged into becoming combatants. Others become soldiers as a means of escaping poverty. One newspaper article reporting on the civil war in Congo claimed:

> It is one thing to pull children out of the army, quite another to keep them out. Many join up to escape the poverty in a country ravaged by war: at least four boys have passed through the demob centre twice . . . The only people guaranteed not to starve in Congo are those with guns. (Astill 2001, p. 25)

But, as with the adult population, there is little sense in which children freely choose to go to war. Brett and McCallin (1998) also refer to children in conflict situations being press-ganged into taking up arms. Nevertheless, research suggests that not all children automatically suffer similarly from the experiences of war, with some taking a degree of control over the situations in which they find themselves. The context within which children become involved in armed conflict is significant. Bettelheim (cited in Garbarino, Kostelny and Dubrow 1991, pp. 23–4), in his work on life in Nazi concentration camps, comments that child 'victims' of war with ideological and religious convictions were often able to insulate themselves from some of the negative effects of war. Punamaki (1996) concludes that child soldiers with a strong political commitment to nation or community are less likely to feel traumatised than those children suddenly confronted by war. As with many adult combatants, children are motivated by the particular set of ideas that pull a country or community into armed struggle. Prospective child soldiers are rarely shielded from problems that a civilian population faces, such as arbitrary arrests and beatings, rape and restrictions of movement. Many are driven by a sense of injustice sometimes allied to strong ideological commitments. Thus many children were at the forefront of the struggle against apartheid in South Africa in the 1980s. Beirens (2001) adds that children here saw themselves as having a responsibility towards their people and communities to fight inequality.

As with other child-related issues, the problem with our understanding of child soldiers lies in the absence of accounts from the child soldiers themselves. Research with child soldiers demonstrates their ability to account for their involvement in reasonable terms, in terms that go beyond the rather simplistic 'child as victim' narrative. Beirens (2001) cites the case of Mozambiquan girls joining the fight against the colonial authorities and thus escaping the restricted lives that are mapped out for them in their villages:

> Upon joining the Destacamento Feminino, many told me, they delighted in the fact that their lives would not be limited to tending agricultural fields, carrying water, cooking and caring for children. Life as a DF would give them greater range of movement across social and geographical landscapes. (Beirens 2001, pp. 13–14)

The post-conflict period brings a range of problems around children's reintegration into peaceful society. Again there are tensions between what children should be doing and children's own conceptions of their social situations. The need for international organisations to impose a model that revolves around dependence, play and individual development does not satisfactorily address questions of 'normality' where children may play a more prominent role within the family or community. At the same time, where children have joined the army to escape poverty or family break-down, a return to a pre-conflict situation within the community does nothing to change the conditions that pushed them into the army. Brett and McCallin (1998) argue for a twin-track approach: first, the underlying reasons for children's involvement in war must be addressed; secondly, localised rather than Western concerns must dictate the form that this reintegration takes.

The post-conflict period also poses problems for the treatment of children suspected of war crimes. The civil conflict in Sierra Leone was prominent for its use of child soldiers, some as young as eight years old. In the post-war period the UN set up a commission to try and bring those responsible for war crimes to court. One dilemma they faced was whether to prosecute an estimated three thousand child soldiers accused of committing some of the worst atrocities. In the end it was felt that children could not be held responsible for their actions, with the UN favouring rehabilitation for child soldiers (Wilson 2002). According to Wilson, the tension here is between the international community's attempts to impose a Western solution on the problem – favouring a Western welfarist construction of childhood over an African conception that emphasises the individual responsibilities of the child soldiers.

Case Study 2 – Child Carers

This second illustration of reconstruction focuses again on children's involvement within the adult world, this time in the 'working' role as carers. There are some interesting links with the child-soldier theme, with children's experiences of war sometimes involving them having to replace a parent and take on the role of caring for younger siblings. For example, one of the consequences of the genocide in Rwanda in the mid-1990s is the phenomenon of the child-headed family, with children having to take the place of a murdered parent (Mann and Ledward 2000). As with the child soldier, these new roles for children are not seen as legitimate because they do not fit the Western conception of childhood. Consequently, they tend to be ignored by AID agencies, which ironically makes the child–parents even more vulnerable.

Child carers of a less dramatic sort can be found in more politically stable contexts. Becker, Dearden and Aldridge (2001, p. 75) have written widely on this issue, taking the line that young carers in the UK suffer developmentally and educationally as a result of having to look after a sick relative, particularly those who take on 'substantial or regular care'. For the purposes of this chapter I want to concentrate on the possibilities for conceptualising childhood in terms of their competence as carers. Recent research from various European contexts highlights the significance of children's domestic responsibilities (Morrow 1994; Solberg 1997). Nevertheless, caring is something that children are commonly thought to learn about in the home, it is not something normally attributed to them as a set of roles or responsibilities.[3] In the West we think primarily in terms of 'child care' rather than 'child carers'. As I argued earlier, placing the child in the home and school as dependent social apprentices strengthens the integrity of concepts such as childhood innocence and dependence (Moss and Petrie 2002, p. 84).

The juxtaposition of 'child' and 'carer' is not just a problem in terms of the 'generational' status of the carer. The term 'carer' itself conjures up the 'natural', personal attributes of individuals. Caring for some is not a profession or a job or a set of public responsibilities. Sociologists have been concerned to highlight the hidden privatised nature of caring within the home (Barrett and McIntosh 1982). As with more long-standing debates around women's hidden domestic responsibilities, the care of spouses, children and wider kin has largely been defined as a labour of love, work that is done for abstract principles rather than monetary gain or professional status. Sociologists have equated domestic work with paid employment in an attempt to bring into the public domain the way that women can be exploited by spouses, employers and the state (Harris 1983). Children's work within the home, as with that of women, is not formally recognised because of its privatised nature. Nevertheless, the expectation is that the *adult* female within the family has domestic responsibilities. The child carers' dependent status as children, on the other hand, compounds their invisibility. This makes it difficult to think of others depending on them and rules them out from making claims on the state.

As with the child soldiers, we have very rough estimates of the numbers of child carers. Two factors obscure any accuracy: the privatised nature of the work and the fact that children and their parents will often conceal their roles as carers. The second point is worth exploring. The reversal of the carer/cared-for relationship poses all sorts of problems for both parents and children, not least the perception of the child carer that any attempt to make a claim for support will result in them being taken into care (Becker, Aldridge and Dearden 1998, p. 64). While the child may be perfectly capable of looking after a sick parent, the counter-intuitive nature of the idea of 'child carer' generates anxieties among both parents and children as to how exactly the state is likely to view their domestic situation.

According to what is known to researchers, there are between 19,000 and 51,000 child carers in the UK. Carers have an average age of 12, with more than half living in lone-parent families (Becker, Dearden and Aldridge 2001). Most of them are caring for someone with a physical disability or illness, but significant minorities are working with kin with mental health problems and learning difficulties. Care ranges from the general to the more intimate. In the latter case around 20 per cent of young carers have toileting and bathing responsibilities.

As with the child soldiers, the young carers' 'adult' responsibilities are a consequence of poverty and lack of choice. These circumstances are maintained because of the inadequate treatment of both recipient and carer. In particular, the latter have little access to benefits and rights, their caring skills are not recognised by any vocational accreditation scheme, and schools tend not to recognise carers as having special education needs. (Dearden and Becker 2000). Moreover, the invisibility of the young carer is reinforced in the way that any formal and informal support is aimed at the recipients rather than the carer. Carers often come to the attention of agencies for more punitive reasons. In Aldridge and Becker's (1993) study, Jimmy, aged 16, had been looking after his father 24 hours a day. He had been given a social worker because of his lack of attendance at school: 'When they did find out I was looking after him and that he had a brain tumour, social workers didn't really do much about it. Then I was taken to court and threatened to be put into care' (Jimmy, aged 16). Whilst we need to highlight the limited opportunities for child carers and their families, it is also important to identify the ways in which child carers adjust to these circumstances. In Aldridge and Becker's (1993) study of 15 carers in Nottingham, the carers had adjusted to some very difficult, often embarrassing circumstances. Fifteen-year-old Sarah, who had been caring for her mother who had multiple sclerosis, had the added complication that her older sibling took no responsibility for their mother's care:

> After a while I just got used to showering my mum. Just one more thing you've got to do. I was embarrassed when she first asked me and for a bit I thought, you know, Tessa's older [sister], why didn't she ask her, but I just I said all right then. You've got to help out. (Sarah, aged 15)

The recipients of care were ambivalent about their carers' status. The various domestic responsibilities of the young carers were seen as central to the maintenance of family life. And young carers' knowledge and skills were a taken-for-granted part of what Morgan (1996) calls 'family practices'. As with the young carers themselves, parents sometimes affirmed their children's responsibilities as primary-care-givers as rights over and above any perceived intrusions from the outside.

Whilst parents were quite protective of their children's responsibilities, there was also an awareness of some of the problems that their young carers were facing (Walker 1996, p. 10): 'Because she felt there weren't many of her peers with a parent with a life-threatening illness, she felt quite isolated and worried' (disabled mother of Helen, aged 17). From the same study there were other recipients who referred to a reversal of parenting roles: 'Sometimes I feel that I am dependent on them and I feel they should be dependent on me. I think it's all topsy-turvy, not how it should be' (disabled mother of Christine, aged 16). The Nottingham study picked up on the loyalty the carers felt towards their parents, with none of the 15 carers wanting a social worker. There was also a sense in which they felt that the caring skills, which they had developed, often over a period of some years, were not recognised:

> I will sit there and they will ask me questions and everything and talk to me like I'm a kid – at that point I wasn't a child because I was doing exactly the same things as they were at home, you know what I mean, like when they went home they was putting the dinner on and I was, and they made me really mad because they used to talk to me like I was a child and I used to feel like getting up and saying, 'Don't talk to me like that!' (Debra, who had been caring for her mother since she was 13)

There are important parallels with the plight of street children here. As I argued earlier, state intervention has often been a rather blunt instrument in supporting street children who are significant contributors to their respective domestic economies. The same can be said for child carers. Whilst it would be wrong to caricature the social services as intent on labelling families with child carers as dysfunctional, there is a perception that children with primary caring responsibilities require considerable state support, which threatens the relationship that the child carer has with the parent.

The anxieties here revolve around two issues: Aldridge and Becker (1993, p. 39) refer to a need for both carers and recipients to 'create an aversion' to any authority figure who could potentially threaten the caring routines that have been established. Whilst this might be seen as a psychological mechanism leading unintentionally to the ghettoising of child-carer families, the researchers also refer to a social reality whereby social workers often err on the side of breaking up families. Carers and recipients are concerned that any fine distinctions made between intervention and help might be overridden by agencies in attempts to 'rescue' children.

There were more positive views expressed towards formal support in the study conducted by Walker (1996), with around half of the sample of 29 carers expressing a desire for support from outside agencies. Yet this stopped well short of them wanting to give up their roles. Money, time and the relevant knowledge were needed to make life easier for them as carers. Giving up their caring was not seen as an option. As illustrated earlier by Debra, many of the families had a difficult relationship with the social services. Some carers simply needed more practical support: 'Instead of sending me a load of letters . . . I wish someone would come out and see me, come and help fill in the forms there and then' (disabled father of Joan, aged 12).

As I stated earlier, our knowledge of child soldiers and child carers is still very limited. Yet these children are a very small minority of the child population. We cannot be certain that broader global or national social trends are intimately connected with a rise in the numbers of children occupying these 'adult' spaces. As with many 'new' child-related phenomena, armed conflict and family responsibilities are contexts within which children have participated for centuries (Aldridge and Becker 1993). As our mechanisms for monitoring and regulating children's welfare have become more sophisticated, so we are gradually becoming aware of these different child-related contexts. Both these phenomena have been much more widely publicised in the past few years as child welfare has become a global and national priority. However, I want to speculate briefly on possible relationships between recent social change and the case of child carers. That is, in spite of our heightened awareness of these child phenomena, we may also be witnessing a rise in the numbers of children with adult-type responsibilities. In relation to family restructuring within the UK and USA, there is clearly a shift away from the nuclear family as the sole moral and social frame of reference for child-rearing. The trebling of the numbers of lone-parent families in the UK since the mid-1970s now means that they account for a quarter of all families with dependent children (Social Trends 2000). Out of necessity, children within this kind of family play more prominent domestic roles.

I referred earlier to research that suggested that around half of child carers were from lone-parent families. If we take these two social phenomena together, then we can see the child carer in less negative terms. Within the childhood-in-crisis framework, children are incapable of taking on these roles. Moreover, the notion of children as responsible domestic agents undermines childhood innocence. An alternative reading of child carers within lone-parent families is that they are more formative, more able to adapt to their given social circumstances. As we saw in Chapter 3, the children of separated and divorced parents demonstrate a degree of resilience. One possible outcome of this resilience is a greater ability to adapt to a one-parent household and take more responsibility for household tasks. Questions of vulnerability need to be set against the coping strategies utilised by children, in many cases out of necessity. Children demonstrate their social competence because they often have to.

Conclusion

Undoubtedly the case studies referred to in the second half of the chapter are significant additions to the catalogue of problems which children constantly face. In one sense they broaden and deepen the crisis that societies appear to be facing over the position of children. Yet I have argued that the retention of a well-established but narrowly conceived framework through which we view children filters out other ways of thinking about children and childhood. I argue that the crisis theme presupposes a universal and 'naturalised' view of the child. I have set out this crisis at both national and global levels. As I shall argue in Chapter 10, the United Nations Convention on the Rights of the Child was drafted as a statement on the condition of the world's children. For the most part this was a legal and political response to the perceived problems facing children in a variety of distinct cultural contexts. But by implication this was also a legal document that restated and reaffirmed a particular conception of childhood, a conception sometimes at odds with children's experiences. I will come back to this. At this stage I simply want to signal the importance attached to the crisis of childhood at global as well as national levels and the mobilisation of governmental and, to a lesser extent, non-governmental responses around a Western conception of childhood.

Paradoxically, the salience of the discourse around childhood is matched by the invisibility of children themselves in terms of their social status. Children are dominated by adults in terms of agenda-setting, in terms of social expectations and in relation to conceptions of social action. Whilst there is lots of talk about children and childhood, until relatively recently very little dialogue has taken place with children. In relation to the crisis theme, childhood has become a key issue in public debate, largely owing to the fact that children's position as provisional, semi-social, 'silent' beings can no longer be taken for granted. The problems of children out of place – on the street and on the web – are viewed as children shifting from their marginal social positions towards the public realm occupied by adults.

I argue that children can and do occupy different social positions. I also contend that a careful examination of these variable positions and the accounts that children give reveal a complex pattern of social relations, commitments and social competence. It is with this in mind that I draw on the cases of child soldiers and child carers. My purpose in drawing on child soldiers is not to reject the growing international lobby to outlaw children involved in armed conflict.[4] Nor am I trying to underestimate the economic and social problems that child carers face. What we are doing is questioning some of the assumptions built into the idea that the 'child carer' along with the 'child soldier' is a contradiction in terms (Beirens 2001). We are suggesting that children have a degree of agency in these situations. Children are acting with others, making and taking decisions, and demonstrating commitments and responsibilities that at the very least confound a 'care and control' model of childhood.

5

Children, Family and the State: Policing Childhood

Introduction

The previous chapter identified public and sociological commentary on a perceived crisis of childhood. I examined this in terms of the idea that children are structurally in the wrong place, that is, children cannot now be quite so easily positioned as generational inferiors or social apprentices. There is undoubtedly an element of romanticism here, with commentators invoking a golden period of social and moral tranquility (Foley, Roche and Tucker 2001, p. 1). Tackling the current crisis for some thus amounts to rescuing childhood, with political and social forces deployed to restore the correct balance of 'care and control' within homes and schools. In this chapter I draw on two interrelated recent child problems, child abuse and child crime, in addressing institutional and political responses to the perceived crisis. Whilst issues of care and control are ultimately bound up with the moral integrity of childhood, I will argue that the political realm has a more complex relationship with children and their families.

In the first section I set out this relationship in terms of the state and other 'external' agencies being instrumental in shaping modern family relations and the social positions of children. Whilst we conventionally associate family as a sphere of social action separate from the activities we associate with the public realm of politics and policy, I will argue that state and family are intimately connected in the process of what we call the privatising of childhood. Whilst we accentuate the complexity of relations between child, family and state, political cultures, at least in Western, English-speaking countries, tend to separate family from state as competing realms of child support. In this section I draw on the problem of child abuse in highlighting this separateness. I will examine recent policy innovations that attempt to restructure a public system of child care and at the same time find a balance between the proprietorial interests of the family and the collective interests of the state.

In the third section I stay with the problem of child abuse but move away from a predominantly child-care or welfare context and examine the involvement of the criminal justice system. Concentrating more on practice than principle, I will examine the extent to which child protection is irrevocably associated with notions of legal and criminal responsibility. I argue in this chapter that relations between family and state have developed in such a way that issues of abuse, neglect and delinquency are inextricably linked. In sections two and three I concentrate on child abuse. In the final section I address delinquency alongside abuse as social problems that generate possibilities for viewing children as competent social actors. Systems of child protection and welfare have tended to subsume children within the family. However, I also contend that children in their own terms have become more central in considerations over their care and development.

The Privatisation of Childhood

In the previous chapter I argued that locating children within family effectively excludes them from what we might call the public sphere. Children's natural and primary social environment is family, commonly seen as the personal and private sphere. According to this way of thinking, the realm of politics and economics resides 'outside' in the public sphere. The family acts as an 'incubator' for the public sphere, with children dependent on their parents for physical, emotional and moral support (Roche 1992, p. 94). These dependency relations are supposed to provide children with moral and social stability, which in turn propel them out into the wider society at an appropriate time as moral and purposeful citizens. Childcare, then, is best undertaken within a relatively detached and privatised environment where parents have a degree of autonomy. In effect, what we are saying is that we tend to attach a great deal of importance to child care and parenting because it is perceived to be a supremely personal and private bundle of responsibilities.

What we are thinking about here is a separate-spheres model of childhood. Children incrementally move into the public sphere as they head towards adulthood. This public/private framework has acquired a degree of social and historical invariance within social scientific thought (Cheal 1991). However, various authors have re-examined this dichotomy, arguing for a more constructed notion of the private realm. Moreover, if we think of 'childhood' in terms of its historical and cultural roots, the shaping of family both parallels and is implicated in the construction of childhood. Hendrick (1997), for example, refers to the way that from around the middle of the nineteenth century in England, the concept of childhood developed as children were progressively removed from the street and workplace. Children's gradual prominence within a domesticated and 'psychologised' family was accompanied by ideas of responsibility for children's moral and social development. Out of this developed tensions around the 'ownership' of the child with notions of parental responsibility strengthening the idea of both the particular interests of parents and the general and collective interests of the state for the wellbeing of children as a future generation (Dingwall, Eekelaar and Murray 1995, p. 220).

Donzelot (1979, p. x), from a French perspective, talks about modern conceptions of childhood arising out of a social, moral and legal space known as 'the social', a 'hybrid domain' made up of governmental and non-governmental sectors. He argues along similar lines to Hendrick that a range of economic, political and moral forces converged on mothers and their children to produce childhood as a period of prolonged seclusion from the adult world of politics, employment and responsibility. Donzelot emphasises the disciplinary role of mothers in nineteenth-century France. Welfare professionals from the state and the voluntary sector worked with the bourgeois mother in helping to provide her children with a degree of 'protected liberation'. Mothers here became the means through which new ideas about psychosocial development were tested out. The assumption here was that children's autonomy would be best nurtured through 'discreet (maternal) observation' (p. 47). Donzelot offers a subtle shift in emphasis when discussing the position of working-class mothers and their children. Given the public concerns over delinquency and street crime throughout the nineteenth century, mothers' responsibilities here were to be more physical and overtly controlling: surveillance of their children's whereabouts produced a degree of 'supervised freedom' (p. 46).

A myriad of external supports from the school, the media and the health profession created the family as an inner sanctum by positioning woman as domestic responsible agents. Rose (1992) makes the same point in outlining the way that models of the 'delinquent' child and the 'neglected' child are presented to parents as part of a loose causal chain that strengthens notions of care and control within the family. Perfidy and wickedness were replaced by neglect as the professional and commonsensical grounds for assessing children's delinquency. As Harris astutely observes, 'one of the characteristics of twentieth-century family culture is that, whereas in the past a bad child was seen as a misfortune and the parent deserving sympathy, it now symbolises a character defect on the part of the parent' (Harris 1983, p. 240). Delinquency started to be viewed as a problem with its roots within the family. What were seen as natural bonds of love and affection between mother and child were also likely to be seen as an insurance against criminality. In the twentieth century mother/child relations were dominated by the 'psy' complex and the rise of consumerism (Donzelot 1979). The new psychological professions worked on the assumption that early mother/child relations were natural, with mothers laying down the child's psychic structures through physical bonding or attachments. At the same time, images of the nuclear family began to dominate advertising through the mass media presenting women as domestic, autonomous agents responsible for the development of children. Domesticity was a pivotal feature of the nuclear family, which became a dominant and idealised reference point for child-rearing. Childhood was thus gradually constructed as a private terrain within which close intimate relations organised by the mother underpinned children's lives and served as a basis for their future moral and social careers in adulthood. In effect, cultural and historical forces privatised childhood.

Privatisation in these terms presents us with a paradox: 'external' forces in the shape of state agencies, voluntary bodies and developments within the social sciences drew a perimeter around the nuclear family. The family was to be an emotionally and economically self-sufficient unit relying heavily on the mother as a moral and domestic focal point. Children were contained within the family. Yet this notion of privacy was contingent on external forces. The state does not simply act as a backdrop to the private business of child-rearing. Ideas of privacy need to be introduced and reinforced. As the twentieth century progressed, mothers had to be seen to be developing their children's futures appropriately. The state thus performs a significant policing role, intervening where there are problems. In these terms it is not whether the state disrupts the 'natural' flow of emotional resources or undermines the authority of parents. As state agencies grow and as we become more knowledgeable about family and child affairs, child professionals accumulate more responsibility for maintaining family relations. The latter point is clearer when we look at notions of family privacy from the professional and institutional perspective, and here we diverge from the idea of the public shaping the private. The aspects of the state and voluntary sector that impinge on family life are more and more dependent on the integrity of the private nuclear family. The issue cannot be couched in terms of the 'public' clashing with the 'private' but of both realms presupposing each other (Asquith 1996). Thus public institutions with an interest in children have a significant impact on relations within families and the dominant ways for thinking about family and childhood. At the same time, any notion of state-building and policy-formation is also a response to changing conceptions of family and childhood.

Modern Protectionist Strategies: The Problem of Child Abuse

In this section I set out one of the key social problems of the late twentieth and early twenty-first centuries: the failure of the state to provide a secure and clearly structured system of child protection. A series of high-profile cases of abuse in the 1970s and 1980s brought to the fore the inadequacies of the existing system of child protection, as well as highlighting the dominance of the 'private' nature of family life. There had been earlier periods in Britain and North America when child-protection issues were brought to public attention. By 1880, 33 Societies for the Prevention of Cruelty to Children (SPCC) had been set up across the USA. At about the same time in the UK, charities such as Barnardo's and the Royal Society for the Prevention of Cruelty to Children (RSPCC) were formed in response to perceived problems within working-class families (Parton 1985; Gordon 1985). Yet by the end of the first decade of the twentieth century these concerns over child protection had died down. The presumption from then until the post-Second-World-War period was very much in favour of the private nuclear family and the proprietorial interests of parents. The development of the welfare state during this period revolved around health, education and social insurance; child-care issues were linked to the problems of crime and delinquency rather than any notion of child protection.

The origins of the present problems with the child-protection system in the UK and the USA can be traced back to the work of the medical professions in the USA in the 1950s and 1960s. Parton (1985), for example, points to the way that paediatric radiologists came across injuries to children that could not easily be explained as accidents. Researchers and practitioners within this field started to think of these injuries as instances of physical abuse, attributing a range of social and medical conditions to the offending parents. The naming of the problem 'baby-battering syndrome' in the USA during this period was an important moment in opening up families to public scrutiny: it provided child professionals, politicians and moral entrepreneurs with a highly emotive label through which the abuse of children by their parents could be articulated as a national social problem. Yet, as Parton argues, the idea of a syndrome helped to steer attention away from the 'agency' of parents, implying a form of medical or social pathology. Within the context of a more benign relationship between the individual and the state, parents who abused their children were to be treated and families were to be held together wherever possible. During this period there was a more benevolent relationship between family and state, with the latter playing a supportive role in situations where parents were having difficulties (Parton 1985). Dingwall, Eekelaar and Murray (1995) talk in terms of the 'rule of optimism': welfare professionals in the majority of cases erring on the side of the parent, subject to a number of conditions being met where there are allegations of abuse. In broader political terms, abuse is defined within what has been termed a 'welfarist' paradigm.

It was a decade or so before the battered-baby syndrome was recognised in the UK, with the Baby Battering Research Unit being set up by the

NSPCC in the late 1960s. And it was not until the Maria Colwell case in 1973 and the subsequent report the following year that the British government and the media became involved. Maria Colwell, a 7-year-old English girl, was killed by her stepfather who was subsequently convicted of her manslaughter and sent to prison for eight years. The media furore that followed the murder and the enquiry a year later concentrated on alleged lapses within the child-protection system that allowed Maria Colwell to be abused. Particular emphasis was placed on the social services for taking Maria away from her 'loving' foster parents with whom she had spent most of her life and placing her with her birth mother and stepfather who were characterised as feckless and dangerous (Parton 1985). Much was also made of the knowledge that the social workers had of Maria's circumstances immediately prior to Maria's death, and the concerns expressed by neighbours and teachers, which apparently went unheeded by the social services. In effect, the social services were blamed for Maria's death.

Whilst notions of professional neglect and 'under-intervention' dominated the Colwell case and others that followed, from the late 1980s onwards the debate on child protection focused more on how the state was seen to be overpowerful and 'over-interventionist'. Events in Cleveland and Rochdale in England and in Orkney in Scotland in the mid-1980s concentrated on the ways that the police, social services and medical profession were able to make professional judgements on clusters of families, resulting in children being separated from their parents and placed in institutional care. The problem here was heightened by a shift in concern from physical abuse and neglect to child sexual abuse. One of the great social taboos, incest, had resurfaced as a national problem.[1] The role of the media was important here, with two national television channels publicising child sexual abuse in 1986 and instigating national surveys on the subject (La Fontaine 1990). The Cleveland affair, a year later, seemed to crystallise the crisis in child care, with a group of parents being accused of sexually abusing their children and welfare professionals accused of professional arrogance.

From the late 1970s Britain's social democratic consensus broke down, with a shift towards a more antagonistic relationship between individual and state, a mixture of neoliberal thinking on the economy and a more conservative approach to cultural and political issues (Hall 1983). This meant that the liberal and potentially amoral elements of individualism generated through the discourse on the free market were obscured by conflating the 'individual' with the moral 'family' – producing rhetoric on the 'freeing' of families from the 'nanny state'. As with education in this period, child-protection issues were played out within this context, with child professionals, as in the Cleveland case, accused of acting in their own professional interests rather than those of their clients, the parents.

Within this political climate the press concentrated more on the power of the state. Headlines such as 'HAND OVER OUR CHILD' (*Daily Mail*, 23 June 1987) and 'OUR CHILDREN'S HELL IN THE HANDS OF DR HIGGS' (*News of the World*, 28 June 1987) illustrated the dominant view that social workers and medical practitioners had the power to 'break up' families.[2] The report that looked into the Cleveland affair the following year targeted overzealous professionals and the lack of inter-agency communication in cases of abuse, and reasserted the proprietorial rights of parents (Home Office 1988). In response to these problems, the 1989 England and Wales Children Act and the 1995 Children Act of Scotland were legislative attempts to provide clear lines of responsibility for parents, children and professionals in both public and private law (criminal and civil cases). In the case of the 1989 Act, Freeman (1992, p. 5) argues that this amounts to 'reconciling the 'irreconcilable', trying to manage the tensions between family and state. Two of the key features of the act attempt to deal with these tensions: the 'paramountcy' principle and the reassertion of parental responsibility.

Paramountcy

The Children Act states that the welfare of the child is the paramount consideration of parents and professionals. In theory, paramountcy can be equated with the 'best interests of the child' principle. Irrespective of the position of the child's family and the interests of individual parents, the child's future care is based on what is taken to be in the child's best interests. The principle separates the child from his or her 'natural' environment, becoming the dominant frame of reference when decisions are made regarding a child's care. In theory this opens up the possibility for children to be removed from their families if it is felt that their welfare is best ensured elsewhere. The act is also a departure from previous policy in that it moves beyond the competing adult parties bringing into focus a previously hidden third party, the child. I will come back to the implications paramountcy has for children's agency later.

Parental Responsibility

In turning to this second key feature of the act, I revisit the uneasy relationship between family and state. Parental responsibility is an ambiguous concept (Wyness 2000). It can be equated with rights or powers, parents having more space to manoeuvre in and against a minimal state. A presumption here is that children use their powers benevolently in discharging their responsibilities within the private nuclear family. Any movement from the outside in the form of intervention is argued to have a negative effect on the child's development (Goldstein, Freud and Solnit 1980). Parental responsibility can also mean something quite different. Responsibilities can be invoked to restrict parents' powers in that society delegates duties and obligations to parents to socialise their children. The presumption here is on parents to do right by their children, to discharge their responsibilities as duties as if they had been delegated to them by external sources. The external world and the state form a shadowy presence sometimes generating amorphous sets of social expectations, sometimes generating more specific notions of good or adequate parenting.

The Children Act reflects the ambiguous nature of parental responsibility. On the one hand, family is still seen as the most appropriate and effective child institution. For example, the presumption is still on the courts to justify a care order that would remove the child from the family and the latter is invoked as a natural 'child' institution set against the artificial arrangements put in place by the social services.[3] On the other hand, the act starts off by defining parental responsibilities with reference to 'all the rights, duties, power, responsibilities and authority which by law a parent of a child has in relation to the child and his property' (Part I, section 3). Responsibilities here are couched in terms of minimum requirements for meeting the child's needs. These requirements are unremitting as parents cannot be relieved of their responsibilities: 'responsibility . . . is never lost by parents even where it may seem that they have behaved without it' (Freeman 1992, p. 4). Moreover, these requirements or duties can be used by child professionals to monitor parents' future as well as current relations with their children. Another of the act's key phrases, 'likely significant harm', challenges the biological and natural basis to parenthood in that social workers can break the bond of permanency between parent and child. The social services have to be satisfied that the child's future integrity is secured within the family, that the parents are likely to discharge their obligations. Thus rather than concentrate on prior acts that constitute abuse, professionals are in a stronger position to assess the quality of future care arrangements for children within families. In these terms the idea of parental responsibility bears down on some parents as an imposition from the outside.

Child Protection and the Criminal Justice System

I have set out the Children Act in terms of two principles: children rather than families or parents as the main frame of reference for thinking and practice related to child support, and an emphasis on parental responsibility, which could be seen as shifting the balance of power from parents in favour of more co-operative relations between families and the state. In turning to the implementation of the act, I can address these principles by asking two questions: has the child's welfare become the central concern for child professionals? Do the same professionals offer a more supportive environment within which parents can carry out their caring responsibilities? In addressing these questions I argue that issues of welfare have become inextricably linked to issues of control.

A conventional reading of child/family/state affairs would map 'welfare' on to child care/child abuse issues, and 'control' on to issues relating to child criminality. However, things are not quite so simple. In the first instance, we have already seen how family acts to bring welfare and control issues together, supported by an external network that inextricably ties neglect to delinquency (Rose 1992). Secondly, as I have already argued, family/state relations have polarised. Benevolence gave way to conflict in the 1980s as the integrity of the individual and 'his' family was undermined by an overarching state bureaucracy.[4]

In the post-Children-Act period in England and Wales, child support has shifted from welfare to control (Parton 1996). 'Child welfare' has now become 'child protection', absorbed within the criminal justice system. Within a context of diminishing public resources, a breakdown of trust between welfare professionals and the general public, and a political culture that renders public services more accountable, social workers err on the side of pessimism when assessing a child's welfare. Parton refers to social workers as risk-assessors, who invoke 'likely significant harm' as a basis for identifying the child's future welfare. Thus the concepts of welfare and needs are calculated in terms of possible risks to the child from within the family. Alongside this the police and courts play a more central role in supporting this 'forensic' approach, whilst structuring explanations of child abuse in terms of criminal responsibility. Links are therefore more likely to be made between abuse and criminality. This is not simply confined to linking the adult abuser as criminal and the abused child as victim. To come back to Rose, the neglected child is likely to become, if not one already, a delinquent child. Researchers are sceptical of the 'inter-generational transmission' of sexual abuse. Nevertheless, theorising within professional circles seems to assume that adult abusers are more likely to have been abused in their childhoods (Saraga 1993). Whilst statistical correlations between the background and propensities of abusers hardly qualifies as a theory, it has acquired an almost 'paradigmatic' status in professional circles. In so far as there is some connection, what I want to argue in this section is that the complex relationship between welfare and control puts the child in an ambiguous position within the criminal justice system. The child here is both a victim and a potential offender.

An International Comparison

Parton, Thorpe and Wattan (1997) make links between the English/Welsh child-protection system and systems from other English-speaking countries such as Canada, the USA and parts of Australia. Whilst there are important differences in the legal systems in each of these countries, there appear to be similarities in the way that each child-protection system prioritises high-profile cases of abuse such as sexual and physical abuse at the expense of other forms of abuse such as neglect. One of the key findings from research commissioned by the British government, *Messages from Research* (DoH 1995), is that the criminalisation of child welfare has led to the targeting of abusers from 'extreme' cases rather than supporting parents having difficulties with their children. Child-protection systems in these other English-speaking countries are characterised as 'filters'; the majority of cases that come to the attention of the authorities are filtered out of the system as they progress from the initial point of entry to the later stages of children being registered 'at risk'. For example, in Western Australia a small minority of cases reported were substantiated as abused children (Parton, Thorpe and Wattan 1977, pp. 6–7). The stark 'message from the research' is that the majority of vulnerable children, those from 'environments low in warmth and high in criticism' ((DoH 1995, p. 19) are ignored, with approximately a seventh of all cases being fully processed. Sexual and physical abuse figure highly in this minority of cases. These are instances of abuse that are more likely to fit a criminalised model of perpetrator and victim than the more amorphous and legally ambiguous cases of neglect. Moreover, Parton (1996) refers to the way that certain types of family are more likely to be criminalised than others. Citing Denham and Thorpe's contribution *to Messages from Research* from their small sample of families, almost half (48 per cent) of reported cases of abuse involved lone-parent families.

In introducing a European dimension, the 'criminalised' or child-protection model competes with a dominant European 'family-support' model.[5] In various Northern and Western European countries, abuse is viewed much in the same way that it was viewed in the post-war period in Britain, as a symptom of a dysfunctional family. Pringle (1998), for example, discusses the Dutch and German systems where cases of abuse are referred to specialist medical teams. In the Dutch case, the assumption 'is that where abuse occurs, families need help rather than coercion if they are to change damaging modes of behaviour' (Armstrong and Hollows, cited in Pringle 1998, p. 161). The emphasis is on the non-punitive attention of the state on the whole family, rather than those directly involved in the abuse being treated for the problem. While there are differences between Northern and Southern European countries, there is still the same emphasis on support rather than intervention (Harder and Pringle 1997). In Italy, for instance, very little importance is attached to child abuse. In France state and family have joint responsibility for children. There are state-run centres for families which, unlike in the UK, do not carry a stigma for families involved. In general there are more optimistic and trusting relations between parents and child professionals.

Criticisms of both models revolve around their failure to protect children (Pringle 1998). In England very few cases are detected and, as we have seen, even fewer are fully processed through the system. The ones that are likely to come to the attention of the state are those families most economically vulnerable, those most vulnerable to processes of criminalisation. In Europe the focus is on the family rather than the abused child or perpetrator. This is grounded in two ways. First, the family-support approach draws on a family-systems theory. Unlike the child-protection model, abuse is explained as a symptom of systemic failure, with family viewed as a self-contained microsocial system. Thus sexual abuse is not differentiated from other forms of abuse; all problems relating to the care and control of children within family are viewed as indicators of family/systemic failure and the 'system' becomes the focus of the state's attention.

Secondly, unlike the English system, the family-support model is based on the principles of 'social solidarity' where there is a much weaker sense of the individual and his or her rights and responsibilities. The state plays a more integrative role through welfare payments and social support for families. There is also much less of a stigma attached to professional support for families and their children in most European countries than there is in England/Wales and the USA. To a much greater extent, the state is seen as more of an extension of family ties. I referred earlier to Donzelot's concept of 'the social' in France. Whilst the characterisation of state/family relations in terms of 'policing' leaves a much darker and more negative impression, social solidarity suggests more organic and productive relations between the individual, family and state.

If we compare this situation with that in England and Wales, whilst only a minority of cases are processed, child abuse, nevertheless, has a much higher political and public profile. The criminalisation of sexual abuse has sharpened our awareness of the problem. It is effectively now a national problem, with public child-care institutions being brought into the category of potentially dangerous sites for children.[6] In Europe, on the other hand, the problem is more diffuse. This diffusion means that there is much less concentration on children as individual victims. A less conflict-driven relationship between state and family and an emphasis on the principle of subsidiarity, the maintenance of problems at the local level, means that family and community are more likely to be regulated internally. Policy-makers in European states are less likely to think in terms of individuals including children having rights within families. Pringle argues that the cultural and theoretical bases to the system makes it less likely that individual cases of abuse will come to light.

Childhood, Agency and the State

There is a marked absence of any examination of underlying power relations in the family-support model of state support of children (Pringle 1998). This is because family relations are unlikely to be disaggregated in terms of conflict, leaving children with a weak sense of autonomy or rights. In turning to the child-protection model, the sharpening of relations between various actors involved in child-care proceedings has led to some re-evaluation of generational power at the 'micro' and 'macro' level. The discourse on child protection has rather ironically 'challenge[d] us to re-assess our own use of authority as parents, strangers, friends and teachers' (Kitzinger 1997, p. 177). In the following I want to examine this reassessment in terms of the position of children within the criminal justice and legal systems. In turning to one of the central themes of the book, the relationship between children, childhood and agency, we need to link policy and practice on child care and child crime, the latter discussed more substantively here, to developing notions of competence, consultation and children's voice.

We saw in the last chapter that child crime was one of the focal points within the crisis discourse. Children illegitimately enter the public realm as delinquents and child criminals. I also referred earlier in this chapter to the kinds of links that are made between delinquency and neglect. These have formed the basis of an alternative approach to child crime commonly referred to as the juvenile justice system. In the UK there has been little political or academic consensus on the treatment of delinquents. The debate has pitched justice models of juvenile crime against more liberal welfare models (Muncie 2004). In the former case, children are to be processed through the criminal justice system as if they were adults, with few concessions made to their age and with punishment, deterrence and due process taking precedence. In the latter case, children are defined as a separate legal category, with an emphasis on treatment and rehabilitation. The assumption here is that the younger the offenders are, the more impressionable they are and the more they are in need of forms of correction. The antecedents of this latter approach go back to the early part of the nineteenth century where attempts were made to discourage delinquents from a life of crime by restricting their time with adult offenders and providing alternative institutional arrangements for their reform.[7]

The debate has polarised issues of justice and welfare. At the same time, a third recurring theme throughout the last two centuries has been the attempt to balance the interests of justice with the needs of children and young people. Any attempt to find a compromise position has tended to concentrate on how justice can be administered locally through the family, what Donzelot (1979) calls 'government through the family'. If we set the issues of child crime and delinquency alongside child abuse, the overriding public problem is to tighten up mechanisms for the care and control of children, with a stronger accent on the latter. Commentary on the problems of children and childhood still has a tendency to focus on what should and should not be done to children. This lack of child agency is evident in criminal justice policy that targets parents as blameworthy. For example, the 1981 Criminal Justice Act and the 1998 Crime and Disorder Act of England and Wales specifically refer to parents' culpability in controlling their 'delinquent' children. The courts can bind the parents over for their children's misdemeanours. They can also be forced to undertake parenting classes, with the threat hanging over them of the local state taking over through the introduction of curfews (James and James 2001). At the same time, we can discern trends that place more emphasis on the position and disposition of children themselves processed through the criminal justice system as both victims and offenders. I want now to illustrate four ways in which the social problems of child crime and child abuse have generated conceptions of childhood in terms of agency.

Individual Responsibility

Notions of 'justice' generate models of children's criminal responsibilities. In a recent article, Goldson (2001) argues that the focus on parents and their responsibilities obscures the way that the criminal justice system generates notions of the 'responsibilised child', that is, child criminals are treated by the police and the courts as responsible agents. Whilst I have some reservations as to the extent to which children are targeted rather than their parents, this argument does generate conceptions of childhood that, at the very least, complicate an adult-oriented legal and criminal justice system. A starting point here is the age of criminal responsibility. With the exception of Scotland (8), England and Wales has the lowest age of criminal responsibility (10) within Europe (Muncie 2004).

Since the 1960s in the UK considerable pressure has been put on successive governments to raise the age of criminal responsibility. The 1969 Children and Young Person's Act, a key legislative moment for juvenile justice, sought to raise the age to 14. This was never implemented, partly because of an incoming Conservative government that wanted to retain a punitive element to juvenile justice, partly because of the 'youth as problem' theme discussed in the previous chapter, where young people were seen as a potential threat within the public realm. Yet countervailing pressures from within a welfare perspective persist, not least the recent recommendation from the United Nations that reinforces the paramountcy of the 'child's welfare' (Muncie 2004; Goldson 2001). The recent Crime and Disorder Act (1998) in the UK reinforces a punitive approach, drawing children both under and over the age of criminal responsibility within the system. Children under the age of ten are placed in 'at risk' categories through the introduction of curfews. Here we have a recurring historical trend that brings *prospective* juvenile delinquents within the criminal justice system.

The murder of James Bulger was an exceptional event. It was exceptional in the sense that it was an exception or aberration, with only 27 child murders by children recorded in the past two and a half centuries in England and Wales (Franklin and Petley 1996, p. 135). It was exceptional in the sense of being out of the ordinary, for James Bulger was murdered by two 10-year-old boys, barely old enough to take part in criminal proceedings. It was also exceptional owing to the amount of public commentary surrounding the case, particularly just after the two boys, Jon Venables and Robert Thompson, were convicted. Much of the controversy was over their treatment as child criminals. While the two boys have now been released, they spent much of their sentence in a special unit, where the emphasis was on rehabilitation and education. Much of the furore over their treatment centres on the way that the criminal justice system processed their cases in adult terms. The media carefully followed the progress of the case through an adult court where Venables and Thompson were felt to be competent enough to stand trial.

For many commentators, the 'responsibilising' of the two boys did not go far enough. The courts were perceived to be too lenient. This was the view of the Home Secretary, who intervened and increased their sentences from 10 to 15 years.[8] To some extent, the issue was one of just deserts. The feeling was that the two boys would serve their sentences in rehabilitative rather than punitive surroundings and that the boys would not pay for their wrongdoing. There was also a concern that they would serve out their time before they reached adulthood, thus lessening their sentence. 'Doing time' here does not mean the same thing for children as it does for adults. What we have here is an illustration of children's time not being seen as real time. The notion of childhood as a period of play, innocence and 'irresponsibility' cannot be equated with the way that adults' time is measured. Thus we can see the Home Secretary's intervention as a means of stretching their punishments into early adulthood and thus into the appropriate timeframe for serving their sentences. Effectively what he was saying was that children really only start to serve their sentences once they reach adulthood.

The Bulger situation has rather overshadowed other cases where children have been convicted of adult-type crimes. At about the same time as the Bulger trial, the Sexual Offences Act (1993) in England and Wales was passed, abolishing the presumption that boys under the age of 14 were incapable of intending to have sexual intercourse. The presumption in favour of younger boys being aware of their sexual capacities effectively draws 13-year-old boys into the category of rape. Following this legislation there have been several notable examples of children being processed through the system as rapists.[9] Thus legislation has been chipping away at the idea that children's welfare comes before any notion of justice. Paraphrasing Muncie (2004), youth justice seems to concentrate more on young people's 'deeds' than on their 'needs'.

It is difficult to think of the child as a social agent within the context of the criminalisation of children. The trend has been towards pathologising social problems, with individual families, parents and children viewed as culpable agents. Nevertheless, we can discern a limited notion of children's sociality and competence through the idea of individual responsibility. In some instances, children are being viewed as agents in terms of their capacity to know that they have broken a moral code and can accept a limited conception of 'just deserts'.

The Reliable Legal Witness

Up until now I have concentrated on negative notions of children being incorporated within the criminal justice system as offenders. A more positive conception of childhood agency can be found in the way that the legal system is starting to view children as reliable legal witnesses (Wyness 2000). In returning to the problem of abuse, one outcome of the process of criminalisation is the greater involvement of the legal system in searching for more effective ways to identify cases of abuse. This process of identification has been fraught with difficulty. First of all, I referred to the various political and cultural obstacles to detecting sexual abuse across Europe. We might add to this a more deep-rooted problem that affects all child-protection systems. That is, sexual abuse has to be seen as a 'family secret' (La Fontaine 1990). There is still no incontrovertible evidence as to the extent of sexual abuse in any given historical period or geographical area. There are also no clear-cut predictors as to where abuse is likely to take place and with whom. Nevertheless, researchers argue that abuse is more likely to take place in private than in public settings and an abused child is more likely to know the abuser.

In these terms, family has become more of a focus for making sense of abuse. However, the position of modern families within the social structure, the cultural norm of privacy and the power of the 'stranger-danger' theme discussed in the previous chapter make it difficult for us to know about cases of abuse. First of all, there are unlikely to be any witnesses to abusive incidents; potential allies to abused children are ambivalent about involving the state. I have already examined the subordinate position of children within families. This puts them on the defensive about coming forward and discussing any abuse with others outside of the family. Considerable physical, emotional and moral pressure can be put on the child to conceal the abuse from others. The secret nature of the abuse thus becomes a crucial obstacle within the criminal justice system. Few cases are likely to become public and any cases that are made have limited prospects, owing to lack of witnesses and evidence.

Secondly, Spencer and Flyn (1993) estimate that there is an average wait of 10.5 months between allegations of abuse being made and any subsequent court appearance. This lengthy judicial process gives ample opportunity for pressure to be put on child witnesses to retract allegations made. Thirdly, the child is commonly viewed as an unreliable and incompetent legal actor.[10] Theory and practice within the legal system have assumed that children do not have the psychological or moral resources to withstand the various pressures from the system. Child witnesses are thus unlikely to be in a position to give evidence. Where there is a likelihood of testimony, they have difficulty substantiating their claims of abuse.

Given the high political and public profile of child sexual abuse, demands made on professionals to deal with the problem, and the equally pressing case to protect children more effectively, the legal system has loosened its rigid definitions of evidence and due process. Children are now partially incorporated into the system. I argued earlier that very few children in vulnerable situations are brought fully within the child protection system in England and Wales. At the same time, the criminalising of the process has led to children being individualised, being seen as legal entities that need to be treated separately from their more organic family ties. In the government report commissioned after the Cleveland abuse cases, this 'separateness' was to be endorsed by professionals working with child witnesses whose accounts were to be taken seriously (DfSS 1988). The emphasis on children as 'human subjects rather than objects of concern' percolates through the legal system, influencing social work practice and court procedure. First of all, ideas of legal competence in theory are less pressing in cases involving children now. The Criminal Justice Acts of 1988 and 1991 both make it easier for judges to accept the child as a competent legal actor. Secondly, the 1991 Criminal Justice Act has made it easier for children to give evidence in court. Thus taped interviews between children and investigators recorded at an earlier stage in the proceedings can be used in court. Experiments with video link-ups, which were first used in Canada and the USA, are used in British courts in order that children can avoid appearing in court. Court officials can interrogate child witnesses via a television screen, with the child in a separate, adjoining room. There is an element of exceptionalism here as children are excused the full rigour of a court appearance. Nevertheless, there is a tendency to treat all sex cases in exceptional terms now, irrespective of the age of the victim (Spencer and Flyn 1993). More importantly, by producing the right conditions and the appropriate support from child professionals, children's accounts of traumatic events are more likely to be believed.

Correspondent in Child-Care Proceedings

As I mentioned earlier, the 1989 Children Act views the child as a third party in family/state affairs. The act covers private as well as public cases involving children. This includes divorce cases as well as cases of abuse. Whilst children's 'welfare' can be defined by adults in terms of a 'best interests' clause, one interpretation of the paramountcy principle is that children themselves are the best judges of their own welfare. Moreover, the act also states that considerations about the care of children have to take account of children's 'wishes and feelings' before decisions are taken which affect their relations with their parents and siblings (section 8). There is a degree of inclusion, with children being consulted through case conferences. There is also an elaborate system of checks and balances that position children as responsible agents. Emergency protection orders, the summary separation of children from their families, and medical examinations can be contested by children. Recent research suggests that adults still dictate the timing, the location and the agenda relating to encounters with children. Despite this, children are more routinely consulted on a range of issues relating to their care (Thomas 2001).

Finally, the notion of children's voice has a more literal meaning in the Children Act through the use of children's guardians (formerly known as guardian ad litems) who mediate between young children and the courts. These child professionals will relay to the court the interests and feelings of child clients, normally those very young clients who are not always in a position to speak for themselves. Other attempts to strengthen the voice of children being processed through the welfare system have followed. Among others, organisations such as the Children Society have been set up and children's rights officers have been introduced in some regions within the UK, offering advocacy services for children in care.

The Challenging Child Victim

Our first three models of agency develop out of changing state theory and practice. This last model to some extent challenges the adult structures of support. One of the dominant images running through the discourse of child abuse is the child as a passive and helpless victim in the face of attacks from an all-powerful adult abuser. Kitzinger's (1997) data from a group of adults recounting their abuse as children uncovered a range of strategies adopted by the 'children' in trying to fend off these attacks. These ranged from children trying to make themselves unappealing and unattractive to the abuser to developing strategies that limited the opportunities for abuse. These strategies were, for the most part, unable to stop the abuse. Nevertheless, Kitzinger (1997) demonstrates that far from being 'lifeless' and dependent victims, these children were active in blocking out the worst effects of the abuse.

The notion of the active child victim underlies attempts to give young children the resources to deal with any potential abusive advances. Programmes such as Kidscape in Britain and Right to Security in Holland are geared towards giving children knowledge and psychological skills (Elliott 1989; Taal and Edelaar 1997). In the USA child abuse prevention programmes have been set up, with around 60 per cent of children being affected. Whilst there are limits to the extent to which children can prevent abuse in practice (See Wyness 2000, pp. 68–73), a combination of teaching and role-play puts children in a more active role in being able to recognise sexual abuse and take some steps towards avoiding it.

Conclusion

Child abuse and child crime are issues that have complicated family/state relations. I have concentrated rather more on the former in setting out policy principles that aim to provide supportive links between families and child professionals. At the same time, political commentary on child abuse opens up children's relations within their families to more public scrutiny. In turn this has generated more ambiguous perceptions of relations between family and state agencies. Our brief discussion of the underclass in the previous chapter focused on the way that certain families were allegedly unable to provide children with moral boundaries. The welfare state is a key frame of reference here, with underclass parents allegedly rejecting the moral bedrocks of marriage and work because of the existence of a welfare safety net that provides parents with financial and social support. In these terms the state is culpable in the process of weakening the generational boundary within families by encouraging dependency-type relations between parents and the state. At the same time, within a context of rising concern over child abuse, child professionals are expected to play a more central role in protecting and controlling children. This has inevitably led to child professionals playing a more proactive role *within* families.

I have also argued that both welfare and criminal justice systems work on a privatised model of childhood whereby children become central figures in modern private families. Children's centrality within the family has little to do with notions of autonomy or independence, with family life constructed around the need for parents to take a proprietorial interest in their children through processes of socialisation and powerful notions of parental responsibility. Whilst family and state presuppose each other, liberal Western cultures are dominated by the proprietorial relationship of parents with their children which separates the interests of the family from the interests of the state. Privatisation here implies that families have an antagonistic relationship with the state. Recent changes in child policy have sought to bring these interests together through the notion of children's welfare being paramount.

I also argued that, in English-speaking countries such as the UK and the USA, child 'welfare' has become synonymous with child 'protection'. Thus child protection narrows the public focus to children who have been abused and does little to deal with the wider issues such as child poverty and educational failure. Moreover, recent research suggests that welfare/protection systems fail to protect the majority of children at risk, with particular forms of child abuse having a much higher priority than others. However, if we compare this conception of childhood with an alternative European model, there is at least the beginning of a social ontology for children. Within neoliberal societies the accent is on the individual parent. I offset this by briefly referring to an alternative model of public child support, the family-support model, which characterises much of the rest of Europe. We saw that the principles of social solidarity subsumed the child within the family, thus negating any 'individual' status for children. Following the United Nations Convention on the Rights of the Child, we can discern what Lee (2001) calls children as 'dependent beings', a construction of childhood that recognises their limited capacities as social actors.

Whether we are talking about responsibility or welfare, the central official models of family/state relations still emphasise the adult as caretaker of the child's 'best interests'. However, in setting out a series of models of child agency we have shifted the focus away from parent/professional and family/state relations towards seeing children as important constituent elements in policy-related considerations. As I have maintained throughout this book, conceptualisations of childhood now incorporate the child as an active determining subject. Despite the neglect of broader child-related issues, an emphasis on child protection has opened up other possibilities for viewing children as responsible social actors.

Part Three

Regulating Children and Childhood

6

Theories of Growing Up: Developmentalism and Socialisation Theory

Introduction

In Chapter 1 I discussed the significance of social constructionism as a theoretical approach within the sociology of childhood. I compared this with commonsensical thinking on childhood, that social and cultural features of childhood were inferred from children's biological immaturity. In this chapter I want to turn to the latter in more substantive terms. That is, I want to set out the social-scientific basis for the popular idea that childhood is a universal and natural phenomenon largely because, irrespective of context, children are smaller, weaker and less physiologically developed than adults are. This chapter will consider a range of ideas, practices and representations of childhood that until recently have underpinned the work of the two dominant 'child'-related disciplines within the social sciences: psychology and sociology. While these disciplines have often been at odds with each other in theoretical and methodological terms, they converge on a series of broad principles as to how we view the essential nature of childhood. These principles make up what Prout and James (1997, pp. 10–14) call the dominant framework.

In the first section I outline the key features of the 'dominant framework' that bring psychologists and sociologists together in the pursuit of conceptualising and researching childhood. I will discuss the central principles that have for most of the last century governed research, social policy, professional practice and in many ways commonsense thinking about the nature of adult/child relations. In this section I want to address the influence of socialisation and development as frames of reference for measuring and evaluating childhood. Reference will be made to scientific conventions, sociological and psychological prescription and the legitimating power of

117

the dominant framework that serve to render childhood as a universal fact of life. In the following two sections I go on to discuss the dominant framework in terms of its two central disciplinary approaches: developmental psychology and socialisation theory. The second section is concerned with the key concepts and methodologies that govern the way in which psychologists have tended to treat the topic of childhood and the positions of children. I will also examine the origins of this approach, known hereafter as developmentalism, and briefly refer to its influence in broader social scientific, professional and commonsense terms.

Whilst the dominant framework brings psychology and sociology together in terms of general principles relating to children and childhood, developmentalism tends to deal with the process of growing up from within, that is, growing up consists of a series of intrapsychic processes that affect individual children. Socialisation theory, on the other hand, deals more with the social realm and the ambiguous position of children within society. The third section will thus be taken up with the sociological counterpart, and examine the influence of socialisation theory. The final section will aim to do two things: offer a critical appraisal of the dominant framework and, in the light of this critique, examine more recent work within the new sociology of childhood that views children as accomplished social actors. In other words, this final section moves outside of the dominant framework and explores a different set of assumptions in relation to researching children and childhood.

The Dominant Framework

In this first section I want to refer to four key features of the dominant framework, the dichotomising of childhood and adulthood, children's lack of ontology, the child as a proto-individual, and the role of the state. First, there are a number of ways of describing and conceptualising childhood that clearly distinguish it from adulthood in oppositional or binary terms. Throughout most of the twentieth century these ideas were working assumptions for social scientists, structuring our thinking about childhood and the end state of adulthood. These assumptions are collectively contained within what Prout and James (1997) call the dominant framework and are set out in diagrammatic form in Figure 6.1.

Let us take the nature/culture dichotomy, for example. Children are viewed as being closer to nature, adults as closer to culture. There are significant historical and philosophical approaches flowing from this binary opposition. Historically, the regulation of children in England came about in the nineteenth century partly because of the need to clear children from the streets and provide regulated populations for a developing education

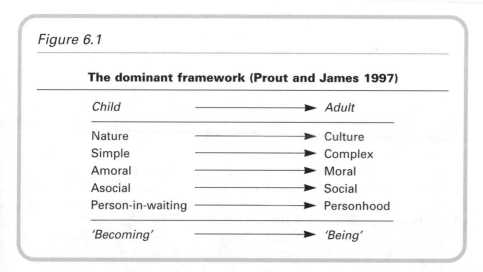

Figure 6.1

The dominant framework (Prout and James 1997)

Child		Adult
Nature	⟶	Culture
Simple	⟶	Complex
Amoral	⟶	Moral
Asocial	⟶	Social
Person-in-waiting	⟶	Personhood
'Becoming'	⟶	'Being'

system (Hendrick 1997). Children's association with nature was rooted in assumptions about their precocity and undisciplined nature. Whilst there was an important social-class dimension to this trend, children were to be domesticated, more firmly located within the family, and educated, gradually positioned in the classroom as pupils. Both family and school acted as disciplinary structures through which children would eventually become more 'cultured'.

Philosophically, there are links made between the child and 'primitive' or 'uncivilised' species through what has been called recapitulation theory. In essence, child development recapitulates history. Early anthropology and social science equated the development of 'mankind' with the development of the child towards adulthood. Thus just as societies developed ever more sophisticated signs and symbols, children, in a parallel way, developed the capacity for language and more complex ways of relating to the world (Burman 1994, p. 10).

If we take the simple/complex dichotomy, again there is a hierarchical comparison with the psychological characteristics of adulthood more superior and complete, adults' behaviour and dispositions more sophisticated. However, the notion of children's simplicity can take many forms. If we are thinking about the measurement of childhood, and a range of appropriate methodologies, then the child as a less complicated organism becomes easier to work with. Thus the tendency for developmental psychologists to experiment on children in laboratory settings partially reflects the assumption that children are less complex organisms than adults are, making it easier to control for 'external' environmental factors. If we equate simplicity with purity and innocence, on the other hand, children's essential nature is viewed more positively as something that children eventually lose as they move into adulthood. Complexity, on the other hand, describes the fully developed, cognitively and emotionally sophisticated adult. In social terms complexity might refer to the shifting allegiances and relationships and the breadth of choices which determine the judgements that adults have to make on a daily basis. Interestingly, in these terms the child as a simple entity reverses the developmental process and at the same time transposes recapitulation theory. Childhood, innocence and closeness to nature are all personified through Rousseau's 'noble savage'. The subsequent social processes that are supposed to constrain the child's irrational state and lead to the 'civilised' status of adulthood, according to Rousseau, rob the child of his or her purity. Thus the social is equated with barbarism; culture and civilisation are equated with cynicism and duplicity.

A second key feature of the dominant framework is the child's lack of ontology, that is, children are conceptualised in terms of what they will become rather than who they are. In terms of the previous discussion of binarism, children are incomplete becomings, whereas adults are fully constituted social beings, persons in their own right. I will discuss socialisation theory later in the chapter. However, as with developmental theory, the work of structural functionalists neglects the social position of children, other than to see them as carriers of social resources and forces that project them forward in time as a future generation of adults. In Chapter 2 I examined the structuralist approach which locates children within society as social inferiors. The emphasis is quite different here, with children rendered visible in categorical terms, occupying a social space within a system of social stratification. The dominant framework, on the other hand, implies that children are invisible, they cannot be understood in their own terms. They lack an ontology because social scientists have tended to look at children simply in terms of the adults that they will become. Hence the forward-looking nature of socialisation is concerned with how children will fit in to society as adults (Inkeles, cited in Corsaro 1997, p. 9). There is much less concern for children's situation in the here and now as children.

Children are compared with adults, with the latter the standard model that children work their way towards throughout childhood. As I set out in Chapter 2, childhood is thus a deficit model of adulthood, with the language of 'need' being invoked to bring children up to adulthood. The arrows in Figure 6.1 suggest a series of pathways or journeys that children must follow in order to reach a state of completion. Whilst these binary differences form the basis of the dominant framework, the key concepts, research conventions and professional practices that flow from these differences, as exemplified by both developmental psychologists and sociologists, are concerned with the pathways or careers that link the binary opposites together. As we shall see in the following chapter, primary schooling in England and Wales is heavily influenced by carefully choreo-graphed movement along a developmental pathway. Thus, like the sociali-sation theorist, child professionals tend to be future-oriented, with children plotted along one of these carefully structured pathways. Children are thus transitional objects; as Jenks (1982, p. 14) argues, the 'child is never onto-logically established in its own right'.

In turning to individualism, processes of development and socialisation largely reflect the cultural expectations of advanced Western societies. Childhood as a transitional process projects children into the future as ratio-nal, centred individuals. We will come back to this point later in our discus-sion of cultural bias. What is important at this juncture is that the dominant framework takes for granted that children are being viewed as discreet abstract entities, with problems of growing up couched in terms of intra-psychic processes found within the individual child or the effects of the envi-ronment on the individual child. The emphasis is on the singular *child* rather than children and their collective practices. As Corsaro (1997, p. 17) notes, "there is little if any consideration of how interpersonal relations reflect cultural systems, or how *children* through their participation in communica-tive events, become part of these interpersonal relations and cultural patterns and reproduce themselves collectively [author's emphasis]."

This abstracting of children as individualised projects further strength-ens the idea that children are not of society. Children are seen as unfinished projects who require the continuous involvement of socialising adults before they are complete and can enter society as full members. This abstracting of children is reflected in social scientific practice, particularly within development psychology. Clinical interviews and sustained obser-vation of children's behaviour often take place in laboratory conditions as psychologists attempt to identify, isolate and measure the transitional process of growing up (Smith and Cowie 2003). Children are abstracted from their social environments in an attempt to isolate and regulate the factors that impede the process of growing up. And whilst children are often observed together within friendship networks, the main focus is on the influence of these friends as external stimuli that trigger aspects of the child's internal cognitive and emotional make-up.

A fourth feature of the dominant framework is the intimate relationship between the growing child as a proto-individual and the expanding role of the state. One key feature of modernity discussed in Chapter 3 was the search for rational control of physical and social environments. In trying to control the social environment, more defined and precise techniques and policies have been developed through the tutelage of the state, particularly the welfare state, throughout most of the last century. As we saw in the previous chapter, this quest for control extended into the formerly private domain of the home, with children and predominantly their mothers subject to a range of health, educational and social technologies. Lee (2001, p. 27) refers to this as the 'developmental state': '[R]ulers identified the investment in and training of the young as a central concern of statesmanship. The young were being identified as embodiments of the future and, thus, in need of special treatment . . . Reasons of state guided the treatment of children.' We may be talking about changes in hospital policy that allow mothers to stay overnight with children receiving prolonged treatment. We may simply be thinking about the different ways that parents can be held criminally responsible for their children's misdemeanours (Muncie 2004). Whatever the policy domain and the reasons for more intensive scrutinisation of the process of growing up, the incorporation of parents within more statutory frameworks of care and control signifies a far more influential role for the state in underwriting the pathway between childhood and adulthood.

The dominant framework has considerable legitimising power: we can refer again to the discourse of 'needs', the moral demands made on adults who oversee children's development and socialisation processes. Oakley (1972) in an early feminist critique of 'need' refers to the mythological status of attachment theory. Directing her critique at the work of Bowlby, she argues that the language of need is at its most potent when addressing the relationship between the mother and the young child. Bowlby's attachment theory emphasises the necessity of close, continuous physical bonding with the child for the first eighteen months or so of the child's life (Bowlby 1952). In popular terms this has been translated as the injunction that children need their mothers. Oakley (1972, p. 203) argues that there are three parts to this assertion: 'The first is that children need their biological mothers. The second is that children need mothers rather than any other kind of caretaker. The third is that children need to be reared in the context of a one-to-one relationship.' In the early part of the twenty-first century, this notion of need has been revised considerably, with fathers, mother figures and professional child workers now in a much stronger position to act as proxies for mothers. However, for much of the second half of the twentieth century, this notion of need achieved the status of both scientific fact and 'natural' state, and, as Barrett (1998) argues, many of the most popular current child-rearing manuals still promote early maternal bonding and breast-feeding.

Developmentalism

Universality and rationality are underpinning features of developmentalism, the dominant means of measuring and assessing the transition from becoming to being. What we will refer to as the 'ages and stages' model of childhood has for many constituted childhood as a theory, as a practice and a dominant mode of common sense when talking about children and childhood. Children are routinely positioned along the pathway to completion by connecting their chronological age with a clearly defined stage of development. We need to see this pathway more accurately as a gradated hierarchy, with children moving vertically upwards as they move between ages and stages.

Throughout the latter half of the last century Piaget was dominant in child-development approaches, providing a more sophisticated version of the ages and stages model. His 'genetic epistemology' is, strictly speaking, an attempt to explain the origins and development of knowledge rather than to provide a theory of how children learn (Burman 1994, p. 153). However he is best known for producing a framework for measuring children's cognitive growth and providing a common language for talking about children as transitional objects.

Whilst the new sociology of childhood has been heavily critical of his influence (we will come to this later in the chapter), it is worth bearing in mind that Piaget concentrated on the child's capacity to adapt to his or her social surroundings; that, within limits, children are active in trying overcome their environments. Thus in one sense, as we shall see in the following section, Piaget had a more developed sense of the child's abilities than the work of socialisation theorists. However, whereas socialisation theory directs us to thinking about the ways in which the environment has a differential impact on children's development, developmental theory views the environment as a fixed backdrop; we simply measure a child's ability to adapt to his or her environment at a given age.

Development, according to Piaget (1932), unfolds naturally and universally. Children by virtue of their biological growth will develop cognitively and emotionally at the same pace. Children's behaviour and social skills will inevitably follow on from biological and psychological growth. Whilst children are active in this process in the sense that they have to adapt to and make sense of their environments, the social acts as a relatively fixed and stable backdrop. The psychologist's focus is the individual child, not the social context (Morss 1996, p. 5). His model takes us from the birth of the child through to mid-adolescence (see Figure 6.2). The early sensorimotor stage emphasises the child drawing on his or her physical and sensory experiences in making sense of the world. Gradually, as the child grows older, this early exploratory period gives way to cognitive skills that are more abstract and three-dimensional. By children's early teens they are capable of much more abstract reasoning; children can theorise and hypothesise about their environments and the worlds of others.

This is a fairly simply sketch of the general direction that cognitive development takes: what has given developmental thinking its paradigmatic

Figure 6.2

Cognitive development

Ages	ADULT Stages
12–14	*Formal operative*
7–12	*Concrete operations*
2–7	*Pre-operational*
	[the problems of egocentrism and conservation]
0–2	*Sensorimotor*
	CHILD

power is its more graduated structure within which children can be located. Thus the process of becoming is one of gradually acquiring cognitive skills by moving upwards from one stage to the next as illustrated in Figure 6.2. This is done through a continuous process of what Piaget called assimilation and accommodation. The child gradually learns more sophisticated skills by first of all assimilating new ideas and experiences. At the same time, the child's existing cognitive structures incorporate these new ideas through forms of accommodation. There is a strong evolutionary influence here, with both assimilation and accommodation acting to stabilise the child's cognitive structures, what Piaget referred to as 'equilibration'. This is a ceaseless process as equilibrium presupposes disequilibrium. Further action on the child's part being assimilated and accommodated with a consequent movement further up the developmental scale.

It is important to state that this theory of development presupposes that all children will go through these stages and that they have to go through them in a predetermined way. The process of development is 'invariant': children can only move in one direction and have to go through each stage in order before they reach completion. For example, children cannot think hypothetically about a particular problem until they have grappled with a concrete version of the problem. In Piagetian terms, children must work through the concrete operations stage before they can move on to the formal operations stage.

Subsequent attempts were made to try and contextualise Piaget's 'proto-individual' (See Morss's (1996) review of Vygotsky). However, Piaget's insistence on biological growth as the key variable, and an emphasis on the children's mastery of their social contexts, foregrounds the child as a 'rugged individual', gradually overcoming the unpredictability of the environment: 'Piaget's commitment to the modern project can be seen in his depiction of the developing child as a budding scientist systematically encountering problems in the material world, developing hypotheses and learning by discovery and activity' (Burman 1994, p. 157).

Origins and Influence

The origins of socialisation theory as well as developmentalism can be traced back to the late nineteenth century and the development of a positivist social science. As I shall outline in the following section, Durkheim's aim was to locate socialisation within a corpus of work that emphasised the social over other individualistic influences. The work of Darwin and the 'child study' movement, in the latter half of the nineteenth century, on the other hand, grounded child development within a more individualistic methodology which viewed children as subject to law like biological forces. Whilst Darwin's methods for arriving at his theory of child development rested largely on observation of his own children, his work presaged the move to more systematic observation of children within laboratory conditions in an attempt to isolate environmental factors and measure individual growth as an independent variable.[1]

In returning to social constructionism, 'naturalising' was about conflating mental age with biological growth, creating a mythical child, in effect an image of the child that lay within the minds of developmental psychologists. As Burman comments,

> The normal child the ideal type, distilled from the comparative scores of age-graded populations is . . . a fiction or myth. No individual or real child lies at its basis. It is an abstraction, a fantasy, a fiction a production of testing apparatus that incorporates, that constructs the child, by virtue of its gaze. (1994, pp. 16–17)

Interestingly the emphasis on social production incorporates technological changes in the research and assessment of young children that alters our understanding of children's capabilities. Burman (1994, p. 234) refers to the way that changes in medical technology over time allowed practitioners to work with ever younger children's cognitive and emotional abilities. By the 1960s the ability to test infants' development, had altered our conception of childhood because experiments allowed us to make judgements about the competence of infants. Piaget's claims that children are active more or less from birth were thus strengthened and provided a challenge to the view that the child was a tabula rasa, or blank slate, which was more dominant in the first half of the twentieth century.

Through the establishing of developmental psychology as a dominant set of truths about children and childhood, certain standards or norms were being created and this had significant implications for parents, child professionals, children and latterly manufacturers of child paraphernalia. Growing up as a process became naturalised, with observation a powerful tool in the measurement of children and their subsequent regulation as human 'becomings'. Childhood was both standardised and normalised: techniques and practices created norms and, by implication, theories of the abnormal or deviant child (Walkerdine 1983; Burman 1994). As we shall see in the following chapter, these ideas and methods became an important resource in developing a language within education for answering questions about how we measure what children know and learn. Parents similarly draw on the ages and stages theory and are keenly aware of their children's development, actively seeking out signs from their children that they are conforming to their appropriate age-related stages. The influence of developmentalism is far more pervasive, with manufacturers producing toys, games and child paraphernalia in more nuanced ways as marketers utilise developmental scales in expanding consumer markets One trend here is the use of high-profile psychologists in endorsing products. For example, Miriam Stoppard, a well-respected British psychologist, endorses a range of baby-care products for Mothercare, a large chain of high-street stores. Parents and professionals are locked into a powerful consumer culture where developmental ideas are simplified and applied by companies in trying to expand their markets in child-related paraphernalia.

The Story of Socialisation

Much has been written about developmental psychology in terms of the influence it has on the study and science of childhood. Sociology has probably been less influential in structuring modern understandings of childhood. I nevertheless want to concentrate on the way that sociology through the concept of socialisation has played a role within the social sciences in establishing the importance of family and other determining agencies and the position of children as 'becomings'. Durkheim established very early on that children were incomplete social actors. The child was seen as 'fickle, changeable and capricious . . . intellectually weak and fragile with limited faculties' (1982, p. 148). At the same time, Durkheim clearly sets out the binary model of childhood, in the process offering a version of recapitulation theory referred to earlier:

> We can see what a gulf there is between the child's point of departure and the goal toward which he must be led: on the one hand a mind endlessly moving, a

veritable kaleidoscope that changes from one moment to the next, emotional behaviour that drives straight ahead to the point of exhaustion; and on the other hand, the preference for regular moderate behaviour. It has taken centuries for man to travel this distance. Education must enable the child to cover it in a few years. (Durkheim 1961, pp. 133–4)

Thus Durkheim (1961) took the view that children were socially unformed. Children were a bundle of primitive instincts, a potentially dangerous force within society that had to be brought within the structures of the social system. These primitive instincts needed to be constrained and channelled by the forces of socialisation. Durkheim was writing within a context of considerable political and social turmoil. French society in the late nineteenth century was divided by conflicting religious, political and social conflicts (Giddens 1971). Durkheim's chief aim was thus to construct a science of both society and morality, providing an informed understanding of social structures and bringing a much-needed consensus to French society. For Durkheim, moral education was a particularly powerful means of achieving this end. The asocial child was a starting point in creating social stability and, by implication, a moral consensus. With childhood such a powerful alien and asocial force, one might ask how exactly children are to be constrained. How are children to be brought within the confines of society? Durkheim argued that children are predisposed to socialisation in two ways. First, they are naturally habit-forming, a child will endlessly repeat particular modes of behaviour; the child is imitative and repetitive. There is no pattern to this behaviour; habit-forming for the child is unpredictable, with behaviour fluctuating from the stable to the volatile without any warning. The child, according to Durkheim (1982, p. 149), is 'an anarchist, ignorant of the ruler yet soon becomes a traditionalist . . . stuck in his ways . . . habit forming'. However, it is this very inconsistency and volatility that acts as a pretext for adult intervention. According to Durkheim, children's 'irrational' behaviour can be channelled and disciplined.

A second predisposition is the child's suggestible nature. Children's limited cognitive capacities make it easier for adults to 'plant' ideas and actions in the child's head. Children are receptive to the suggestions of others, again an opening for the socialiser to shape the child's tastes and hint at the boundaries of normative behaviour. Interestingly, Durkheim's theory of socialisation was at odds with later sociological orthodoxy. He was suspicious of the family as the main socialising agency. Whilst parents were important in 'developing regular habits' within the child, they were also seen as being too particular and partial, less likely to instil in the child a broader and universalistic moral framework (1961, p. 146). Durkheim's approach highlighted the importance of the teacher as a professional authority figure. However, as we shall see in the following, his emphasis on external constraints in the guise of fully socialised adults was necessary to bring children fully into an ordered society. This principle underpinned the work of American structural functionalism, the dominant theoretical approach within sociology from the 1940s to the 1970s.

Drawing on Freudian theory and Durkheim's earlier formulations, the work of Parsons was central to socialisation theory in the 1960s. His work on the social system and how it can be subdivided into subsystems followed on from Durkheim's totalising concept of the social, with the assumption that everything within society can be explained and understood primarily in terms of social factors. The key issue for Parsons, as it was for Durkheim, was how social order could be maintained. Parsons (1951) constructed an elaborate and highly abstract account of the social structure. In addressing the 'problem of order', one of the core ideas was socialisation. For Parsons the social system and its subsystems consisted of a series of ordered constraints on the individual. The theory of socialisation is effectively a theory of how these constraints, as primary social forces, act on individuals. This determinism suggests that rather than seeing 'socialisation' as something that inheres in the adult/child relationship, it is something that the socialiser brings to adult/child relations – it is imposed on children by adults (Thorne 1993, p. 5). Socialisation is thus a unilateral imposition of the adult world on children. Powerful adult figures, namely parents from the nuclear family, take on the responsibility of bringing the social to the child. Children here are a relatively powerless and passive force, reliant on the actions of significant adult others.

Socialisation implies a dependency-type relationship between parents and child. Adults over time instil in children the capacity to be independent entities. There is here the same emphasis on the individual child found within developmental theory. The Western liberal model of growing up presupposes a paradox: the end point of rational independence is based on an earlier period of dependence. We can refer back to Figure 6.1 and the binary model of childhood. Parsons draws on Freud in constructing his model of children as becomings: the child as a bundle of primitive 'erotic' instincts has to capitulate to the all-powerful figure of the parent. A period of physical and emotional dependence ensues as children start to make sense of the world around them; they gradually internalise the dominant norms and acquire the capacity to become independent. Through this process children become social beings.

One classic example of socialisation theory is Frederick Elkin's *The Child in Society*, published in 1960. It is worth setting out his work in some detail as it provides us with a 'modern' and popular version of the work of Durkheim and Parsons. First of all, there are the initial biological connections, what Elkin refers to as the child's 'biological inheritance'. This is taken as a precondition for socialisation. By this the author is referring to the child having the 'normal' capacity to learn and develop. Following Durkheim, children are predisposed to being socialised. This means two things: children are in an absolute sense helpless and dependent and by necessity must rely on others to bring them within society, and they must be in a position to take advantage of the support of a range of socialising agencies. Elkin, for example, refers to children with serious brain injuries as being helpless and dependent but not in a position to be socialised.

Secondly, socialisation is what differentiates children from the 'lower' animal species. Here we are thinking of the ability that humans have to reflect on the situations of others. There is a more sophisticated idea of socialisation in which humans go beyond Garfinkel's (1967) caricature of functionalism as a blueprint for producing 'cultural dopes'. Socialisation thus produces adults with the capacity for self-reflection. Thirdly, socialisation is an important means of maintaining social order and continuity. Children are born into an ongoing society. This effectively means that children have to fit in to a pre-existing order. As Elkin (1960, p. 7) states, 'the function of socialisation is to transmit the culture, and motivation to participate in established social relationships to new members'.

Fourthly, the constraints on children, the larger 'macro' forces that bring children into society, are institutionally recognised and sanctioned. They are commonly known as the 'agencies of socialisation' and are listed in the contents page of Elkin's book in order of temporal and spatial influence. So we start with the family, moving outwards and upwards into the school and peer group.

- *The Family*: While Durkheim viewed the professional educator as a more suitable socialiser, Elkin reflects the dominant trend in post-war functionalist thought that the parent is the most significant influence on the child. Drawing on Freudian and small-group theory, the nuclear family is seen as being the primary means of socialisation (Parsons and Bales 1956). This has two meanings: primary in the temporal sense that mothers and fathers come first in the child's life – they are the first point of contact that the child has with the social structure, and primary in the sense that the family is the most important agency of socialisation. The relations that the child establishes within the family are the most enduring and most formative. Parents mediate between the child and the wider community. They are the primary decision-makers within the home, chief interpreters of the wider community and society, in effect children learn about the world and its combination of roles, rituals, responsibilities and relationships through their parents.

- *The School*: As with the family, the school is a powerful determining force within society. For socialisation to be effective within the classroom, the expectation is that both family and school play a complementary and mutually reinforcing role in guiding the child towards full social membership as an adult. In some cases the teacher plays a similar role to the parent, introducing the child to the complex and varied aspects of the wider society. However, there are substantial differences in the kinds of responsibilities that the teacher discharges and the kinds of orderings that the child encounters in school. First, the school offers the child a more formal structure of rules and regulations. Whilst there may be a degree of give and take within the family, the school introduces the child to relatively fixed practices and procedures. Secondly, relations with authority figures are more formal: teachers have a professional responsibility of care for the children in their classroom. Thirdly, learning is much more explicit within the school, with teachers transmitting knowledge and skills within an environment dictated by the curriculum, the timetable and the end-of-year examination. Having said this, the hidden curriculum in school – the incidental, routine norms and practices that permeate the school – reinforce what Elkin (1960, p. 59) calls 'status, expectations and values'.

- *The Peer Group*: Whilst the peer group works alongside the other agencies in structuring the pathway between childhood and adulthood, it differs from the family and school in a number of ways. First, the democratic appeal of friendship networks gives children some experience of less authoritarian relationships. Secondly, the informal nature of peer relations allows a wider range of subject matter to be tackled. Elkin (1960, p. 64) refers to sex education, a taboo subject within the home and classroom, but more likely to be broached in playgrounds, bedrooms and street corners. Thirdly, the peer group is more likely to be familiar with changes within popular culture than the older, parent generation. Friends become a testing ground for new ideas and values generated in periods of rapid social change.

Finally, the peer group is the site for the exploration of independence, particularly where the child has formerly been dependent on adult authority figures. Elkin thus follows the classic structural functionalist line in viewing a symbiotic relationship between the hierarchical structures of the family and school on the one side and the relatively informal and egalitarian form of the peer group on the other. The latter becomes the more visible and obvious manifestation of the child's journey along the pathway towards independence. While reference is made to the potential for peer groups to become more powerful than other socialising agencies, friendship networks and gang membership is viewed benignly as a 'comforting collective cushion in the face of demands of authority' (Elkin 1960, p. 66). Thus, whereas the significance of 'other children' might imply that in certain contexts children play a more formative role in their own socialisation, Elkin follows the conventional functionalist line that the peer group is a legitimate influence on children that does not threaten the proprietorial interests of parents as primary socialisers.[2]

In Chapter 2 I argued that feminism was instrumental in drawing our attention to the invisibility of children and thus provided us with some of the conceptual tools for the new childhood studies. I also identified some of the ways in which feminism might restrict a fuller understanding of children's structural position within society. A feminist perspective is critical of the conflict-free and apolitical nature of socialisation. The emphasis on patriarchy rather than the 'social system' or 'modern society', and 'gendering' rather than 'socialisation', clearly challenges assumptions made by structural functionalists about the child, the socialiser and the social structure. Feminists in the 1970s and 1980s were keen to reinforce Dennis Wrong's claim that sociological orthodoxy had created an 'oversocialised conception of man' (Wrong 1961; Stanley and Wise 1983). However, there are a few 'family' resemblances between an emphasis on structure and the asocial child, and the feminists' concern to elicit the gendered implications of the process of socialisation. There is, as it were, the same top-down view of socialisation, with adults tending to the needs of children as asocial incompetents (Mayall 2002, p. 168).

Thorne (1987, p. 89) makes this point when discussing the feminist movement: 'like the traditional theorists such as Marx and Parsons, from whom we borrowed analytical tools while also rebelling, feminist theorists have assumed the standpoints of adults'. Thus children follow separate gendered pathways as they move from childhood to adulthood: the various agencies of socialisation have differential effects on boys and girls growing up, with the process having fateful consequences for girls. For example, Oakley's (1981b) reliance on social learning theory points to a range of processes that project boys and girls along different trajectories towards adulthood.

Similarly, Marxism is normally in contraposition to structural functionalism: the former emphasises material constraints that differentiate the process of socialisation. Yet there are similarities between the two. Basil Bernstein (1971), a Marxist heavily influenced by Durkheim, produced a more sophisticated conception of socialisation, but one nevertheless that emphasises constraints being imposed on the asocial child as he or she moves progressively into society. Socialisation is

> a process whereby a child acquires a specific cultural identity, and to his [sic] responses to such an identity. Socialisation refers to the process whereby the biological is transformed into a specific cultural being. It follows from this that the process of socialisation is a complex process of control, whereby a particular

moral, cognitive and affective awareness is evoked in the child and given a specific form and content. Socialisation sensitises the child to the various orderings of society as these are made substantive in the various roles he is expected to play. (Bernstein 1971, p. 174)

Corsaro (1997, pp. 9–11) refers to this as a 'reproductive' model of socialisation: agencies of socialisation function to reproduce social class differences within society. There is the same level of determinism here, but whereas functionalism has less to say about different outcomes of socialisation for children, reproductive approaches emphasise 'completion' taking different forms depending on the material and cultural investments of parents.

Moving outside the Frame

In moving outside the dominant framework, researchers are challenging several features of both socialisation theory and developmentalism. These features have in turn generated some new ways of thinking about children and childhood. We have encountered some of these approaches in previous chapters. Nevertheless, it is worth bringing them together here as a more general response to key features of the dominant framework.

The Bias of Biology

First of all, there is the centrality of biology, particularly within developmental psychology and the way that children's lives are determined by the relationship of chronological age to stages of development. Socialisation theory works from the social in terms of external constraints on the child. At the same time, it also has recourse to the child's inner state in trying to outline how exactly children are made social. Thus Durkheim, Parsons and Elkin all refer to psychological concepts when demonstrating the mechanisms that bring children into line. As I have demonstrated in previous chapters, new thinking on childhood has challenged this emphasis on biology by locating children fully within the social world. Thus whilst biology tells us something about the differences between children and adults, there is no necessary relationship between biological immaturity and childhood as a social and cultural phenomenon.

The Overdetermined Child

Despite Piaget's attempt to incorporate a degree of voluntarism in his theory, the dominant framework holds an overdeterministic conception of children's lives. In the case of developmentalism, biology is the determining factor. Moreover, as we have seen, biology is conflated with what is natural, thus providing a taken-for-granted legitimation of what counts as an independent variable. Children's growing up is predominantly talked about in terms of biological age. Their accomplishments and their problems are understood in terms of phases in the biological life-cycle. In turning to socialisation theory, the emphasis on childhood as a transitional state and children as provisional 'beings' in one sense suggests that this is not a theory of children. The insistence on external constraints ensures that children, if they are at all conceptualised, are viewed as either passive recipients of socialisation processes or simply the bearers of forces as they move from childhood to adulthood (Jenks 1982). In short, the dominant framework has endorsed the view that children's lives are necessarily subject to intense control if they are to grow into adulthood.

Challenges from an 'emergent paradigm' here assume that adult/child relations are far more dynamic and complex, with children often viewed as formative social actors. Whilst the dominant framework categorises children having power and agency as forms of child deviance or abnormality (cf. Chapter 4), a social constructionist approach takes children's influence as an immanent possibility and a constituent element within a range of social contexts. Whilst the sociology of childhood uncovers a range of situations where children's lives are overdetermined, there is now ample evidence to suggest that in situations where children have a degree of autonomy and space, their social competence belies their developmental age. I will return to this point later in the section.

Cultural Biases

The dominant framework is clouded by a Euro- or Anglo-centrism (Hart 1997). That is, the conceptual tools drawn on by social science in researching children and childhood are culturally specific. The 'scientific' tendency to generalise, and the emphasis on childhood as a universal and natural form, has often meant that Western modes of thought about childhood are assumed to have currency in non-Western cultures. This cultural bias takes several forms. The ages and stages model and the significance of agencies of socialisation are assumed to dominate processes of growing up in all cultures and societies. As I argued in Chapter 1, social constructionism uncovers the cultural biases in developmental psychology. Childhood is more a way of seeing children, and these perspectives are shaped by a range of cultural, social and political factors. In response to this, the new sociology of childhood frees children from a biological essentialism, opening up the possibility for viewing the process of growing up in a number of culturally distinct ways.

Cultural bias within the dominant framework is also inherent in the concern to uncover the processes through which the child as a proto-individual becomes social. This reflects the interests and structures of Western welfare societies and, within these societies, the interests of more affluent sectors. The child here is the product of an affluent Western background, moving through the developmental stages with relative ease on his or her way to becoming a rational, free-thinking individual.[3] In coming back to Piaget, the child 'is like the pilgrim, the cowboy, and the detective on television – is invariably seen as a free-standing isolable being who moves through development as a self-contained and complete individual' (Kessen, in Morss 1996, pp. 43–4). Burman (1994, p. 157) views Piaget's proto-individual in cultural and gendered terms. Thus Piaget's pioneer and explorer of the environment is assumed to be white and male. She draws parallels between the colonial exploits of dominant white cultures and the emphasis that Piaget places on children's need to overcome their environments. Just as children apply a nascent scientific rationality in solving the various obstacles placed in their path by their surrounding environment, Western scientific principles form the basis of a cultural imperialism, with Western values dominating in a global sense. Piaget's child was also a masculine pioneer, with manufacturers of educational toys encouraging mothers to make sure that their male children use the various toys to demonstrate their physical prowess and emotional development (Burman 1994, p. 156).

One of the key features of the new sociology of childhood is the focus on the different ways that children collectively become more experienced and accomplished members of society. I discuss the significance of 'other children' in Chapter 8. But whereas functionalism views the peer group as an adjunct to the dominant institutions of family and school, the work of Corsaro (1997), James (1993) and many others argues that peers constitute an important focus for studying children as contributing members of society.

I have so far concentrated on the new sociology of childhood. But, as this chapter has also concentrated on dominant psychological approaches and as some sociologists have acknowledged the early influence of a critical psychology within the more general field of childhood studies, it is worth briefly referring to developments within psychology (James and Prout 1997; Mayall 1996). Whilst constructionists and critical psychologists still inhabit the margins within the psychological community, they have nevertheless, produced a potent critique of the cultural biases within developmental psychology.

Morss (1996), in his excellent text on critical psychology, sets out a fourfold typology of the field. He starts with the 'hard positivism' of traditional Piagetian approaches which take as read the natural unfolding of the individual child's development, drawing on controlled experimental methods designed to produce generalisable results. He goes on to typify a second 'development-in-context' approach, which sees social factors as having some explanatory value. The influence of Vygotsky is central here with his insistence that the environment plays a more influential role in pushing the child along the developmental pathway. The third approach emphasises the constructed nature of child development. The work of Harre (1986) is pivotal here. He challenges the biological, factual basis to development, arguing that all human life arises out of interaction and is thus quintessentially social. Child development is thus no exception, with exchanges between adults and children providing the focus for research.

Morss (1996) aligns himself with a fourth approach. He argues that constructionism presupposes an individualism in the way that communication arises out of voluntaristic exchanges between rational beings and thus fails to challenge the individualism implicit within developmental psychology. Here the distinctions between psychology and sociology are blurred as critical psychologists draw on the work of Marx, Freud and Foucault in contesting the ontological basis of the individual. Thus, rather than assuming children are either proto-individuals or full individuals interacting with their environments, they attempt to uncover the grounds for claiming that the individual exists.

The Absence of the Here and Now

The final problem with the dominant framework is the reticence to acknowledge problems that affect children as children. This neglect has largely come about because of their lack of ontology. Throughout the book we have noted a range of problems that affect children's lives. I have argued that poverty is more likely to affect children than adults, and children are probably more likely to suffer mental health problems and in a global sense are more likely to be exploited in the workplace than their adult counterparts. We might even refer to child-specific problems such as physical and sexual abuse. Whilst the analyses of these problems undoubtedly focuses on the effects on children, there is also a tendency to project these effects into the future; to talk predominantly about the long-term effects of these problems in adulthood. Children are constantly referred to as the 'next generation', which is of course shorthand for the next generation of adults. Kitzinger (1997) refers to this as 'adult-centrism'. In discussing the problems that children experience as a consequence of abuse, she argues that the suffering which children go through as children is often less important to analysts of abuse than the problems that abused children will experience as adults. Adult-centrism is evident in the calls to help children because they are 'the parents of tomorrow' and 'our most valuable human resource': 'Children are valued because of the adults they will become and their pain is evaluated in terms of its effect on adult functioning. It is almost as if, on one level, childhood suffering is discounted because it is only a "passing phase", an oppression that you literally "out grow" ' (Kitzinger 1997, p. 186).

Interestingly, Prout and James (1997, p. 28) argue that children are often projected backwards as well as forwards in time. Just as we are concerned to read into the future what children currently do, we also want to try and make sense of adults' social problems with reference to what happened to children in the past. This is particularly the case with the application of socialisation theory. Sociological explanations of crime, for example, are usually based on a retrospective account of offenders' early childhood and their experiences within the family.[4] 'Inadequate socialisation' is often used as a catch-all explanatory device in assessments of crime and delinquency and, as I discussed in Chapter 5, these assessments have often influenced 'child' policy.

Social Experience rather than Biological Age

Sociologists such as Berry Mayall (1996, 2002) and Bill Corsaro (1997) have been telling us for several years now that children's daily lives do not correspond to the morally inferior status attributed to them through the all-embracing construct of childhood. Parent–child relations routinely involve more open negotiations, with children regularly demonstrating their social competence. In part this disjunction comes about because the research on and with children tends to take place in school, where children's lives are heavily regulated and where there are many fewer opportunities to demonstrate agency and competence (more of this in the following chapter). Despite this disjunction, commonsense thinking still tends to take for granted that biological age is the key criterion for judgements about children's abilities and notions of normality. As has been repeatedly pointed out, the dominant framework makes it difficult to think outside of an ages and stages approach to childhood.

Solberg's (1997) research on Norwegian children's independence provides us with a fairly recent illustration of how we might make judgements about children drawing on factors other than biological age.[5] In the UK and USA biological age is the dominant factor in judgements made about children's independence. Thus the general idea is that children cannot be left on their own at home until they reach an age when they are capable of looking after themselves. Recent cases of children who have been left on their own by their parents seem to highlight dramatically the child descriptors discussed earlier of vulnerability and dependence. In the USA one of the most popular films of the early 1990s was *Home Alone*, involving a 9-year-old boy who was accidentally left at home as his parents went on a fortnight's holiday.

Whilst this was a humorous and unrealistic take on the phenomenon of child abandonment, at around that time there was a series of high-media-profile cases of children left to fend for themselves at home:

'Home Alone' Mother Sought (*Guardian*, 13 February 1993).

Home Alone Parents are Found; Dublin Couple who left Toddlers at Home are Found (*The People*, 2 October 1994)

More recently the home-alone syndrome has been linked to the phenomenon of teenage killers, with links made between their crimes and the absence of parental supervision (Eberstadt 2001). These public perceptions can be located within the dominant framework: children here are too young and immature to be left on their own.

Solberg's analysis of Norwegian family life, on the other hand, suggests that in different cultural contexts the home-alone syndrome is not so powerful in situations where children spend substantial periods of time on their own. She argues that children accused of being neglected might just as easily be viewed as domestically competent. The Norwegian context is important. First of all, the great majority of mothers in Norway work. By the mid-1980s only about a sixth of all mothers were classified as house-wives. However, according to Solberg there has been no concomitant increase in day care or after-school services for families with children of school age. Thus there are increasing numbers of young, school-age children having to fend for themselves once they get home from school until their parents return from work.

In the UK the home-alone phenomenon was similarly viewed in terms of the rising numbers of mothers going back into the workforce. Claims were made that around 20 per cent of all children aged between 5 and 10 were likely to spend some time on their own after returning home from school. This was seen as a major problem, with calls made to try and improve the quantity and quality of child care for children (Wainwright 1994). However, according to Solberg, Norwegian parents are less likely to worry, more likely to negotiate degrees of independence with their young children. A second, cultural factor suggests that, unlike in the UK and USA, the home-alone syndrome is much weaker in Norway. At the age of 10, children are considered to be quite capable of looking after themselves without adult supervision. Many Norwegian children become independent from a much earlier age than is acceptable in other countries.

Social geography is a third factor: Norway is a less urbanised country. Although Solberg is rather vague here, she seems to imply that parents' perceptions of the public sphere are more generous and optimistic compared with the UK. Public spaces are perceived to be much safer because 'Norway can be seen as a collection of villages' (Solberg 1997, p. 130). In other words, whether children are playing with their friends in the parks and streets or at home on their own taking care of their domestic responsibilities, parents are less anxious. According to Solberg, domestic responsibilities are not simply based on the Norwegian children becoming older and therefore progressively more independent. The level of work done by children within the home and the extent to which they are left on their own are not straightforwardly related to the age of the child. Thus, irrespective of age, those children who 'take possession of the home' for parts of the day when their parents are absent and are often seen as being 'independent collaborators of their mothers' are more likely to be seen as 'big' and 'responsible' (1997, p. 142). These children seem to grow in relation to their domestic responsibilities. Here then we have an example of children's abilities not simply being assessed against a relatively static ages and stages model. Children, along with their parents, are able actively to negotiate their status within the home. Culture and circumstance interact with age to produce a more variable model of children growing up.

A second example revolves around children's imputed inability to make sense of their own situation and thus take some responsibility for their own future. Particularly in situations where children are under pressure or suffer from life-threatening illnesses, the tendency is for adults to protect children, and insulate them from the stress that decision-making is supposed to generate. If we take the example of children suffering from long-term illness or life-threatening diseases, Priscilla Alderson's (1994) study of children's rights within a medical context nicely illustrates the contrast between the dominant framework and the new sociology of childhood. On the one hand, there is the power of ideas from within the dominant framework that restrict children's access to knowledge until they are developmentally 'ready'. Children's assumed lack of understanding forms the basis for their social and political exclusion as health service clients. On the other hand, there is the possibility of seeing children with limited rights to self-determination, which would imply that decisions regarding children's treatment should be shared by professionals, parents and child patients.

Alderson (1994) does not understate the problems that parents of children with life-threatening diseases have in deciding whether to tell their children of the seriousness of their condition. However, one of the unintentional consequences of this lack of consultation is that children refuse treatment because their ignorance of their condition often makes the treatment seem far worse. Some of her sample of young patients, aged between 8 and 15, and their parents were happy to let the professionals take responsibility for treatment on the grounds that the patients were under the age of consent (16). However, as with the previous example of domestic competence,

Alderson (1994) argues that children's capabilities and competences develop through personal experiences. Many of the children in her sample of those suffering from chronic or life-threatening conditions were often seen as experienced patients, children who were growing up with their conditions. There was often conflict in the way that parents, children and professionals understood the young patients' competence. There were also instances where the closeness of the relationship between the children and their parents led the latter to believe that their children were competent enough to understand the implications of transplants and potentially life-saving surgery and were happy for them to make the final decision.

Interestingly, this closeness between parent and child challenges the dominant framework in that independence and the maturity to make informed decisions comes as a consequence of closer relations with parents rather than the loosening of generational ties as children get older (Alderson 1994, p. 58). In these terms, the abstracted model of the isolated individual child developing autonomy tells us much less about the process of growing up than children's own social experiences and the closeness of relations within the family.

Conclusion

In drawing on two examples of research that challenge the ages and stages model of childhood, the analysis moved outside of the dominant framework. These are illustrations of Western childhoods, but they do demonstrate the limits of relying on biological and psychological growth as indicators of agency and competence.[6] The bulk of this chapter, however, has been concerned with outlining the key features of the dominant framework and, in particular, the significance of developmental psychology and socialisation theory. Various authors have seen the latter as central to the project of modernity (Jenks 1996; Lee 2001). Whilst Piaget claimed that all children, irrespective of their cultural or social background, would go through these stages, the staged theory presupposes a modern Western model of the completed adult or 'being': Piaget and his followers are theorising the development of the rational, centred individual. In Chapter 3 I discussed the links between late modernity and the regulation of children. If we locate Piaget's work within this theoretical framework, then Piaget's influence is potentially even more far-reaching. The need to take more control of children as future generations of employees and citizens relies on ever more precise measures of child development. Thus more sophisticated and gradated indicators of a child's performance are drawn on in the classroom and the doctor's surgery in bringing the child up to a normal standard.

Socialisation theory does not offer the same degree of precision in accounting for the process of growing up. Nevertheless, it contains the same assumptions about children as persons-in-waiting rather than persons in their own right. In one sense, socialisation theory provides us with a corrective to the overly abstract model of the child as an isolated proto-individual biologically programmed to overcome his or her own immediate environments. The emphasis on social context, the significance of social institutions through the process of growing up, opens up possibilities for seeing children as constituent members of the social world. However, apart from children's limited involvement in peer groups, the socialised child suffers the same fate as the developing child, inhabiting the social periphery as a transitional object or project. Children's social invisibility is a key feature of the dominant framework, providing a powerful rationale for institutions and, by implication, adults to regulate their lives. In the following chapter I continue the theme of regulation and control and turn to the relationship between education, schooling and childhood.

7

Schooling Childhood

Introduction

The focus in this chapter is both schooling and education. In commonsense terms there is a tendency to conflate the two: we tend to assume that school is the natural and inevitable setting for a child's education. Whether we are talking about the passing down of generational skills or the passing of formal exams, in one way or another education is pretty much part of all children's lives. Whilst education might be thought of in terms of learning and developing skills in more formal situations, the historical and global contexts to childhood inform us that education goes way beyond a modern Western conception of schooling. Quite simply, children from developing countries are likely to be educated outside of any system of compulsory schooling (Illich 1971). One of the key characteristics that differentiates conceptions of childhood in developing and developed countries is the absence of a compulsory system of schooling in the former. Thus when we come, as we do in this chapter, to examine the relationship between education and modern Western childhood, we are really talking about the significance of schooling.

I take up this point in more detail in the first section when I argue that schooling, in particular mass compulsory schooling, has been influential in shaping our understandings of childhood. When addressing children and their schooling, I contend that their structural location, their social status, is most clearly demonstrated through an examination of their school status. Research into family life has uncovered quite complex relations between children, their parents and their siblings (see Chapters 3 and 5). When turning to children's experiences in school, we encounter relatively clear and unambiguous lines of responsibility and authority that marginalise children's agency and powers of negotiation. Children learn, develop and acquire a range of skills within the home; in the broad sense children are educated by others around them. There is, if you like, a much stronger idea of give and take between children and their parents and siblings. Rather ironically for an institution that promotes individualism and independence, the school, on the other hand, formalises and fixes children's positions within the social hierarchy. I examine children, schooling and social structure in the second section.

School structure also forms the basis of the discussion in the third section. Along with the curriculum, organisational issues have focused the attention of educationalists from many Western societies over the past couple of decades or so. Consequently, significant reforms to the curriculum and school organisation have been made. I examine these with respect to the position and experience of schoolchildren. In the final section I set out what I think are two challenges to the 'schooled child'. In both cases I am referring to forms of school absence. In the first instance, truancy has presented educationalists and politicians with a series of questions about the nature of schooling since the introduction of mass compulsory schooling throughout Europe in the nineteenth century (Paterson 1989). Truancy also has much wider ramifications, not least in the way it threatens the various formal and informal mechanisms that hold children in place. I will tease out the implications that truancy has for childhood. A second form of school absence comes from a far more legitimate source, the family. To be more specific, the imperceptible but gradual increase in parents 'schooling' their children at home illustrates the limitations of conflating education with schooling. We will look at this 'hidden' phenomenon in rather more detail. I use home schooling to exemplify the significance of schooling for our understanding of childhood. This will bring us back to our original distinction between schooling and education.

Mass Schooling and the Production of Childhood

One of the common themes that runs through more historically grounded work on childhood is the significance imputed to the development of mass compulsory schooling. Hugh Cunningham's (1995) history of Western childhood documents the significance of schooling in transforming the lives of children and our understandings of childhood. Whilst schooling had been around in one form or another throughout the medieval and early modern periods, it was not until the introduction of mass compulsory schooling that modern childhood started to take shape. To take the example of Europe: throughout the period of the introduction of compulsory schooling, the numbers of children attending school steadily increased from around a quarter of the child population in 1870 to around three-quarters by 1900 (Cunningham 1995, pp. 157–9). In the process, children's status was changing from productive family members to economic liabilities. In an earlier chapter I argued that, from the limited evidence gathered, in the late nineteenth century children were working partly through custom but mainly through economic necessity. There was little enthusiasm among members of working-class families for children's factory employment. Yet economic necessity and parents' concerns over the quality of schooling on offer were at the heart of tensions between agencies that regulated school attendance and the interests of parents and employers. Nevertheless, by the 1920s there seemed to be a general acceptance of compulsory schooling in most European states.

If we turn to the USA, schooling had little to do with children or childhood until the early nineteenth century (Bowles and Gintis 1976). Families were taken to be the significant units of production and, along with the Church, the main source of education. Up until 1870 fewer than 50 per cent of children aged between 5 and 17 attended school and, for those who did attend, the school year lasted on average for 78 days, the equivalent of around 15 school weeks (1976, p. 153). Bowles and Gintis argue that the development of a modern education system characterised by 'bureaucratisation, tracking and test-orientation' (1976, p. 2) was not evident until the 1930s. Thus the attendant idea of schools as both factories for the production of future workers and laboratories for the measurement and refinement of nascent adult identities is a relatively recent development.

Hendrick (1997) goes along with the significance of schooling for childhood in arguing that key features of a modern British childhood were crystallised through the introduction of compulsory education. Children's innocence, dependence and incompetence were all reinforced through the demands made on parents, educationalists and employers to exclude children from the workforce. Compulsory schooling meant children's economic dependence, whilst the naturalising of schooling took place as children working began to sound like a contradiction in terms. Children were seen to be incapable of earning money because of their innocence and incompetence, what were taken to be core characteristics of childhood. Hendrick argued that child labour was seen as a problem not simply in terms of the existence of exploitative employers but because children were seen as both incapable and naive, constitutionally unsuited to inhabiting the world of employment and dealing with the rapacious demands of employers.

Children's dependent status was compounded in schools during this early period through the introduction of a curriculum that defined children's needs in moral terms. The school was charged with the responsibility of shaping the child's character through physical and moral discipline. Childhood was also being equated with a state of ignorance. As Hendrick (1997, p. 46) notes, '[The school] threw aside the child's knowledge derived from parents, community, peer group and personal experience. Instead it demanded a state of ignorance.' Children were being ranked in social and moral terms as subordinates. The equating of childhood with ignorance underpinned this ranking which took place *within* childhood as children were propelled up through a hierarchy of knowledge ordered in terms of age-grading. This idea of a state of ignorance became the basis of another key feature of childhood, which we referred to in an earlier chapter, their ambiguous ontological status. Schools began to institutionalise the idea that children's identities were future-oriented. Through the ordering of the curriculum, children were to become relatively less ignorant as they moved in incremental fashion towards a state of full social membership.

We encountered the work of Illich (1971) in Chapter 2. His critique of schooling – his 'deschooling' of society – is important here because it is a critique of the institution of childhood that developed in industrialised countries in the nineteenth and twentieth centuries. Illich (1971) refers to the cultural and historical specificity of childhood. Childhood is tied to the taken-for-granted compulsory nature of schooling. Thus mass schooling is not seen as being inevitable, just as childhood is argued to be a minority feature in historical as well as global terms. His critique rests on a clear distinction between children as members of society on the one hand, and what he sees as the artificial and stultifying institution of childhood on the other hand. Illich points to the way that childhood is manufactured out of adult, bureaucratic and institutional needs to control children, whether this takes the form of learning, indoctrination or what he calls 'custodial care' (1971, p. 32.) He defines schooling as 'the age specific teacher-related process requiring full-time attendance at an obligatory curriculum.' (1971, p. 32). Thus children are positioned in schools according to age, dominated by teachers who demand of them their undivided attention to a body of knowledge called a curriculum. His 'phenomenology' of school is an attempt to bracket off any natural or commonsensical relationship between schooling and education; in other words, his definition of the school is an attempt to strip schools of any educational functions.

Locating Children

In the first section I suggest that a constructionist approach concentrates on the symbolic world of meaning: childhood is located in this symbolic world within a broader backdrop of political, economic and cultural change. One key historical trend is the introduction of mass compulsory schooling. In these terms an understanding of schooling is central to a conception of childhood. In particular, in Western industrialised societies our under-standings of childhood are bound up with the development of mass compulsory schooling. In turning now to structuralist attempts at making sense of childhood, the rise of schooling is a significant factor within a much more materialist analysis. Instead of asking what we mean by childhood, a structuralist is more concerned with what flesh-and-blood children do and how this affects our understanding of childhood. I return to the 'child labour' debate referred to in Chapter 2. The groundbreaking Childhood as a Social Phenomenon project distinguishes between different types of work carried out by children (Qvortrup 1994). Central to any understanding of the relationship between childhood and schooling is the shift in forms of labour from classical economic child labour as typified by child workers in the early industrial period and the modern notion of children's work within the classroom. Qvortrup refers to this change as the 'scholarization' of childhood (1994, p. 12). Thus changes in the form of children's labour are crucial to an understanding of modern conceptions of childhood. Both early and later forms of child labour are 'socially necessary' forms of labour; the difference lies in the role that the school plays in producing children as future economic assets.

A second structuralist line of argument locates children in social and temporal space; children are positioned within schools as recipients of structural forces. Schools are environments where children eventually take on routines and form habits that determine their broader social position as well as provide a structure for their formal education. Thus, just as schooling and childhood are inextricably linked, children's structural position in school illuminates their broader social status. Structuralist accounts here rest on the relationship between the child and adult populations within schools. The school reinforces the subordinate status of children in the way that rules, values and working routines are oriented around the need to act on and position children. Clearly there are important differences in terms of the effects that schools have on children. For example, we saw in Chapter 2 how school disciplines have a differential impact on working-class and middle-class children (Bowles and Gintis 1976). And, as we saw in Chapter 3, a range of other dimensions of stratification are important and offer a more complex picture of children in society. Yet the emphasis on structure here refers to constraints that all children more or less experience in their roles as pupils. James, Jenks and Prout (1998) refer to schools as structures in terms of fairly rigid time disciplines: 'schooling imposes complex temporal schedules which, through their intersection, structure daily, weekly and yearly cycles and create, for children, different spatial and temporal constraints and possibilities in relation to their school work which must be negotiated with parents and teachers' (1998, p. 75). We can take one example of this, the timetable. Children's day-to-day activities – their use of time and space – are determined by the timetable. From the pupils' perspective there is a strong sense of temporal structuring in that, within the timetable, pupils are supposed to know where they are, what they are doing and when they are allowed to act in particular formal and informal ways. Pupils are physically located in school through the timetable. Yet the timetable does more than this. It acts as a social and cultural map, determining the quality and quantity of social relations and pupils' abilities to establish themselves in relation to curricular and extra-curricular activities.

A second mechanism for structuring children's school experiences is the curriculum. Historically in England and Wales there have been 'exceptional' schools that gained a reputation for pupil involvement in curricular matters, for example A.S. Neill's Summerhill School based in south-east England (Neill 1968). It is also worth mentioning that the trend in primary schooling in the 1970s and 1980s was for education to be more 'child-centred', with children on occasion able to initiate classroom activities (Wyness, 2000). Yet any child-focused initiatives in school have always taken place within a broader context of teachers, bureaucrats and governments shaping the content of what is taught in classrooms. As we shall see in the following section, in countries such as England, Wales, Australia and New Zealand, the determining of the curriculum by those outside of schools has been a defining feature of education reform. In general, what children learn is more or less determined by the school curriculum. There is some variation in the form and content of curricula across geographical areas. In Europe, for instance, different educational traditions inform the curriculum in specific countries, with different emphases placed on the humanities the sciences, social studies and vocational courses (Mclean, 1990). Yet whether the curriculum is structured by moral, economic or social imperatives, knowledge is handed down to children. A structural emphasis here focuses on the way that the curriculum constrains pupils' activities in class.

Classroom management is a taken-for-granted generic term drawn on to denote a range of teaching styles used to control the form that the curriculum takes in class. It is also part of what we might call a teaching culture in the way that it regulates the way in which teachers think of each other professionally (Walkerdine 1983). Pupils' moral and intellectual commitments and abilities are therefore also determined by the regulative strategies adopted by teachers in conveying this knowledge. A third element that overlays the timetable and the curriculum is the school's code of conduct, the rules and regulations imposed by head teachers, often formalised as school policy. These rules not only govern what is expected from pupils in the classroom, they also extend into the playground, traditionally a relatively free space for children. In recent years behaviour has become a global concern, with education systems making more concerted efforts to cope with a perceived increase in disruption inside and outside classrooms (Parsons 1999). School policies on discipline are sharpened; surveillance around the perimeters of some schools and playgrounds has increased. The general tendency to control the activities of pupils has intensified, adding to the burden of constraints placed on pupils in school.

A final determining factor is the increasingly expanding network of responsibilities that incorporates the involvement of parents. Much has been said of the shift towards parental choice in education in countries such as England and Wales, New Zealand and the USA (Fine 1997; Ball 1994; Brown 1990). Whilst parents' powers in relation to the school depend largely on their access to 'cultural capital' (Ball, Bowe and Gewirtz 1995), parents are central as responsible educational agents. Among other things, we can refer to parents' legal obligations for their children's school attendance, their rights to a range of information on schools through the parents' charter, the widening of parental choice of schools, and the formalising of parental involvement with their children's schooling. Thus in some countries the parent has become a more significant reference point for educational professionals.

One powerful if complicating factor within a structuralist account of schooling and childhood is age. Ariès's description of the typical modern classroom discussed in Chapter 1 is not only a site for the regulation and control of children but the place for the incremental segregation of children by biological age. Thus, whilst all children's school experiences are more or less determined by external forces, an 'ideology of immaturity' dominates educational thinking in school with differential effects on children as they get older (Rudduck, Wallace and Day 1997). Age-grading complicates things in that as children get progressively older and move through the various 'developmental' stages, they become progressively more integrated into society. Age in these terms is a significant variable that positions children differently. Children are well able to confirm this in the way that they locate younger and older children on a hierarchy based on sometimes quite minute age differences.[1]

Nevertheless, there is still an important sense in which we can divide the school inhabitants up into two groups with differential access to a range of social, economic and political goods: to refer again to Qvortrup (1994), the adult population of 'human beings' and the child population of 'human becomings'. Age in these terms is not so significant a criterion for differentiating the child population; it becomes a measure of a child's progress towards the completed status of adulthood. We might think of this as the social apprenticeship model of childhood, with the school offering us vivid examples. We might even go so far as to say that the child as school pupil is the social apprentice proving his or her social worth incrementally through the age-graded acquisition of knowledge. Thus children follow a developmental pathway: children are supposed to reach appropriate incremental changes in knowledge and skill as they become progressively older. In these terms the teacher is the finished article, with the child always progressing incrementally towards this end state.

If we refer back to Illich's critique of schooling, he asserts that '[s]chools are designed on the assumption that there is a secret to everything in life; that the quality of life depends on knowing that secret; that secrets can be known only in orderly succession; and that only teachers can properly reveal these secrets' (1971, p. 78). What this means is that children start from a position of relative ignorance in schools, with knowledge and skills carefully accumulated through a series of incremental stages from the teacher until they reach the last stage of completion. Within most schools, age is the main organising criterion for the transmission of this knowledge. This incremental acquisition of knowledge is validated through formal assessments. At each stage, children are tested. In France this takes place at ages 8, 11 and 15. In England and Wales pupils are tested at 7, 11, 14 and 16. The various techniques for assessment tell us more or less whether the child is making 'normal' progress towards a chronological end-point. The maturation process within schools is an involuntary one. Prout and James (1997) refer to an age class system whereby, irrespective of their personal and social characteristics, children are propelled up the system via the National Curriculum as they get older.

Schooling and Post-Structuralism

Within structuralist accounts relations are more or less given, with children located towards the bottom of the social hierarchy. In turning to post-structuralist accounts, fewer assumptions are made about relations in school. The emphasis is very much on the production of relations and positions in classrooms. Power is more diffuse, with cultural resources interacting to produce identities for both adults and children. There is also more stress placed on the construction of childhood here, with children being located within conceptual and cultural frameworks. Identities in the classroom are shaped with reference to particular sets of ideas that gain a foothold within a teaching culture and structure the practices of teachers. Walkerdine (1983) offers an example of this. Focusing on primary schools in England and Wales, she argues that the classroom becomes a 'site of production' of both knowledge and social identities. Children are intimately involved in this process. Rather than see children passively internalising blocks of knowledge, Walkerdine argues that routine classroom interactions between pupils and teachers transform scientific ideas about child development into forms of educational knowledge. The primary-school classroom is thus viewed as a child laboratory where pupils are viewed as children rather than the more formal status of pupils. We can go further and think of the primary classroom as a child-centred laboratory. Children's development is closely monitored and measured against education norms that have been transposed from developmental psychology. From the 1960s onwards, the work of Piaget shaped primary-school culture, with an emphasis on children acquiring cognitive and social skills (Walkerdine 1983). The accent here is on the social and emotional aspects of the child's development, with children expected to reach certain levels by certain ages. Teaching becomes a process of monitoring and observing this development of skills. Child-centredness here means that teachers play a more enabling than didactic role in guiding and measuring children to the appropriate level.

The application of a developmental scale introduces all sorts of concepts and terms that are used to classify the child's educational development. Educational measures are transposed from scientific concepts that measure children's essential being, their core state of development. We are not talking here of educational wellbeing separated from other aspects of the child's welfare; we are talking about 'education' as the umbrella term for the child's overall welfare. In effect, developmental psychology frames primary-school activities for both teachers and pupils and primary-school activities locate teachers and pupils within school structures. Thus, whereas structuralism implies adult power over pupils, post-structuralist approaches demonstrate the contingent nature of both teachers' and pupils' positions. Teachers are locked into the processes of the monitoring and evaluation of skills such that their own professional identities become dependent on them.

Normalisation is a key concept here. As was stated earlier, teachers' normal practices are located within a 'child-centred' discourse. More significantly, the normalisation of childhood takes place (Donzelot 1979). This is not simply the outcome of a prolonged set of value judgements made by the teachers; it suffuses the teachers' common practices, becoming a built-in feature of their professional vocabulary. Children's 'natural' or normal state of development is taken from a range of assessments instigated by the teacher. There is a continuous process of comparison going on here. Children are expected to have acquired certain skills and capacities by a certain stage, the ages and stages approach to childhood discussed in the previous chapter. Children are thus measured against developmental norms. Those children who do not measure up, those who do not conform to a normal childhood, for example those designated as having 'special educational needs', are seen as problematic.

Epstein's (1993) work on young children and racism offers us an example of this process of normalising. The conjunction of what she calls 'ideologies of childhood', developmental psychology and the ideology of innocence assume that children in the first few years of schooling are incompetent. In the first case, incompetence refers to the child's cognitive and moral inabilities. In the second case, incompetence refers to the general expectation that very young children need to be protected from 'older' discourses such as sexuality and 'race'. She argues that these ideas influence the way that teachers view these children. Teachers view normal children up until the age of seven in terms of learning to be social rather than having any capacity to think and act socially. Children at this age are thus incapable of knowing about the world and knowing how others feel. In other words, these children are unable to form full social relations with others in class. Several things follow. First, children's serious or challenging questions in class are either ignored or trivialised. Epstein argues that this is partly as a result of their imputed incompetence and partly to do with children learning to be pupils: learning to be subordinate and accepting of the teachers' authority. Secondly, teachers view the children as being incapable of understanding the consequences of their actions. In Piagetian terms they cannot 'de-centre', cannot understand the world from the perspectives of others. Teachers thus have difficulty acknowledging that their pupils can be held responsible for actions that might be construed as racist. Children, in effect, cannot be seen as racist until they reach a certain age of maturity. Epstein argues that, on these grounds, education policy excludes primary school children from 'grown-up' subjects such as anti-racist education and sex education.

Reforming Schooling, Reforming Childhood?

I discuss children's rights and children's citizenship status in Chapter 10. Yet it is pretty clear from a perusal of policy and research in England and Wales in the first few years of the twenty-first century that little account has been taken of pupils as social agents or that there is any notion of pupils having collective interests. There are a few counter-examples in other countries. In France, for example, children are consulted by central government on education policy and there is a much more concerted attempt to involve children in school policy-making through school and local community councils (Dubet 2000). Nevertheless, the general tendency in Western cultures is for responsible adults to set educational agendas at national and local levels. If we return to the situation in England and Wales, historically children have had little say in school matters. What we find in current policy are trends that strengthen this state of affairs. If anything, reform tightens the grip that professionals have over children's school experiences. In the following I examine two of these trends in England and Wales: the emphasis on standards, and the tendency towards tightening relations between key school actors through networks of accountability.

Standardisation

One of the key areas of reform here is the National Curriculum. Economic recession in the 1970s concentrated educational minds on the form and content of the curriculum (Chitty and Dunford 1999). The need to link education more firmly to economic output, and central government pressure on schools and teachers to provide children with a standardised educational experience provided the grounds for the introduction of the National Curriculum in the late 1980s. As I mentioned earlier, the National Curriculum is divided up into four key stages: Key Stage 1 for 5–7-year-olds, Key Stage 2 for 8–11-year-olds, Key Stage 3 for 12–14-year-olds and Key Stage 4 up until the age of 16. Up until the mid-1990s, with the exception of Key Stage 4, children took the same ten subjects throughout the key stages. The Labour government in the late 1990s modified this by focusing on basic skills in English, mathematics and sciences for Key Stages 1 and 2. This allowed teachers in primary schools to suspend the teaching of other National Curriculum subjects such as geography, art and music. Having said this, the broad of thrust of the curriculum is to provide all pupils of all ages with a standardised curriculum experience. As well as the content being standardised, assessment is the same over the school life-cycle, with children, in theory, being tested from the earliest days in primary school (KS1) through to the age of 16, the first point at which they can leave school.

In the immediate post-reform period, reference was made to the National Curriculum as an 'entitlements curriculum' (Barber 1992; National Curriculum Council 1992). If we think of entitlements in terms of opportunities, then the attempt to standardise educational experiences for all pupils has had some beneficial effects, for example in narrowing the 'gender gap' between male and female take-up of subjects, particularly the more highly valued subjects such as mathematics and science (Arnot, David and Weiner 1999). Others have argued equally forcefully that the curriculum has done little to equalise the chances of academic success for other groups of pupils, such as those with learning difficulties and those from ethnic minority backgrounds (Troyna 1993). If we view entitlements as rights, children have little sense that the school offers them the prospect of any redress where the curriculum does not provide them with the right opportunities. The idea of entitlements suggests rights that can be taken up by certain groups; it also implies that there are channels through which these rights can be reinforced. In these terms, children's entitlements are largely rhetorical. Unlike British child-care policy, there are as yet few opportunities for pupils to express an opinion on the quality of their schooling.

It is only in the past few years that anything has been made of the effects of these new measures on pupils, particularly in primary schools. Pollard's (1996) earlier research points to teachers in English and Welsh primary schools being able to cushion the effects of the National Curriculum by, among other things, holding on to more informal teaching methods in protecting pupils from the pressures of school assessment. However, more recent findings seem to go along with the idea that the National Curriculum fosters greater continuity between primary and secondary sectors, with primary schooling becoming a more structured and formal experience for young children. In a more recent book on children's experiences of primary schooling, Pollard and Trigg (2000) note a complex relationship between pupils and their school work. There is, first of all, a growing awareness among the pupils of teaching and learning as a performance.[2] Pupils, especially those in the later primary years, understand that continual teacher and school assessment puts more pressure on teachers to induce pupils to produce high test scores. The pupils also view their own performance in terms of their educational careers. High-achieving pupils are more instrumental in their views of assessment, with some performing well despite their dislike of core subjects such as English and maths. The low-achieving pupils, on the other hand, experience more frustration and anxiety as they try to grapple with what is being asked of them. These latter pupils have difficulties coping with an emphasis on achievement. According to Pollard and Trigg (2000), primary school pupils experience degrees of individualisation with the 'risk' of failure a more significant feature of their school lives. In this respect England and Wales is unique in that an emphasis on measurable outcomes in class seems to be taking place at an increasingly younger age compared with other Western countries (Dixon 2000). To sum up here: whilst there appears to be little rejection of the National Curriculum and associated assessment practices in schools by pupils, the research seems to suggest that there are fewer ways now for teachers to protect younger pupils from the full effects of classroom assessment.

Accountability

The introduction of the National Curriculum in England and Wales is part of a more complex network of accountability, granting limited autonomy to key actors and at the same time constraining this autonomy by accentuating notions of performance and responsibility. What is significant here is the limited role that pupils play. The Labour government emphasises the need for pupils to take more responsibility for their learning (DfE, 2001). Provisions for children with learning problems emphasise the need to consult children involved in the assessment process (Armstrong and Galloway 1996). There are also some research grounds for thinking that children play an informal role in choosing their secondary school and in mediating home/school relations (Gorard 1996; Carroll and Walford 1997; Edwards and Alldred 2000). But, as with the National Curriculum, there are few policy strategies designed explicitly to treat children as responsible agents.

This neglect of the pupils' perspective is reflected in the way that the

National Curriculum has been framed almost exclusively in terms of the role of the teacher. As Pollard and Filer (1999, p. 23) state, ' "children" and "pupils" are mentioned solely as an adjunct of the dominant discourse about standards'. The teacher here is supposed to mediate between demands for improvements in academic and behavioural standards and children's attempts to come to terms with a highly prescriptive curriculum and a more intensive system of assessment. This has sharpened the focus on teachers. Vic Kelly (1994, p. 65), for example, states that 'a prime purpose, perhaps *the* prime purpose, of assessment in the National Curriculum is teacher appraisal and accountability' (author's emphasis). Pupil assessment at the key stages of the National Curriculum provides an important framework for measuring the input of teachers. The notion of accountability is quite powerful within education as far as the quality of teaching goes, with teachers under intense pressure to standardise their teaching and concentrate more on pupils as 'output'. Teachers and heads are more susceptible to outside influence now. School inspection was reformed in 1993, with the introduction of Ofsted giving much more prominence to a school's performance over a predetermined period of time.[3] The results of school inspections are publicly available, often becoming the focus of local and national media coverage. If we take this, along with the publication of league tables that rank schools according to academic performance and levels of absenteeism, then schools and teachers are under much more pressure now to perform.

As I mentioned earlier, parents rather than pupils have a degree of agency through their educational status as consumers. Parents, in theory, can make a more informed choice of school through the parents' charter that puts schools under pressure to produce more information. At the same time, parents are also accountable through a range of recent measures that strengthen the idea of parental responsibility for their children's performance in school. Home–school contracts, homework policies and a range of initiatives geared towards bringing parents into the educational equation all place the onus on parents to play a more formative educational role. A final significant 'reformed' educational actor is the school governor. School governing bodies are much more clearly implicated in school policy as responsibility for budgets has been devolved to them. Interestingly, school governing bodies became more significant just at the point where the pupils' 'consultative' role has been withdrawn. Pupil governors were summarily dismissed from school governing bodies through the 1986 Education Reform Act. Pupils have little or no means to make themselves heard in relation to the curriculum, the conduct of teachers and school policy. In recent years a debate has emerged within the educational academic community as to the relevance and efficacy of 'student voice', and the introduction of citizenship education within the National Curriculum in 2002 has put school councils on the educational agenda (Rudduck,

Chaplain and Wallace 1996; Fielding 2001). This is discussed in more detail in Chapter 10. However, it is worth stating here that as yet children are at best peripheral actors within an educational network of accountability.

Deschooling Childhood: Truancy

The key characteristics of modern Western schooling are the minute and well-defined techniques for regulating children's use of time and space. As I stated earlier, one taken-for-granted aspect of this is the compulsory nature of schooling. Regulation within school is only really effective if we can safely assume that children attend school on a daily basis. Debates around children's absence from school have been framed in the negative with reference to the idea of truancy. Truants may be said to be challenging the norms of childhood in three ways. First, children who truant are no longer safely confined within the perimeters of the school and are likely to stray into non-child territory. I will discuss the child's relationship with the public realm in a later chapter. The general perception of Western childhood is of children's movements and experiences being heavily circumscribed until they reach an age at which they are able to take care of themselves. Children in public spaces are normally expected to be accompanied by responsible adults, and greater fears over public spaces have placed a much higher premium on parental or, more generally, adult supervision (Corsaro 1997, p. 38). Secondly, truants are out of position in the structural sense in that they are no longer positioned in relation to the teacher's authority. Here truancy becomes a key feature of the discourse on crisis referred to in Chapter 4, with the teacher as the responsible agent acting in loco parentis. Notions of childhood disappearance suggest that children are less likely to approximate to a bounded and constrained conception of childhood (Wyness, 2000). Children straying unaccompanied into the public realm have implications for the concepts of care and protection. This also has implications for the issue of control. Whilst there is more to schooling than a simple custodial or 'baby-sitting' role, one of the most powerful norms of Western childhood is that children be in the right place at the right time. Children on the street or in shopping malls are at best seen as being 'on' the street rather than 'of' the street, a 'highly visible and contained but unacceptable presence' (Matthews et al. 1999, p. 283). At worst they are seen as a threat and in constant danger of criminalisation.[4] As I have already argued, schooling becomes one of the key normative reference points for positioning children. The implications for children being out of place are not simply geographical or physical. The school provides rules and structures, sets of expectations which enmesh children in networks of authority and responsibility.

Truancy is a threat, thirdly, because truants are less likely to conform to the idea of the social apprenticeship model discussed earlier. That is, a central problem of truancy is the absence of school experiences that are taken to be a necessary part of growing up. Interestingly, the largest survey so far conducted in English schools concludes that the majority of truants do not reject schooling outright; they miss specific lessons and renounce certain features of their schooling (O'Keeffe 1994). They make rational choices about whether to attend a particular class on the basis of what it has to offer them. Nevertheless, truancy as a social problem is associated with groups of children missing out on experiences that are supposed to prepare them for their future as adults, citizens and workers.

Deschooling Childhood – Home Schooling

Debates around children's absence from school overwhelmingly emphasise the negative or deviant in terms of truancy. When we come to look at the case of children who do not attend school because parents have made alternative arrangements for their education, we have a quite different version of school absence. With the exception of Germany, parents across Europe are entitled to 'school' their children at home. If we return briefly to truancy, in a legal sense truancy is not so much the absence of schooling but the absence of education. I return to the distinction made between schooling and education at the beginning of the chapter. Most of us would take truancy to be the absence of a child from school. Yet Section 7 of the 1996 Education Act in England Wales implies that truancy is bound up with the much broader project of education: "The parent of every child of compulsory school age shall cause him to receive efficient full-time education suitable (a) to his age, ability and aptitude, and (b) to any ... special educational needs he may have, *either by regular attendance at school or otherwise* [my emphasis]."

Technically, truancy results from parents failing to provide their children with a formal education, either by ensuring that their children attend school or by educating them at home. It is the latter form of education that concerns us here. Whilst the 'noise' of education reform has dominated thinking within educational circles in many Western countries over the past 15 years, Meighan (1995) refers to home schooling as a 'quiet revolution'. Parents have quietly gone about the business of taking their children out of school and educating them at home. This stealth is reflected in the hidden, almost invisible nature of the subject within the public realm. Petrie (1995) refers to the variable levels of regulation across Europe. When focusing on England and Wales, she refers to the absence of any policy or practice guidelines on dealing with children schooled at home and to a marked reluctance by administrators to discuss the quality of education received by children out of school. There is also little consensus among researchers as to the numbers of children schooled at home (Lowden and Bennett 1995). Local Education Authorities (LEAs), who have a range of administrative responsibilities for English and Welsh schools, have some records based on children who were known to them before being taken out of school. But parents are under no obligation to inform LEAs that they are educating their children if their children have not previously been in school. Consequently, there are no national statistics on home schooling. However, according to very rough estimates, home education is on the increase. Meighan (1995), for example, refers to 20 families of home schoolers in 1977 rising to around 10,000 in 1994.[5]

There are two dominant issues relating to home schooling. First, the main findings of research in this area are that children's academic performance improves as a consequence of the shift from school to home (Meighan 1995, p. 278). This may not be an altogether surprising finding, given the level of individual attention paid to home-schooled children. Secondly, what has always been more contested and more open to debate is the extent to which the home can offer the kinds of social contact found within the school. Does the absence of interaction with peers, as well as the more formal social contacts with teaching staff, seriously restrict children's social development? Does home schooling offer children the same opportunities to be socialised as schools? As I argued in the previous chapter, socialisation is a key framing device for understanding modern Western childhood. So far in this chapter I have alluded to socialisation within a school context by referring to the social apprenticeship model of childhood. In the following I address this idea in relation to home schooling. We see the significance of home schooling in the way that it brings into sharp relief not only taken-for-granted aspects of children's lives, but dominant assumptions about Western childhood. Our examination focuses on three of these aspects of childhood: age segregation, schooling as a 'secondary' form of socialisation and the hierarchical nature of adult/child relations. They correspond to three key aspects of home schooling: desegregation, continuity between home and education, and the fluid nature of relations between adult and child respectively.

Desegregation

As I discussed in the previous chapter, a dominant concept within sociology is socialisation. Following the influence of Durkheim (1961), one of the mainstays of introductory sociology is the idea of the school as an agency of socialisation.[6] This is usually expressed in two forms: the various informal ways that teachers help shape pupils' social characters, and the broadening of children's social contacts through peer relations. With reference to the latter, notions of emotional and social development are predicated on children getting on with their peers in school. In one sense, home schooling challenges a key function of schools in that children educated at home are excluded from regular playground and classroom contact with friends and other children. We need to be more specific here. Schools structure peer relations in such a way that this broadening of experience amounts to contact with other same-age children. There is some variation in the age that children start school across European and North American education systems. Yet, through the school system, most children are, at around the age of 5 or 6, introduced to same-age children, children reputed to be going through the similar stages of biological and psychological development. Socialisation here is not simply about loosening children's dependency ties within the family by propelling them out into the wider world *through* the school. For socialisation at school both separates and segregates children into clearly defined age groups. Proponents of home schooling are not so much challenging the idea of socialisation, but the narrowly conceived notion that the school forces children to develop friendships within a very limited circle of same-age children. They contend that this produces unrealistic expectations, sometimes leading to conflict within the peer group (Thomas 1998, p. 116). According to this argument, then, the school hampers rather than facilitates children's social development. Proponents go on to argue that children schooled at home have a much wider social frame of reference, with more opportunities to interact with adults and children of different ages. Thus what home schooling produces is the potential for desegregation. We need to be careful when drawing inferences from the documented research. As yet there is no evidence that home schooling actually broadens children's social networks. Nevertheless, there is the potential here for children to move beyond the age-segregated forms of contact which dominate children's lives in and out of school.

Continuity with Preschool Learning

The automatic link between school and socialisation can be questioned in a second way. If we examine socialisation theory more closely, the crux of education rests on the function that the school plays as a *secondary* form of socialisation (Parsons 1961). As I argued in the previous chapter, social scientists in the latter half of the twentieth century emphasised the family as the primary socialising agency in terms of parents being the most formative influence on their children. This view is clearly supported by educationalists in theory and in practice in the way that teachers continually refer to their pupils as the products of more significant others, namely parents. As Sharp and Green (1975, p. 86) argue in their analysis of primary schooling, teachers generally expect parents to provide them with 'school trained child[ren]', children who have been appropriately socialised by their parents and can slot into the role of pupil.

The influence that parents have over children is said largely to determine their social character. However, the contact that parents have with their children is by its very nature informal and incidental.[7] The preschool years are formative, with an emphasis on close, loving and affective relations between parents and children. Schools are important partly because they act as an institutional means through which children can break away from the 'particularistic' features of family life. We are referring here to a shift from primary to secondary forms of socialisation. In order for children to develop a sense of independence, they have to make a transition from the less structured environment within the home to a quite different set of rules and practices within the school (Parsons 1961). There is a general expectation that children will generate their own rules through peer-group interaction in class. Yet the formal and structural features of the school loom large as children encounter rules and practices that eventually position them as pupils. To simplify here: we might see the secondary socialisation as the process through which children take on the more public role of pupil. Children sometimes have difficulties making this transition. To make this easier, primary schools will often encourage parents to bring their children into class and stay with them for the first hour or so of the school day. This allows children to settle into their new environment, gently easing them away from the dependency-type links that they have with their parents.

Children schooled at home, on the other hand, particularly those with no experience of school, make few major adjustments to their daily routines as they enter the formal school age. According to the home schoolers there is a much greater continuity between preschool and school ages. Interestingly, Thomas (1998, p. 42) states that home schoolers start out by following a school model, with parents providing much more structured lessons in a didactic teaching style. Yet they gradually move towards a less formal approach as they become more confident in their own abilities as educators. Secondary socialisation does not play a large part in the lives of these children.

Fluidity of Adult/Child Relations

Parents cite pupil disaffection from school lessons as an important reason for opting for home schooling.[8] British researchers argue that parents taking more control of the curriculum leads to a much stronger pupil commitment to the whole project of education. Home schooling in these terms is child-centred. The curriculum and the style of teaching are tailored to the specific dispositions of individual children. Thomas supports this in arguing that home-schooled children are more actively involved in the form and content of their education than school-based children. Children schooled at home are also more likely overtly to switch off if their parents are not providing them with a relevant, interesting and stimulating curriculum (1998, pp. 58–60). There is thus more potential for negotiation between parents and children as they both search for a happy educational medium. Here it is worth pursuing the different learning environments of home and school. Ethnographic research has paid particular attention to the ways that pupils collectively develop strategies for concealing their dissatisfaction with the curriculum. Hargreaves (1990), for example, identifies pupils' adeptness at impression management in the way that pupils bored or dissatisfied with the lesson are able outwardly to appear to be paying attention in class.

Within the one-to-one situation at home, developing similar strategies becomes much more difficult for home-educated children as they are unable to feed off peers or manipulate the teaching environment in any covert way. We might also speculate that children are less likely to affect an attentive demeanour in front of their parents. Children within the home are less able to develop outward signs of conformity and conciliation. Consequently, they have few alternatives but to express overt dissatisfaction with their education. This has implications for the structural position of children. One way that children contrive a degree of autonomy in school is through the collective hidden strategies that undercut teacher-centred activities. Home-schooled pupils, on the other hand, are unable to develop these kinds of strategies on their own. This potentially produces more confrontational situations, which could give children within the home the upper hand in relation to their education.

What I have identified here are two contradictory trends that characterise both home and school as educational environments and associated relations between adults and children. Schooled children, as I have argued, are largely positioned through all-encompassing structures such as the timetable and the curriculum. At the same time, ethnographic research demonstrates degrees of autonomy for children through age-related peer relations in class.[9] Children schooled at home, on the other hand, have more room to negotiate the form and content of the curriculum yet appear to have fewer options for developing strategies that conceal their feelings towards their education.

In countering the charge that home-educated children suffer socially through the absence of school interaction, Thomas refers to the way that home-schooling parents report levels of confidence and assuredness demonstrated by their children when relating to adults. Interestingly, this confidence borders on social and intellectual precocity. One mother was critical of one home-schooling family:

> There was a family of home education people locally. They put us off. The children were very bright but socially inept. They acted like adults rather than children – not in a way I'd expect children to act. They weren't inept with adults but couldn't fit in with same-age children from the school. (Thomas 1998, p. 116)

Whilst this home-schooling mother was careful to point out that this family was the exception to the rule, we have here an interesting illustration of how home-schooled children might not conform to a dominant social conception of childhood. Children are supposed to learn how to behave and think according to adult-determined conceptions of civility and respect. They are expected to behave as 'normal' children rather than the model of the man-child discussed in Chapter 4. As with truancy, there is some suggestion then that home schooling can produce children 'out of position'.

Conclusion

Home schooling brings us back to our rejection of an automatic link between education and schooling. Whilst home schooling is clearly not the norm, it is not so out of step with conventional thinking on children's education. Concerns expressed over social problems in school may well be a significant factor in the rising numbers of children being schooled at home and the higher levels of truancy. Problems such as bullying, classroom disruption and sexual and racial harassment all feature in parent home schoolers' assessments of the quality of contemporary schooling. Moreover, these problems are currently entertaining the minds of many European educational establishments (Parsons 1999). I am not advocating home schooling here and the paucity of research restricts an informed evaluation. We cannot say whether home schooling produces social misfits. By the same token, there is little systematic evidence to confirm its superiority in terms of the quality and quantity of children's social contact (Thomas 1998, pp. 112–25). What interests us here is the subtraction of school from children's lives and the implications this has for our understanding of the concept of childhood.

I have addressed home schooling as one of four themes that link schooling rather than education to childhood. In bringing all four themes together, we might also argue that home schooling, and to a limited extent truancy, offer levels of autonomy for children, whilst the development of mass compulsory schooling, the positioning of children as pupils and recent school reforms emphasise the regulation and control of children. Regulation is an underlying trend in the first section where I linked the development of a modern Western conception of childhood to the introduction of mass compulsory schooling. Schooling has clearly extended the life chances and enriched the lives of many children. At the same time, schooling has been part of an historical process that excluded children from the public realm and carefully segregated them into age groups. This has produced tensions between school and family as parents and sometimes children have taken issue with official attempts to enforce school attendance. There is a parallel global tension between the schooled child from developed Western countries and the unschooled child from developing countries. As we shall see in Chapter 10, the majority child population from the underdeveloped south is subject to increasing intervention from international bodies and developed 'northern' governments through attempts to introduce compulsory schooling.[10]

Regulation and control is the focus of our second theme. Paradoxically, although children are the majority population in schools, they are 'invisible' in terms of their social status (Oldman 1994). I argued that schools are fundamentally about regulating and positioning children as future social actors. Structural approaches locate children somewhere at the bottom of the school hierarchy. Children are more or less acted upon and not expected to have much influence on school affairs. I hint at the possibility for children's collective social action in class. I take up this idea in the following chapter where I address children's peer relations. Yet, I would argue that this resistance to the all-encompassing nature of schools is partial and, for the most part, contained from within.

Despite recent talk of 'inclusive' schools and greater consultation with pupils, the pupils' voice and any notion of children as social agents are absent from recent educational reforms. The idea of a reformed 'schooled child' is an effect of a series of fairly radical changes to the form and content of schooling. Various commentators have highlighted contradictions within the reforms between the centralising tendencies of a National Curriculum and the individualising thrust of a market or quasi-market in education (Hargreaves and Reynolds 1990). Whilst the latter could be extended to address the child or pupil as an individual, these forces do not really touch on children's worlds. Networks of educational choice and responsibility that develop out of these tensions exclude pupils. Regulation and control is thus an ever-present feature of recent changes. In linking the new schooled child to theories of childhood discussed in earlier chapters, there would appear to be elements of both the 'disappearing child' and the 'exploited child'. In the former case, children on entering primary school have less time to develop and play, less time to exhibit the hallmarks of the protected innocent child. In the latter sense, children become part of a broader economic project whereby schools produce a standardised product for future use.[11] Interestingly, this is at odds with any trend towards home schooling. At one end of the spectrum, parents are taking their children out of school as relations of trust break down between the home and school. At the other end of the spectrum, there are contrary pressures to keep children at school for longer – breakfast clubs, after-school clubs, summer schools all help to deal with the contradictory pressures in families both to 'turn out' high-achieving children and to juggle work and child-care responsibilities.

Part Four

Children as Social Agents

8

Children's Social Worlds: Culture, Play and Technology

Introduction

In the last two chapters I argued that the segregation of children on the basis of age and ability makes the child population more amenable to measurement and analysis in sociological as well as social terms. These forms of regulation and control have formed the basis of a dominant modern and Western understanding of childhood. In the following three chapters I set out various challenges to this conception of childhood. In the following chapter I discuss the methodological and ethical implications to these challenges. In particular, I examine researchers' attempts to engage with children as joint owners of sociological knowledge. In the final chapter I outline the political ramifications of these more radical conceptions of childhood for both adults and children. In this chapter I situate the research process as closely as possible within children's worlds. Rather than seeing these worlds or cultures as part of a process of regulating children's development, we can view them as ways in which children constitute themselves as competent social actors.

In several previous chapters I illustrated the centrality of play to our understanding of modern Western childhood. In the first case, play is conflated with education and provides the grounds for adults to regulate children's activities because of the importance that adults attach to children growing up. In the second case, play is associated with innocence and 'free time' – being childlike – which characterises children's trivial and marginal social position. At the same time, it can be viewed as a potential threat to the adult project of 'growing up', for it is the nearest we come to a natural autonomous realm for children. In this chapter I will take children's play rather more seriously as a socially productive realm of activity. I want to move from child's play and start thinking about children's cultures. The chapter is divided into two sections. In the first section I explore the meaning of children's cultures. To talk about children's cultures is to advance the notion that children are 'of' the social world rather than members-in-the-making. The latter is typified in terms of play, something children rather than adults do, something that denotes childhood both as a form of preparation and as a marginal pursuit that divorces children from the 'real world'. To talk about children's cultures, on the other hand, is to locate children within the real world of norms, values, expectations and responsibilities. Researchers now recognise that children establish themselves as social actors through ongoing interaction with others, particularly their peers. I look at various aspects of these cultures: their quintessentially social character, the significance of conflict and the way that children's cultures become significant spaces for the formation of gender identities.

In the second section of the chapter I look at a range of associated ideas and concepts that strengthen the importance of researching children's social worlds. In particular I focus on the increasing significance of technology in children's lives. In Chapter 4 I addressed one dominant adult concern, that childhood as a social institution is under threat from technological change. I argued that this 'discourse of fear' tells us far more about the way in which adults regard children than it does about the way in which children make sense of their social worlds. In this chapter I concentrate on the latter and provide a more positive conceptualisation of the role technology plays in the lives of children. First I address the social nature of technology in relation to the way that children use television, the video and the internet as a medium through which children's cultures are formed, extended and changed. I go on to outline the way that children's cultures in recent years have been targeted by corporate capitalism through a potent consumer culture. I address this consumer culture with reference to two relatively new constructions of childhood: the consumer child and the cyber child.

Children's Cultures and the 'Dominant Frame'

As we saw in a previous chapter, the dominance of structural functionalism in the mid- to late twentieth century ensured that children's peer groups were seen as an integral part of the socialisation process, with peer relations predominantly 'a rehearsal for adult life' (Schildkrout, cited in Prout and James 1997). The peer group becomes a means of breaking dependency-type links within the family as children gradually grow out of the family. Within the regulated confines of the playground, the youth club or the scout hall, children expanded their social networks, became familiar with more egalitarian and 'horizontal' relations and in general followed a predefined path towards completion and adulthood. The emphasis here is on consensus and conformity, with the peer group a vehicle through which the individual child developed the appropriate norms and values.

One of the most consistent and by now long-standing challenges to this view of peer groups is the ethnographic approach. Within youth studies and the sociology of education the emphasis on the dynamic, two-way nature of relationships within schools and classrooms offers scope for viewing children as active participants within the socialisation process (Prout and James 1997, p. 19). The ethnographic approach relies on a range of research techniques which bring the researcher into close contact with the school community. The observation of children in the playground and classroom, the interviews with groups of pupils on their views of education, and the diaries kept by pupils and teachers for monitoring the daily routines in class make it possible for the researcher to identify the collective nature of children's school experiences.

I will have more to say about method and methodology in the following chapter. It is worth noting here that one of the key themes of these ethnographies was confrontation. In an earlier classic classroom ethnography, Paul Willis (1977) followed the school lives of a small group of working-class boys in Birmingham, England. The 'lads', as they were known, were adept at subverting the authority of teachers through a range of collective strategies, which made it difficult for teachers to manage the classroom. Children's cultures here were viewed as 'counter-cultures' with *Learning to Labour* presaging a steady flow of research into young people's confrontation with the adult world through the analyses of 'subcultures' (Hall and Jefferson 1976; Widdicombe 1995).

From the outside, from an adult vantage point, these assorted groups of skinheads, mods and punks were seen as chaotic, valueless and asocial; from within the researcher identifies rituals, norms and hierarchies that structure the subculture. In addressing children's cultures, sociologists of childhood are adopting the same approach in making sense of the 'senseless' (Harre 1986) Rather than see peer groups as merely developmental or asocial, the 'children's culture' approach takes the view that children are social in and through relations with each other. When given the opportunity, children generate rules and norms which govern their behaviour and their membership of the group. Children's cultures always bring us back to the here and now, to what children do as children rather than as proto-adults. Children's membership of peer groups, friendships and children's cultures is to be viewed as an integral feature of social structures.

The Importance of the Social

Moss and Petrie (2002) view the idea of children's culture as a strength for more general understandings of late modern childhood. In rescuing childhood from the domain of an individualistic psychology, they see it as a quintessentially social phenomenon: children are fully immersed in the social world of relationships and interactions. Citing Corsaro, they argue that '[c]hildren produce and participate in their own unique peer cultures by creatively appropriating information from the adult world to address their own concerns' (2002, p. 124). In emphasising the social nature of children's cultures, we are addressing the various strategies for constructing meaning. Whereas the dominant framework assumes that children's cultures are arenas for developing, refining and rehearsing their social and cognitive skills, in locating children's cultures within the social we are already drawing attention to children as competent meaning-makers.

Corsaro (1997) views this meaning-making in broader terms: children's appropriation of the physical and symbolic world is a productive means of renewing and expanding social relations. What we have here is a continual process of 'interpretive reproduction': 'The term interpretive captures the *innovative* and *creative* aspects of children's participation in society ... The term reproduction captures the idea that children are not simply internalising society and culture, but are actively contributing to *cultural production and change* [author's emphasis] (1997, p. 18).

Two points need to be made here. First, we are establishing children's social ontology through children's cultures. Children are no longer on the social periphery as transitional subjects. Secondly, on the basis of their full social membership, children are offered the same possibilities and are subject to the same limits as other members of society. Thus children are not simply being prepared for a later real world, they actively help to sustain, reproduce and create society as children. Children create and innovate through interaction, particularly among themselves within children's cultures. They are thus competent social collaborators. Corsaro also argues that children, by virtue of being full members of society, are constrained by existing rules, norms and values. At the same time, these constraints are also seen as a cultural framework within which children, like adults, are able to innovate. By highlighting children's roles within the processes of interpretive reproduction, Corsaro implicitly brings children in line with processes of structuration; the rules and boundaries that position people are also resources drawn on by people in making sense of their social worlds (Giddens 1984).

The Normality of Conflict

If we look for a moment at the way children work within these constraints, we can see children attempting to gain control of their lives and share this control with their peers. Adult authority is a significant counter-reference point here. Conflict becomes an important means through which children affirm their social status. In many cases, children explore the various rules that govern their lives. Confrontation with the adult world provides the dramatic element in the examination of subcultures. The flamboyant style, dress and behaviour of, say, the punks in the late 1970s is what caught public imagination as a visible breach of the rules (Brake 1995). Yet conflict can take far more subtle forms as children use adult rules as a cultural resource for shaping and exploring their identities and creating and strengthening group ties.

Thorne (1993) during her observation of elementary school children in class became aware of what she called the 'underground economy of food and objects'. One of the rules of the school she was researching was a prohibition on pupils bringing certain items such as toys, coloured pens and bits of food into the classroom. The children had used these restrictions as a means of creating a subterranean system of exchange, and it needed the children to work together to sustain this system. From the researcher's vantage point at the back of the classroom, she watched the unfolding of this underground economy as children surreptitiously swapped the prohibited items from behind their propped-up desks out of the teacher's purview. Interestingly, sometimes teachers tacitly approved of this deviance. Teachers are put in an ambiguous position. The rules have social and managerial purposes: they affirm the existing social order and are part of the hidden curriculum that structures behaviour and attitude. At the same time, teachers sometimes acknowledge the creative manipulation of these rules and on occasion may 'turn a blind eye'.

Corsaro (1997) draws on Goffman's notion of 'secondary adjustments' in viewing conflict as a more productive feature of children's lives. Thus the bending of rules and the evasion of adult prescriptions are ways for children to gain a degree of autonomy, as well as strengthening group norms within children's cultures. Here we can differentiate 'deviance' from 'secondary adjustments'. The former is often invoked where socialisation has apparently broken down. For example, the recent concern over bullying in the UK has meant that conflict within the group is often diagnosed as a cognitive or social problem (James and Prout 1997, p. 14). Within the dominant frame, children's deviance is seen as a breach of dominant 'adult' norms, a symptom of 'inadequate socialisation', reflecting badly on adults with responsibility for children. The idea of secondary adjustments, on the other hand, locates conflict as a constituent part of being social and being a member of children's worlds. Corsaro (1997) draws on a range of examples, from oppositional talk among Afro-American children to the highly stylised *discussione* in Italian children's cultures, to illustrate the importance of conflict in children's worlds. Connolly's (1995) case study of a group of 5–6-year-old 'bad boys' in an English primary school refers to the way that conflict in class can have serious implications for children's life chances.

Nevertheless, he also identifies the way that the boys draw on a range of sexualised and racialised discourses in the classroom and playground in trying to construct masculine identities. Thus the constant reference in the ethnographic data to girls and other ethnic minorities in derogatory terms made the boys feel bigger and less childlike.

We need to be cautious when viewing young children's confrontations with other children as simply egocentric or selfish. Corsaro (1997), for example, identifies strategies for what he calls the 'protection of interactive space'. Children assert their newly found positions within the group and monitor the access of new members by keeping away anyone who might threaten their ability to share. This leads to potential new members having to develop sophisticated 'access strategies', finding ways to acknowledge existing members' rights as well as their own desire to participate. New members thus hover around the perimeter of where the interactions are taking place, watch carefully what is going on and try to interject at the appropriate moment in an effort to become part of the group scene.

Children's Cultures and Gender Identities

The 'children's culture' approach also allows us to follow the complex inter-actions between children that shape their gender identities. As with other researchers of children's cultures, 'the social' is the medium through which a child's identity is formed. Play here is synonymous with 'the social' in that children develop their gender identities primarily in and through inter-actions with their peers. Thorne (1993) rejects the dominant dualistic approach whereby boys and girls follow different trajectories, mixing in their own gender-specific cultures. Again, 'the social' is important as the collective space through which boys and girls actively construct their gender identities together. Same-sex play is something that children tend to enter into, but there is an element of choice here. For example, children are more likely to choose same-sex peers where they feel they are being judged by others. In more informal and private settings, boys and girls are just as likely to want to play with each other.

The dualistic approach constructs girls' cultures in terms of smaller, inti-mate, more egalitarian groups, which tend to meet in more private surrounding, what McRobbie (1991) has referred to as a 'bedroom culture'. Boys, on the other hand, are more outward-looking, intent on controlling more public space, and drawing on a wider, more hierarchically organised group of peers. Thorne (1993) from her research argues that these same-sex cultures account for a small minority of children. Thus groups of the most visibly popular boys and girls may form separate cultures in these terms. Other less popular children form more unstable groups, some boys form groups that approximate to the bedroom culture, and girls often interact with much larger groups of children. If we address other variables such as ethnicity and social class, then there is more variability in the size, structure and gender characteristics of children's cultures. Moreover, as we shall see in the following section, the rise of the internet, coupled with heightened parental fears of children's use of public space means that a bedroom culture becomes part of a much more inclusive consumer media culture. Both boys and girls are likely to draw on a variety of 'electronic baby-sitters' in creating the home and bedroom as a locus of leisure and relative autonomy (Wyness 1994).

Children's Cultures within the Adult World?

Whilst these collective actions are construed as meaningful and socially 'constructive' in their own terms, there is a danger in viewing children's worlds as hermetically sealed, exotic cultures, products of the ethnographer's or anthropologist's gaze. In order to ground children's meanings and actions with their peers, ethnographic work has viewed children's cultures as microsocieties with their own rules and values. In these terms, children's meanings are in danger of becoming separated from the broader flow of interaction largely dominated by adults, a 'tribalised' version of children's social worlds (James Jenks and Prout 1998). By concentrating on children's interactions with each other in isolation, researchers are implying that children cannot compete with or connect with adults in the broader society, and children as social agents are thus unwittingly consigned to their own fully formed but nevertheless marginal social worlds. James, Jenks and Prout (1998, p. 82) make the point well: 'How far is it sensible or indeed credible to argue that children's daily lives can be understood as separate from, for example, the lives of other family members or, analysed in isolation, as if untouched by an 'adult world' to which, in the end, they must inevitably subscribe?' In the first chapter we referred to the 'play-child' construction as a dominant set of ideas that characterised childhood. And in Chapter 4 play becomes one of the key child domains in crisis. It thus comes as no surprise to find that where children's cultures are being researched, children playing together becomes the focus. Whilst play in these terms does not count as a part of the social, ethnographers have identified the creative and constructive way that children relate to each other. Researchers have wanted to go much further and deeper into 'child's play' and uncover the hidden and quite often illegitimate practices that turn play into culture. In the following chapter I discuss the methodological limits to studying children's cultures. The point I want to make here is that an overemphasis on play, whether it trivialises, 'exoticises' or privileges children's cultures, can take us further away from the myriad ways in which children and adults connect and relate to each other and the mechanisms that underpin the structuring of children's lives.

In advancing the idea that children's relationships should be taken seriously both in terms of the 'tribal' nature of children's cultures and in terms of the contributions that children make within adult-dominated settings, we might refer to Moss and Petrie's (2002) notion of children's space. In a literal sense it refers to children's use of physical space, the broadening of children's physical access to the social world by providing contexts within which they can interact. Thus young people are being incorporated within a range of environmental initiatives that expand their use and control of public space (Matthews et al. 1999; Freeman 1996). Children in the UK, for example, are now routinely consulted by local government officials when play areas and parks are being designed. However, children's space is much more than this. It incorporates 'the social', which expands and enriches children's relationships with each other and with adults. Children's space here goes beyond the conventional adult imperatives to protect and control, towards more reciprocal and negotiable relations between adults and children. Space also refers to a cultural domain of children's rights and practices that privileges the perspectives of children: 'The concept of "children's space" is linked to an ethos, constituted by certain understandings of children, a certain type of relationship between children and adults and certain ethical perspectives' (Moss and Petrie 2002, pp. 9–10). Children's space also has an important discursive dimension, with the emphasis on children having an audible voice. Children effectively have more say in matters that affect them and those surrounding them. Children's space thus provides stronger links between children's and adults worlds.

Whilst it is still difficult to think of children playing formative roles in adult-dominated contexts such as the classroom, the work of Pollard and Filer (1999) pick up on the ethical perspectives referred to by Moss and Petrie (2002). Their ethnographic research is instructive here for it balances the constraints imposed by adults with children's own constructions: children as both determined and determining agents through their relationships with adults as well as with each other. Thus within an adult-regulated and curriculum-driven environment, children are still able to shape what the researchers refer to as their 'strategic biographies', defined as 'their personal histories of adaption, action and interaction regarding the important people, situations and events in their lives' (Pollard and Filer 1999, p. 22).

Their strategic biographies are tracked throughout the children's primary-school years. In the process, the researchers identify the strategic choices made by the young children in the classroom with their peers, their teachers and in some cases their parents. Whilst the methodology rests on case studies of individual children rather than children's cultures, Pollard and Filer (1999) draw out the various strategies adopted by pupils in shaping their identities and 'pupil' careers. These strategies revolve around the relations pupils have with their peers and teachers in class.

One case study worth examining is William, one of four children whose pupil careers were tracked from reception class (age 4) through to the last year of primary school (age 11). Within the classroom William was seen as quite an innovative and creative pupil with an uncompromising attitude to his lessons and his peers. He had a strong sense of his own character, and was confident in the way that he related to teachers and peers. This confidence was very much in evidence when he was in the company of other like-minded pupils. William, particularly in his early pupil career, was able to shine within his peer group and was a popular and witty companion. The authors comment that this was a particularly high-risk strategy in that it occasionally brought him into conflict with peers with whom he was not so friendly, for example the girls in his class. This risk was also evident in the way that his displays of nonconformity in class often allied him with groups of troublesome pupils. He sometimes had to find ways to disengage himself from situations where he would be construed as troublesome by his teachers. Towards the end of his primary-school career William was put in a class with older, more experienced children. This forced him to rethink his strategy as a popular leader in class.

Whilst some teachers interpreted his personality less favourably, William also had a strong sense of his own worth as a student. Interestingly, his relationship with one of his teachers, Mr Brown, illustrates an important conceptual departure in this study from the dominant framework. William had an informal and challenging relationship with Mr Brown, one of his teachers in Year 3 (age 8). This worked well for the teacher, who had a relaxed and interactive approach to teaching. When William returned to Mr Brown's class two years later, the teacher remarked that William had 'calmed down', making more of an effort to please his teachers. This change in attitude was seen by the teacher as a natural part of the maturation process. The researchers, on the other hand, were not quite so sure: 'Indeed it might be judged that this very sudden switch from William's highly interactive, noisy, jokey norm to a quiet teacher-pleasing industriousness looked more like a strategic response to a new context rather than a developmental change in William himself' (Pollard and Filer 1999, p. 149).

The notion of strategy here shifts children away from the developmental model of 'becoming' towards Corsaro's (1997) theory of 'interpretive reproduction'. Whilst William was growing up and becoming a more experienced pupil, he was also using his social skills throughout his pupil career to put himself in a favourable light with regard to his peers and teachers.

Davies (1982), in an early ethnographic study of children's cultures, argues that children, by virtue of their subordinate social positions, inhabit a 'double world', the world of adults and a children's culture. She refers to the 'strangeness' of the early years of schooling where children are thrown together in a quite new and much more formal environment. They are forced to interact with several other children, for the most part probably strangers, who happen to be in close proximity in the classroom. Although children are the majority population in school, they are inhabiting an adult's world where, as we saw previously, decisions, rules and choices are made by adults. Davies (1982) contends that out of this initial strangeness children create their own rules, their own visions, their own ways of making sense of the world. This process of making sense of the world constitutes a child's culture.

As we saw earlier, children's cultures are rooted in the social; friendships are the key to children's meaning-making here. Interestingly, we get a glimpse of the differences between children's and adult's cultures. From an adult perspective, children's friendships illustrate the impressionable and changeable nature of childhood. Thus, referring back to our discussion of the dominant framework in Chapter 6, children are essentially weak and capricious. In these terms, children's friendships are characterised as being fragile, fleeting and riven with conflict. In part this is due to children making sense of the adult world: playing around with the social rules involves a degree of social volatility. More importantly, children take a more pragmatic view of friendship. Many of the children in Davies's study talked about being friendly with someone on the basis of their close proximity to them, someone who would do things with them. Take the following extracts from essays written by Davies's (1982, pp. 68–9) 9-year-old sample:

> 'Why have I got a friend. Because if I dident [sic] have a friend I would have nobody to play with. I think it is good to have a friend don't you. If I had a soccer ball I would give him a game of soccer.'

> My friend is my friend because she looks after me and plays with me and its good to have a friend. A friend is a girl or boy that plays with you.

Adults view this as superficial in that, within the adult world, friendships are of a 'higher level', that is, adults choose their friends because they have intrinsic qualities that appeal to them. 'Being with someone' is an insufficient reason for liking someone. Given that children often have little choice about who they can mix with in the classroom, and given the importance that children attach to not being alone, friends for them were those close by.[1] Moreover, fights among school friends did not simply signify a radical break in a relationship, but were 'manoeuvres within friendships'. Taking the children's perspectives, Davies's (1982) study reveals a range of quite sophisticated rules that need to be followed in maintaining friendships.

Children, New Technologies and Social Relations

Adults' fears and anxieties in relation to children's play and technology were discussed as part of the 'crisis of childhood' in Chapter 4. We might note here in passing that the ambiguity surrounding children's cultures reflects a growing tension between children and their parents and teachers. In revisiting technoplay in this chapter I take a more sanguine line and promote the creative nature of child's play. Cyber children are developing skills that enhance their 'productive' capacities; they are also creating new social spaces for themselves. As was stated previously, the 'disappearing child' can only be sustained if we accept dominant adult conceptions of childhood. In challenging this thesis, I again focus the analysis on the children themselves: their understandings and their relationships with their peers.

The Social Nature of Technology

One of the adult fears discussed in Chapter 4 was that children were being sucked into a technological vortex, which compromised their ability to develop friendship networks. The image of the solitary child creating a virtual network of friends does not really stand up here. Recent research with children makes two counter-claims: first, children see television and computer games as one among a number of leisure pursuits and, secondly, technology opens up more possibilities for social relations for children. Suss et al. (2001) in their comparative analysis of children's consumption of the media in three European countries, Spain, Finland and Switzerland, claim that television does not replace friends or friendships. Children make active choices when, where and with whom to consume media. Most children normally watch television in the home either on their own or with their families. They tend to do other things with their peers. Young children's friendship networks are sometimes based around computer games, whereas older children eschew television in favour of friends and contacts outside of the home. In general, with reference to friendship networks, the internet is just one resource drawn on by children in expanding their repertoire of social encounters (Livingstone 2003).

One associated adult fear that was discussed in Chapter 4 was the assumed relationship between watching violence on television and the imitation of this violence by children in real life. Buckingham (1994) cites the lack of clear evidence to support a causal link between children watching television and subsequent violence, and he also challenges the assumption that children are passive recipients of a more powerful 'external' socialising agency. His research concentrates on children's social uses of television rather than its anti-social effects. In interviews with groups of 9–11-year-old children, Buckingham (1994) argues that children 'appropriate' television for a number of reasons that reflect a much more sophisticated understanding of television than researchers working within a behaviourist paradigm impute to them. Thus children use television as a way of talking about how they are able to evade parental regulation. Watching 'adult' television becomes a way of asserting their grown-up status in relation to other children, and at the same time the television programmes that their peers and younger siblings watch is used to emphasise their 'childish' natures. With reference to the latter, children often adopt the same strategy as adults in displacing the effects of television on to children, with younger children becoming the target of the displacement. Children were also well aware of the 'adult' discourse on the negative effects of the media and how it could be used to position children as incompetents. Interestingly, Buckingham (1994) identified a gender dimension here, with girls often claiming that boys were too immature to watch certain kinds of programmes. This claim was never reciprocated by the boys. Thus the social nature of television is apparent in the way that it is drawn on by children in positioning themselves in relation to their parents, siblings and friends.

In a recent empirical study of children's use of information technology in the classroom, Holloway and Valentine (2003) argue that the computer provides a more relaxed teaching and learning environment. In part this is due to the breakdown of a rigid zero-sum conception of power as knowledge, with pupils working in groups through more self-directed programmes of learning. Technology in this sense clearly breaches Postman's (1982) notion of adults monopolising knowledge. The pupils learn at their own pace, drawing on the teacher for advice and clarification when required. This changing teaching environment is also due to the way that pupils collectively engage with computer learning, thus strengthening the role that pupil cultures play in the classroom. Holloway and Valentine refer to the way that the computer generates four distinct friendship groups, the 'techno boys', the 'lads', the 'computer-competent girls' and the 'luddites'. As the teachers' role becomes less visible in class, so the interactive space is taken up by pupils when they enter the IT classroom and take up computer terminals along peer-group-membership lines. Technology thus helps create new social groups among children.

Children, Technology and Agency

While technology expands children's social networks, it also generates a potent conception of children as agents (Lee 2001). In the following I set out two alternative conceptions of childhood: the child as a consumer and as an internet cyberflâneur.

Children as Consumers

Through links between technology and leisure, the consumer media culture has become a powerful and lucrative feature of the global economy. As with the internet, there are conflicting ways of seeing childhood within this context. First, Kenway and Bullen (2001) emphasise the pleasurable aspects of the media. In particular, advertising in developed societies becomes a source of entertainment and pleasure for an increasingly age-segmented 'youth' market. Surface values relating to the senses generate identifications for children by 'producing a surge of affect, not the reflexive pleasure of knowing what is happening as it happens' (p. 75). Secondly, the market works its way into the lives of children by addressing them much more directly as consumers. Here the issue is partly one of exploitation, with children a more vulnerable target for advertisers and corporations intent on maximising profit. As we saw in Chapter 4, television is one of the main sources of adult discontent. With over 50 per cent of children aged 7 and over watching television in the seclusion of their bedrooms, questions are continually asked as to how parents are able to regulate their children's television consumption (Buckingham 2001, p. 83).

A third view of the consumer child is grounded in empirical research and suggests a more agentic view of childhood, what Buckingham (2001, p. 94) calls the 'media-wise' child. As I argued in the previous section, adults in general tend to read little social meaning into children's play activities. Advertisers, on the other hand, will draw on children's play and children's subjective worlds in marketing their products. In the post-World-War-Two period, marketers were able to second-guess the child's preferences from their mothers. Since around the 1960s in the USA and the UK the focus has shifted away from the mother as the arbiter of children's tastes and preferences as marketers create a symbolic world of identification and fantasy for children. Seiter's (1995, p. 7) definition of consumer culture is apposite here: '[a] shared repository of images, characters, plots and themes: it provides the basis for small talk and play'. Television has become a crucial medium through which this culture is generated. Whilst television allows marketers to shape young people's tastes and preferences through this symbolic world, why and how children prefer one product rather than another has generated demands for much more intensive market research. Kline (1993) notes that from the 1960s onwards much heavier emphasis was placed on researching the children's market for toys. Intensive observation, interviews and focus groups, and a range of child-specific techniques are now deployed in trying to understand the kinds of meanings that children impute to products.

Marketers make several assumptions now about the child consumer. First, children ascribe meaning to the toys with which they play. There is no simple one-to-one correspondence between the child and the toy: in the hands of a child a doll can hold all sorts of hidden meanings, can represent anything from a baby to a friend. Secondly, this meaning is largely constructed through the way that children relate to other children. Children's cultures and friendship networks become an important frame of reference for advertisers. Moreover, when children watch advertising on television they like to watch other children playing with the toys. Children are likely to use their new toy as a means of creating new or reinforcing established symbolic universes which are known to them.

Thirdly, as I noted in the previous section on children's cultures, there is no simple gender dimension to children's play. However, research has identified the gendered nature of advertising (Seiter 1995; Kenway and Bullen 2001). Seiter (1995) points to gender-segregation in terms of the way in which children watch commercials, particularly those that address children as consumers. Boys will not watch commercials with girls in them, whereas girls will identify with products in commercials containing both boys and girls. Seiter (1995) also sets out different categories of children's commercials, among them 'girls at home' and 'boys and toys'. In the former, 'warm and fuzzy' camerawork locates girls together at home playing with toys such as My Little Pony and Barbie. Boys, on the other hand, identify with more action-oriented scenes where boys in the commercial mimic the action roles of racing drivers or fearless soldiers as they play with their toy cars and action men. There are also differences in the forms of communication within each type of commercial. Girls tend to communicate with each other in a more conventional, narrative sense. Boys, on the other hand, communicate through their roles as 'action men' with little or no dialogue between them. Boys, as it were, become their toys in 'boys and toys' commercials (Seiter 1995, p. 131).

Fourthly, as well as gender differences, Seiter's (1995) analysis of children's commercials in the USA identifies ethnic stereotypes. In general, commercials tend to concentrate on WASP (white, Anglo-Saxon, Protestant) children. A few attempts are made to include children from other ethnic backgrounds. If we take the case of African–Caribbean children, advertising tends to conform to the dominant stereotypes of African–Caribbean superiority in music and sports, with 'black' children being used to sell sports gear and musical instruments. Interestingly, McDonald's, the corporate fast-food chain, is a notable exception here, with an ethnic mix of children regularly appearing in their commercials. Advertisers are thus highly sensitive to the interests of children (Corsaro 1997). Children and youth are fertile grounds for market activity, with advertisers developing an increasingly sophisticated approach to children's leisure activities (Kenway and Bullen 2001, pp. 46–9). We could plausibly argue that corporate culture creates demands for products that reflects more nuanced, age-differentiated choices made by children.

Up until now I have concentrated on the toy market and the child as a consumer of toys. A more recent phenomenon in the UK, the 'tweenager', conveys the idea that the teenage group, as a target for companies selling clothes and music, has shifted forward a few years to incorporate the 10–13-year-olds. Recent commentary connects this potential new market to the spending power of children rather than to their pester power. In the latter case, younger children can put pressure on their parents to buy them certain items that they learn about through peers and the media (BBC News, 16 August 2000). These same children or 'tweenagers' are now in a position to use their increase in pocket money to buy some of the items themselves. At the very least, they are able to use this relative economic freedom to put more pressure on parents to buy these items on the basis of more rational arguments. One example of this is the rise in what advertising executives call 'eating individualists'. These are 'tweenagers' who have a degree of autonomy in relation to what they eat, both as consumers of sweets and by influencing the kinds of food that their parents buy on a regular basis (www.datamonitor.com/consumer). Interestingly, the reasons for this reflect the advent of a risk culture discussed in Chapter 3. The rise in divorce, the increase in the numbers of families where both parents have a career, and the increase in the amount of disposable income that parents have, have underpinned this rise in 'tweenager' spending power. Changes in family circumstances are seen as being significant: parents going through a divorce are likely to 'spoil' their children, owing to the guilt they feel as a result of family break-up. Children at the same time may manipulate this situation for their own material ends.

Children are more fully integrated in the consumer culture as sophisticated choosers. This means that they are also apt to display degrees of scepticism with regard to the appropriateness of some forms of advertising. For example, children seem to resist the incursions of a corporate culture into schools, with students regarding the likes of Nike and McDonald's with some suspicion when they advertise their names through investments in computers and food in schools (Kenway and Bullen 2001, pp. 111–16). Kenway and Bullen (2001) in one example refer to a group of Australian 9-year-olds who were aware of the contradictory nature of using McDonald's fast food to sell sports equipment in school:

Boy: Like it's not really sporting equipment, sort of McDonald's sporting equipment. And you would like, expect an Adidas hat or something.
Interviewer: Oh, I see, because McDonald's is not really associated with fitness and sport, you don't think it would be a good idea?
Boy: Yes, it's sort of junk food.
Girl: I think it wouldn't be a very good idea because, like, they sell . . . if they give you sports equipment to get you fit, why would they give you junk food that would make you fat and stuff? (2001, p. 114)

Thus, whilst children are often perceived as being easily led and exploitable in relation to a dominant consumer culture, recent research suggests that children are a more reflexive and wary population of consumers.

The Youthful Cyberflâneur

In their exposition of the 'consumer media culture' Kenway and Bullen (2001, p. 178) see the youthful 'cyberflâneur' as 'the child who transgresses the spatial, physical and temporal boundaries of the corporate world through technology'. Several images of childhood are conflated here, among them the 'nerdy techno-kid' and the 'teenage hacker', but the cyberflâneur is modelled on the nineteenth-century urban streetwalker and observer. The youthful cyberflâneur uses his or her internet skills to make global connections with a range of ideas and movements. Like the urban streetwalker, the cyberflâneur has more latitude to observe and cast a critical eye over what Kenway and Bullen call the 'branded web', the websites dominated by the corporate consumer culture. At the same time, there is a search for other critical spectators, on-line activists as well as other alternative sites. The cyberflâneur also connects with the shift in political affiliations of the young in some European countries (Matthews et al. 1999). The shift from conventional national politics to global environmental issues is partly a result of the way that young people can use the borderless structures of the World Wide Web as an important source of information. This kind of knowledge is not so readily available in conventional learning settings such as the classroom. We might even speculate that this knowledge acquires a certain attraction precisely because it is not covered in sufficient depth in national curriculums. The internet thus allows children to take a far more political stance by, for example, challenging the ubiquitous influence of multinational corporations. Children can gather more information and become more involved with a range of ad hoc activist sites such as McSpotlight, NikeWatch and Adbusters, which seek to restrain corporate practices and uncover any abuses of economic power (Kenway and Bullen 2001, p. 179). Children can become part of a global civil society of pamphleteers and political activists, their membership conditional on internet access rather than age-related political rights.

The World Wide Web has become a powerful alternative and subversive frame of reference for young people. It offers space for a more proactive voice for them. Its anarchic character connects with the young person's desires for freedom from adult authority and regulation. We saw in Chapter 4 how on-line chat rooms have become a source of adult concern. Yet it is the illicit and hidden nature of the internet that attracts children because it provides alternative sources of information and frames of reference outside of the conventional home–school regulatory framework.

Cyberspace also connects with the young person's need for autonomy and privacy. The pressures on children to conform within their friendship networks and cultures, exacerbated by the consumer media culture and the increasing focus on performance through the education system, creates a much greater demand now for children to find their own private spaces. Privacy is not something that is associated with childhood – at best it is a conditional common good given to children by adults as they get older. However, the image of the solitary child communicating from a keyboard, referred to earlier, can be interpreted more positively as the child within an ever more controlling social environment creating for himself or herself a degree of self-control, a space within which he or she can make choices and decisions.

Technology, Consumerism and Social Exclusion

The 'media-wise' child illustrates the different ways that children relate to their social environments. However, the child population in late modernity is a fragmented one: consumerism and new technological media create new forms of social exclusion (Hill et al. 2004). While children are much more implicated in consumer markets now, their actions reinforce existing social and economic divisions and, in the process, generate new means of differentiating and stigmatising groups of children. Children as consumers are more likely to invest in designer labels, clothing that acts to reinforce peer membership and differentiate them from other peer groups. One recent report claimed that more than 50 per cent of 11–19-year-olds think that they are likely to be judged on the basis of what they wear ('Scotland's designer generation that won't play outside', *Scotsman*, 27 April 2005, p. 25). This consumer culture has also generated distinctions between more affluent children who can afford to buy expensive designer clothes and those children who buy cheaper copies of the same clothing. As one commentator stated, 'Couture kids (affluent children) wouldn't be seen dead in the same brands as their council estates counterparts' ('Children who want to have it all', *Sunday Express*, 24 April 2005, p. 11). Interestingly, in this new market for children, gender is reported as becoming less of an issue, with boys becoming just as discerning as girls when buying fashionable clothes. Yet whilst material differences are increasingly highlighted through a children's consumer culture, one of the less obvious effects of the consumer culture, one that cuts across socioeconomic groupings, is the distinction between the 'active' and the 'less active' child. Concerns have been expressed about a generation of sedentary and unfit children as a consequence of poor diet, lack of exercise and the attraction of less active leisure pursuits (James and James 2004, pp. 140–66). One recent report, commissioned by the company that produces the detergent Persil, claims that the obsession with fashion and designer clothing among the young has led to fewer children taking part in traditional leisure activities ('Scotland's designer generation that won't play outside, *Scotsman*, 27 April 2005, p. 25). Children, sometimes on their own account but sometimes under pressure from their parents, are less likely to become involved in ordinary rough-and-tumble games for fear of getting their expensive clothing dirty or torn. This may affect children differently, with groups of affluent, 'designer' children, children who buy the cheaper copies and children with little purchasing power having very different commitments to outdoor pursuits. While there are a number of other key factors such as family routines and access to local amenities, children's access to a consumer culture will also determine the extent to which they conform to 'normal, healthy' childhoods (James and James 2004).

In turning now to the influence of the World Wide Web, at global, national and social levels the 'digital divide', or what some have referred to as forms of 'digital apartheid', differentiates children's access to the new technology in economic terms (Koss 2001). Information technology (IT) is now seen more and more as a prerequisite for growing up. It thus functions to differentiate children, providing the grounds for the powerful popular constructions of 'needy' children in terms of their access to computers (Selwyn 2001). Whilst the internet is becoming a more popular frame of reference for children's identity-formation and their membership of social groups, limited or non-existent access to the new technology has all sorts of negative cultural, social and economic implications for some groups of children. Whilst the school is often seen as a means of redressing these inequalities of access, Livingstone, in her review of research in the field, argues that the digital divide reappears in educational terms with 'info-rich' and 'info-poor' schools (2003, p. 155).

Whilst technology has a differential impact on children's lives at a more mundane level, the internet offers possibilities for altering adult/child relations. The expanding of children's networks includes the possible flattening of relations between children and their significant adult others. National governments in the UK and USA have recently invested money in information technology through their education systems. Notions of equality of access and the linking-up of all schools to an information network are attempts at challenging the 'digital divide'. However, if we take the example of the UK government's initiative on IT, the National Grid for Learning, the assumptions are that computing skills can be transmitted from teacher to learner (the child) in a unidirectional way (Moran-Ellis and Cooper 2000). This neglects the innumerable ways that children are informally 'online' and undermines the research referred to earlier which claims that children are more likely to be working alongside teachers on individualised projects (Somekh 2000; Holloway and Valentine 2003). There is also next to no acknowledgement that the competence that some children already possess from an early age will make it difficult for teachers to take a conventional didactic line in their teaching.

Conclusion

Technological change presents us with a strange juxtaposition of images: children at the video screen drawn into the globalised world of anarchic relations between user and internet; children incorporating IT into their classroom lessons within a context of more traditional and deferential social relations; children drawing on the internet in constructing new, more complex friendship networks. As we saw in a previous chapter, the bewildering nature of technology and the part it plays in children's lives confuses and complicates conceptions that adults have of their children. In one important sense, the internet gives children opportunities to subvert conventional structures that regulate children's lives. One of the key features of Moss and Petrie's (2002) notion of children's spaces is the room to innovate and take risks. In their comparison of these spaces in the UK and Sweden, they argue that adults in the latter case accentuate the need for children to take risks and make mistakes (2002, p. 128–9). They refer to 'free-time centres' for young children in Nordic countries where there is a relative lack of adult supervision. Here children have considerable freedom to explore their physical and social environment. Children are encouraged to confront risky situations and become used to the idea of making choices and weighing up risk.

Within the UK, on the other hand, the range of formal and informal regulatory frameworks within which children are controlled and protected give children little opportunity to make mistakes and learn from them. Children here have fewer opportunities to 'do their own thing', as legislation and convention errs on the side of protection, with young children being excluded from risky environments, and schools minimising the potential for accidents. Research has uncovered similar perceptions of childhood in relation to the virtual world of leisure and technology. 'Risk' is ultimately an adult construction: adults define what is safe, secure and inhabitable for children.

Despite the calculation of risk in favour of 'child protection', children still have their own space in the form of play and ongoing interactions with their peers. Children's play is still an important vehicle for measuring their development. Yet the sociology of childhood tempers this functionalist approach by arguing that children's worlds are also socially constituted domains within which children interact with others and create and reproduce social situations. In this chapter I have highlighted the importance attached to childhood being located within 'the social', particularly children's collective cultures. Children's play with others is a central framing device for growing up and gaining social experience. This assumption has not been lost on a corporate media culture where children are directly addressed as highly interactive social actors and increasingly discerning consumers.

9

Researching Children and Childhood: Methods, Ethics and Politics

Introduction

It should be pretty clear from the foregoing chapters that there is now potential to think of children as active research collaborators. The dominant framework, discussed in Chapter 6, assumes that research is done 'on' children as part of a process of measuring and normalising childhood, evaluating children's socialisation, their progress towards full personhood. I have argued that this kind of research is part of broader social trends that determine children's social characters, positioning them as subordinate and incompetent members within the social structure. The recent reconceptualising of childhood has challenged the basis to adult/child relations and, in the process, led to a reappraisal of relations between adult researchers and child respondents. There has been a prepositional shift from working 'on' children to working 'with' children (Mayall 2002, p. 121). Children viewed as research subjects rather research objects captures a new epistemological interest in children's knowledge and understanding, prioritising the idea that children have subjective worlds worth researching.

In this chapter I set out these interests with reference to the principles and practice of research with children. I want to explore the research process at various levels and from various vantage points. Whilst in this chapter we are going to concern ourselves with approaches that try to uncover children's subjective worlds, there is no monopoly on research innovation within the broad field of qualitative research. In previous chapters I emphasised the structural approach to studying childhood and its significance in rendering children visible as social subjects. This approach pays less attention to children's life worlds. However, it does at the very least establish a social ontology for children. If we can now deploy positivistic methods in measuring and comparing various aspects of children's lives rather than simply their rate of development, then we are starting to recognise children as full members of society. Nevertheless, rather more has been written about qualitative approaches that privilege the understanding of children in local settings. For some, uncovering children's social worlds has become a social as well as sociological imperative. If we take the example of family relations: the increasing diversity of family life makes it much more diffi-cult to infer the quality of parent/child relations from statistical data on birth order or number of parents (Mahon et al. 1996). Children need to be consulted as actors within complex networks of relations between stepfam-ilies and biological families, their views as research subjects are therefore pivotal in gaining an understanding of twenty-first-century family life.

We saw in the last chapter that researchers in recent years have been committed to understanding children's social worlds. Researchers have drawn on a range of techniques for getting at children's meanings and allowing children more participation within the research process. At the same time, they encounter a series of methodological issues that confront most researchers within the field of 'qualitative' research, but which I would argue are magnified and compounded by the involvement of children. In the first section of the chapter I examine some of these issues in terms of methodology. This is followed by a discussion of the ethical dimension to child research. As child professionals have become more sensitive to the needs and interests of children in recent years, so researchers have had to think about how common research practices affect children as respondents. In particular I address one key question: should our conduct within the research process with children follow general ethical guidelines that cover all research within the social sciences, or are there separate moral and legal considerations that affect our research practices with child respondents?

In the final section of the chapter I explore the possibilities for viewing children as researchers. Whilst up-to-date research has tended to assume that children are capable of playing a full research part as meaning-making respondents, a few adult researchers have experimented with using chil-dren in a researching rather than researched capacity. I will draw on some of these projects that illuminate a variety of research roles taken up by chil-dren.

Researching Children's Social Worlds: Methodological Issues

In Chapter 5 I outlined the process of privatisation, whereby children were incorporated within the family as social dependants. If we see the family as a still-dominant setting for children, then it is not so much the status of children that makes research difficult but the nature of contemporary Western family life. Despite an increase in the public surveillance of families, much of our professional and social scientific knowledge of childhood emanates from children's more public personae in the classroom (James, Jenks and Prout 1998, p. 176). Unlike educational ethnography, where the analysis of classroom relations can take place in situ, family researchers have great difficulties in penetrating the domestic interior in order to document family routines. The notion of successfully immersing oneself in the classroom as a 'microculture' (Vásquez and Martínez 1992) and our ability to gain insights into teachers' and pupils' perspectives reflect an ethnographic tradition within education. If we refer back to Pollard and Finer's (1999) concepts of 'strategic biography' and 'pupil career', we have a much more refined version of children's social relations than anything we can glean from family research. A culture of secrecy and privacy still pervades family life. Whether we are talking in professional or research terms, schools, on the other hand, are more open to the public gaze. In sociological terms, then, we probably know much more about children in schools than children within the home.

Having said this, research that tries to capture the routine aspects of family has tended to concentrate on the dominant actors within families, the parents. Anita Lightburn's (1992) ethnographic study of American families with adoptive children and children with special needs was concerned with how the various members of her research families negotiated relations between each other and links with various external agencies. Yet the mothers in each family were assumed to be the key mediators, with much of the researcher's time spent helping and conversing with them as they went about their routine tasks. Thus, even when we are in a position to explore the interior of family life, mothers and fathers are perceived to be the key actors, with routines assumed to flow through the controlling forces of adults. We come up against the perennial problem of 'second-hand data' in child research. That is, researchers in the past have tended to omit from their research proposals the voices of children as crucial mediators of parents' worlds. As with research in other fields such as education and social policy, we learn about how children view their worlds from the perspectives of significant adult figures.

The dominant role of the parent means that much of the action to be observed and documented revolves around the process of socialisation, with parents central. Even where we might anticipate children playing a more formative role, parents as protectors and guardians of their children become significant gatekeepers, shielding their children from the rigorous and potentially intrusive actions of a researcher. I will say more about gatekeeping in the second section of the chapter. An alternative ethnographic strategy is to follow through our instincts about the hidden but formative role that children play. In most instances we will be thinking about children's social worlds that are separate from adults, what was referred to earlier as the 'tribal' worlds of childhood (James, Jenks and Prout 1998). In order for us to bring meaning to children's worlds, children need to be treated as if they were a separate tribe, with their own rules, values, language and thinking.

In the previous chapter we saw ethnographers reporting on children's worlds from the inside through forms of participant observation with children in the playground and the classroom. The ethnographer takes this a step further and immerses himself or herself in children's worlds. Although children can account for themselves, their understandings and their experiences quite adequately through interviews, the ethnographer attempts to experience what the children experience to get a closer view by trying to take the role of the child.

Playing the 'Least Adult' Role

One of the problems with the ethnographic approach, a potentially more intractable problem when working with children, is the multiple and often conflicting roles that researchers play. From the child's perspective, the researcher's adult status can easily be construed as the 'master status'. Especially with younger children, the sheer physical presence of the adult researcher can be a considerable obstacle to entering children's cultures. Mandell (1991) in her research with preschool children tries to overcome this problem by taking the 'least-adult' role. Mandell adopted various strategies in trying to minimise the significant differences between herself and her research subjects. Thus she assumed the role of learner by staying close to the children, watching their movements and initially saying very little until she thought she was being accepted as a child participant. Mandell (1991) eschewed contact with the teachers, gatekeepers or colleagues, preferring to gain entry into the children's worlds via the children themselves. She refused to do what she called 'teacherly' things, often ignoring requests from the children for help, guidance and support, 'suspending all adult-like characteristics except physical size' (1991, p. 40).

Thorne (1993) devotes a chapter of her book, entitled 'Learning from Kids', to try to come to terms with her master status as an adult. Like Mandell (1991), she was attempting to understand children's cultures from the inside. In particular, she was trying to enter the world of the elementary classroom and playground as a way of examining the processes through which children shape their gendered identities. Within the context of the school, Thorne tries at first to conceal a variety of perspectives that she brings to the research as an adult. She goes on in her chapter to talk about her research experiences as a process through which she was forced to reflect on her adult role: if anything, her interactions in the playground with the children magnified her adult status. As an adult she was often mistaken for a teacher. She was sometimes seen as a protector, sometimes a custodian and on occasion an associate of the teachers in school. The very language she used with the children served to heighten her authority:

> During one of my first forays on the Oceanside (school) playground, a boy came over and asked, 'What ya writing?' 'I'm interested in what you children are like', I responded; 'I'm writing down what you are doing. Do you mind?' He warily edged away. 'I didn't do anything', he said. Another of my early explanations – 'I'm interested in the behaviour of children' – also brought defensive responses. I came to see that verbs like 'doing' and 'behaving', which figure centrally in the language of social science, are also used by adults to sanction children. The social sciences and child-rearing are both practices geared to social control. (1993, p. 17)

Thorne also reflects on how the research brought out the 'mothering' aspects of her identity. Thus the physical nature of child's play in the play-ground sometimes generated protective responses. From an adult vantage point, the continual charging of the children into each other and the various ways that they related to each other in physical terms can be seen as an intrinsic part of early childhood but also as an early stage in the process of socialisation. Given that socialisation presupposes that the physical gives way to the verbal, there is also a continual tension between the need to allow children to express themselves in their own physical terms and the demands of a broader social order that emphasises personal individual space. Mandell (1991), for example, found it difficult to shake off her adult/maternal perspective in that she initially found children's interac-tions to be chaotic. Similarly, Thorne documents her urge to intervene and regulate these 'collisions' whilst at the same time becoming sensitive to the notion that the physical in the child's world is part of the social and should simply be seen in these terms. She had to learn to step back and recognise what Cullingford (1991, p. 88) has called the 'volatile underworld of school', that children's worlds are more brutal and physical and that chil-dren have a potentially different and collective sense of what constitutes aggression or bullying than adults. Unlike Mandell, Thorne reflects on the impossibility of trying to pass herself off as a new member of the children's world. Mayall (1996, p. 15) comments on the futility of the least-adult role: we are continually brought back to the power and status differences between adults and children that no amount of effort on the part of the researcher can conceal.

Corsaro and Molinaro (2000) take a quite different approach by using their master statuses as adults as a way of immersing themselves within their cultures. Researchers use their 'foreignness', their distinctiveness from the children, as a means of entering their social worlds. In Corsaro's case, working with groups of Italian children, this meant his nationality as an American as well as his adult status. The children would consciously introduce him to their norms, routines and language as an 'incompetent adult'. Children's familiarity with their school accentuated the researcher's foreignness, with the latter using this as a further pretext for his induction into the group.

Alliances with Respondents

A second role confusion, a perennial one in ethnographic research, is the tension between the researcher as ally and as dispassionate observer of the social scene.[1] In the first case, the ability to enter the researched communities' worlds, or at the very least to get a sense of how others view these worlds, depends on the researcher building up a relationship of trust and empathy between himself or herself and the community being studied. In the latter case, the researcher might have to shift his or her ground to be able to take a more objective line. In the case of researching children, the difficulties are compounded by the 'dispassionate researcher' position being construed as an authoritarian one. John Davis (Davis, Watson and Cunningham-Burley 2000) demonstrates this point in recounting his research experiences with a group of schoolchildren with learning difficulties. Davis consciously eschewed the authority role in trying to build up a rapport with the youngsters. There were two reasons behind this. First, their learning difficulties sometimes made conventional discourse difficult. Davis wanted to learn ways of communicating with these children as a practical means of entering their social worlds. This involved the patient development of friendship-type relations with the children. More significantly for Davis, learning a new language was a way of giving the children a voice within their community. The staff in the school often interpreted the children's lack of linguistic skills to mean that they were incapable of communicating, and they routinely made decisions for them. In relation to the adult staff, Davis became an advocate for the children, constantly reaffirming what they were trying to communicate. In the case of one boy, Bobby, he became the main medium through which communication took place. This rapport with the children was openly if unintentionally undermined by the teachers who would occasionally ask Davis to control or discipline the children, sometimes putting him in an ambiguous position with regard to his young respondents.

As I have already stated, researchers are constantly made aware of their power with regard to child respondents. However, children are in quite a strong position to dictate the flow of interactions with the researcher, especially where he or she is committed to the least-adult role. Mandell (1991) and Thorne (1993) were conscious of the way that their roles were continually being tested by the children, with children intermittently breaking rules in front of them in the playground and in the classroom. These situations were more acute when it became evident to the staff that the researchers were aware of this deviance. In the previous chapter I illustrated the way that children in class can appropriate adult rules through the 'underground economy of food and objects' (Thorne 1993, p. 23). Thorne's vantage point at the back of the class gave her access to children's cultures and on occasion she was drawn in to this underworld as the children were aware of her surveillance. The alliances that researchers are trying to develop with children are often in conflict with the professional and collegiate relations that they have with the teachers. With teachers in the position of ultimate gatekeepers, there is a need to maintain a precarious balance between the demands of the children and the demands of the 'responsible adults'.

Interviewing Children

Ethnographies, as we have seen, rely on the insider role of the researcher as a participating observer of children's cultures. In turning to other less intrusive research techniques such as interviewing, there is less stress placed on the impact of the researcher within the researched community. Scott (2000) refers to a number of ways in which children can be interviewed, including one-to-one encounters, with their parents, in pairs or groups, through focus groups and by using the 'walkman' method. In the last case, Scott used this approach as part of the British Household Panel Survey (BHPS), an annual survey of 'microsocial change in Britain' (Scott 2000, p. 110). This allowed a sample of around 800 children aged between 11 and 15 to respond privately to a series of questions through an audio tape machine in their own homes. The children were 'interviewed' on issues relating to health, family life and leisure.

Other smaller-scale pieces of research have used interview-based techniques in trying to make sense of what it is like to be a child. Mayall (2000) talks about 'conversations' with children as the basis for revealing children's knowledge of their social lives. Her research focus was the 'generational order': how children in a number of different contexts made sense of their social positions as part of the younger subordinate generation. Solberg (1996), similarly, interviewed a sample of Norwegian children as a means of understanding the roles that children played in negotiating the generation order as a series of routines within their families.

However, as with the ethnography, the adult interviewer/child interviewee relationship generates methodological considerations. Various researchers have looked at the interview relationship in terms of power (Oakley 1981b). Thus the typical characteristics of the researcher as educated, white and middle-class influence the nature of the data, with interviewees providing accounts that accord with what they think is expected of them from the interviewer rather than in their own terms. If there is a perceived power relationship between the researcher and researched here, it compromises the sense of ownership that the latter has of their understanding of the world. Power here is attributed to an unequal relationship to knowledge, with the researcher monopolising the situation. Attempts are made to counter this by matching adult interviewees with researchers in terms of gender, ethnicity and social class. In theory, this 'matching' puts the researcher in a better position to empathise with the respondent and gain a more authentic understanding of their social worlds. Whilst it does not and cannot break down the power relationship between researcher and researched, this matching is also less threatening for the respondent.[2] With child interviewees this is much more difficult for, as was mentioned earlier, there is limited scope in presenting oneself in the 'least-adult role'. The power relationship between adult and child is more evident and visible, with physical size providing continual evidence of the power imbalance. Hood, Kelley and Mayall (1996) try to get round this by manipulating other research variables. Children can be interviewed in pairs or in groups – the numerical advantage of the interviewees, to some degree, counteracting the power of the single, adult interviewer. As is well established within the sociology of education, the collective position of peers can wield considerable power within the classroom. We might also return to Mayall's conversations with children on the generational order: in some cases, her young respondents adapted to the interview situation to meet their own conversational needs rather than simply to respond at the appropriate points in the interview to the adult interviewer's requests. When referring to an interview with two 6-year-old girls, she commented, 'they [the two girls] were sufficiently at ease with each other that they could, at some points, set aside the generational order of my conversation with them' (2000, p. 126).

One variable over which the child respondents have little control is the location of the interview. Some researchers have argued that this is a crucial consideration because children's personalities are context-dependent (Scott 2000, p. 103). If we compare their home and school environments, children probably have a different relationship with each other and with adults in these environments. Whether children are any less centred in terms of identity and personality than adults is a moot point. Nevertheless, the location of the research is important because we generally tend to think that the respondent is more likely to feel in control of the research situation where they are familiar with the surroundings and where there is a degree of privacy. In previous chapters I have documented the way that adults are able carefully to regulate children's use of space. Privacy is a common good to which adults have access. Children have to negotiate access according to age-related criteria, determined by their adult caretakers. Older children can expect more private space than younger children. This places considerable limits on children being able to choose an interview location. The researcher's awareness of this problem does not necessarily make things any easier: whilst the adult researcher might think that privacy restricts the direct surveillance of their caretakers, it places more onus on the researcher to act as a surrogate caretaker, thus shifting the 'protective' burden from parent and teacher to researcher. Thus the more private the research context, the more likely adult researchers will have to assume the role of guardian. Nevertheless, having access to some place where there is less adult regulation can help to downplay the 'adultness' of the researcher and provide a less inhibiting context for the research.[3]

Child-Centred Research Techniques

In many cases ethnographers will adopt a multimethod approach in uncovering children's understandings and social worlds. I referred in the previous chapter to Pollard and his colleague's (1999) biographical-case-study approach. Primary school children's school lives were tracked over time – the children were actively involved throughout the research. Among other things they constructed sociometric maps of their friendship networks and kept diaries of their everyday activities, as well as taking part in interviews. In turning to another example, a vignette approach has been used to elicit children's definitions of family. In two separate projects, O'Brien, Alldred and Jones (1996) asked 460 children aged between 7 and 16 to comment on a series of hypothetical family situations in order to elicit their views on the meaning of family.

Conversational techniques are central to a qualitative approach, for they highlight the respondents' understandings of themselves and their social worlds. The general feeling is that the most direct and discursive research techniques allow the respondent a degree of autonomy in producing more authentic accounts of their social worlds. Other researchers have produced innovative methods as a way of engaging with young people and alleviating the power differences between researcher and researched. Samantha Punch (2002) used a 'secret box' (discussed in the following section) and a variety of stimulus material to connect with her young sample, making the research more interesting and relevant to their lives.

However, a child-centred approach to research has often led to child-specific research techniques being deployed, which imply that children are not quite capable of sustaining a more conventional verbal account. The assumption is still that young children can only express complex thoughts and ideas indirectly through role-play, games or drawings. Hill, Laybourn and Borland (1996) were aware of this tension and sought a balance between what they called 'ordinary methods' (interviews) and 'special measures' (child-centred methods). Their research focused on primary-aged children's (5–11) understandings of their emotional well-being. The project was concerned to demonstrate children's social competence through interviews. At the same time, the researchers asserted that younger children are used to child-specific modes of expression in school, such as drawing, games and physical exercises. These more familiar techniques were used to maintain children's interest in the research project.

Ethical Considerations

A key theme in this book is that the neglect of children as research subjects is reflected in their general invisibility. Their lack of personhood has often meant that children simply do not come into the reckoning where organisations involved with research are forced to take account of the dispositions and feelings of certain groups. The ethical dimension to child-focused research is no exception here, with a low priority attached to regulating the general conduct of researchers working with children.

Informed Consent

If we concentrate for the moment on informed consent – a key principle within most professions' ethical guidelines – it is clear that, for many researchers working with children, adult gatekeepers remain the last point at which access to a child population may or may not be granted. Well-established research bodies such as the British Educational Research Association (BERA) are at best ambiguous when discussing research with children. The cursory reference to children makes it clear that consent needs to be sought from schools and parents before interviewing children (see www.bera.ac.uk/guidelines).

A more general statement precedes this, emphasising that research participants need to be fully informed before the research can take place. Thus, whilst parental consent implies that children are not full participants, this is not made explicit anywhere in the guidelines. Given that educational research often involves children, this seems a rather glaring oversight. However, as the field of children and childhood research continues to grow, a number of commentators and organisations are starting to examine the ethical position of children and adult researchers. One important principle established is the ontological status of the child within the research process, with a commitment to allowing children to opt out of participation in a research project. The British Sociological Association makes this clear in its ethical guidelines: 'The consent of the child should be sought in addition to that of the parent' (see www.britsoc.co.uk).

The National Children's Bureau (NCB), a London-based voluntary organisation, has recently set out its 'guidelines for research' in a similar vein. The emphasis here is on ensuring that children have a chance to opt out once the various adult gatekeepers have been informed. Children need to be fully briefed at the beginning of the research. Among other things, children need to know what the research is about, the significance of their roles as respondents and any possible outcomes of the research. Once it has been established that potential child respondents are fully aware of the aims of the research, then they are in a position to decide whether or not to take part.

This does not dispose of the problem of disagreements between child and caretaker, particularly where the caretaker refuses the child access in cases where the child is willing. For example, Mason and Falloon's (2001) research on children's conceptions of child abuse set out to challenge the adult-centred nature of the discourse on abuse. Thus the importance of treating their child sample as the sole 'definers' within their project meant that there was a high premium placed on the children themselves opting into the project. However, their employers, the University of Western Sydney, insisted that they gain consent from the parents as well as the respondents. According to the researchers, this resulted in some children who were willing to take part being excluded from the project.[4]

An analysis of the ethics of child research thus brings to the surface ambiguities surrounding the treatment of children. Children can opt out, but there is a lack of clarity as to whether they can opt in. There is an interesting parallel with the structural approach discussed in Chapter 2. Children are ontologically established as full members of society; at the same time children's status within the social structure is as lesser members of society. In terms of the research process, children are established as agents who can choose to take part in research. Their status as agents assures them of a place within what Hood, Kelley and Mayall (1996) call a 'hierarchy of gatekeepers', but located firmly on the bottom rung. Parents and, to a lesser extent, teachers are still the dominant reference points when negotiating access, reflecting their structurally superior position within the hierarchy.

Formal principles that foreground the child as a key research participant are important in establishing a formal research agenda. However, the organisational structures which researchers have to negotiate and the character of the dynamics between the various participants in the research often determine the outcome of issues of consent. Even where we can establish children's consent, they may feel compelled to take part; the presence of a teacher or parent can imply to the child that they ought to help the researcher. Again I come back to the implicit power of the adult over the child. An illustration from my own experience as a researcher might help here. With a colleague I carried out interviews with primary school children in the mid-1990s. The interviews were part of a broader examination of key educational actors' perceptions of values, choice and accountability in English primary schools (Wyness and Silcock 1999). The pupils were interviewed after we had gained the views of teachers, heads and inspectors. In one of the schools we had developed good relations with the teaching staff, who were quite happy to offer us access to the pupils. We emphasised to the staff how important it was that the pupils should feel free to opt out if they were not happy taking part. On the day of the interviews, the head teacher produced groups of children who were waiting quietly in his office to be interviewed. Before starting the interviews we gave the children the information on the project and the opportunity to opt out. We also assumed that the children had been briefed by the head teacher. Whilst all of the children seemed keen to take part, any of the children in the head's office would have found it very difficult to opt out. We had no reason to think that these children had been forced or even persuaded to take part. Nevertheless, the position of the head, and the knowledge the pupils had that the interviews were taking place in the head's office, probably made it less likely that any of them were in a strong enough position to opt out. It was clearly in our interests to obtain a sample of children. At the same time, our interests in collecting good data needed to be set against the 'right to integrity' of the researched community, a right to be in a position to make a relatively free choice (a child's 'right to integrity' is discussed in more detail in the following chapter).

We need to be careful when assuming that children in school are bound to say yes to researchers even when they want to say no. A culture of obedience may dominate the decision-making processes of young children in school. However, the point that I want to make is that the context within which decisions are made by research participants is important and, in some cases, the presence of an adult researcher may have an opposite effect on the decisions that children make. France, Bendelow and Williams (2000) tried to explain the lack of participation of some pupils in their research on children's perceptions of health because of a more instrumental view among pupils. Hence some pupils refused to become involved in the research because in their opinion there was really nothing in it for them. Moreover, the researchers imply that children view this instrumental culture in school as an unfair exchange, with students continually getting very little back for their deference. As the authors argue, 'Young people are expected to be good citizens but little attention is paid to their own needs as citizens' (France, Bendelow and Williams 2000, p. 158). It may be that the two examples here reflect different school-age populations – a younger, more deferent group in my own case, and an older, more assertive group in the second example. Nevertheless, the context of the school is significant in generating willing and unwilling samples of children.

Confidentiality

It is common practice to assure any sample of adults that what they say and reveal in the research is confidential, with names and places being changed. Where research findings are likely to be read by a much larger or wider audience, consideration has to be given to whether the research community needs to be consulted before publication (BERA ethical guidelines, http://www.bera.ac.uk/guidelines). In turning to child respondents, the same demands are made of researchers to maintain confidentiality. In Sam Punch's (2002) research into how 13–14-year-olds cope with problems, the respondents saw confidentiality as a precondition of their involvement. As I mentioned earlier, one of the author's innovative techniques was a 'secret box' which she used to try and assure her young respondents of the confidentiality of their accounts. Respondents were asked to write down on a blank piece of paper any problems they had experienced or were experiencing. They were to omit their names and post these pieces of paper in a secret box. The researcher assured the respondents that she would not be able to put a name to these problems or trace the handwriting. The researcher was able to collate and categorise the different problems without being able to link them to specific respondents. In one sense there is nothing particularly child-centred about this approach. Adults as well as children experience things that they are unwilling to divulge to an interviewer unless confidentiality is guaranteed. In principle we might use this technique with an adult sample. Where confidentiality is particularly an issue for children is when it can conflict with demands placed on professionals, including researchers, to protect children. Wherever possible, children should be afforded the same level of integrity as adults with reference to the confidential nature of their testimony. In some instances, children are likely to feel inhibited when they feel that what they say to a researcher is likely to be passed on to someone else in authority. This was the case with Punch's sample. Yet Masson (2000) talks here about researchers having limited legal liability. That is, researchers may be legally bound to disclose this testimony to the appropriate agencies when the researcher believes that the child is disclosing information about abuse or exploitation. At a minimum, researchers cannot guarantee child respondents absolute confidentiality because they have a duty to act on any information given to them by the child relating to abuse, irrespective of the effects this has on the integrity of the research.

Some researchers have argued that the ethical dimension goes much further than any legal obligation to inform the appropriate authorities (Alderson 1995). Thus whilst researchers cannot guarantee confidentiality, at the outset they are morally obliged to tell the child respondent that they might have to disclose information given to them. Moreover, where the researcher feels obliged to pass the information to other professionals, wherever possible the researcher will discuss this disclosure with the child first before taking any action. The aim here is to encourage the children themselves to seek help from the appropriate agencies. In some instances, child researchers have a professional background in counselling children. In returning briefly to Mason and Falloon's (2001) research, their own backgrounds in child protection equipped them with the skills to deal with any possible disclosures when interviewing children about child abuse. But balancing the integrity of the interview with the responsibility to protect often makes researching with children a 'risky business'.

The Effects of Research

A third ethical issue, again underpinned by the imperative to protect, is the 'effects' of research on children. Ever since the notorious experiments into obedience conducted by Milgram in the 1960s, researchers have been grappling with the potential impact of certain types of research on their respondents (Baumrind 1964). Will children's participation in a research project harm them in any way? Do we need to debrief children once the interview or experiment has finished? Alderson (1995) goes further in linking 'effects' to the theoretical basis of the research. She argues that the outcomes of the research can be linked to the theoretical assumptions made about the children being researched. As we discussed in Chapter 6, the researcher who makes assumptions about the child's level of social learning or development works within a dominant framework which perpetuates the subordinate position of children. In relation to research that explores the subjective realm, this has often meant that researchers rely on proxy adults for accounts of children's understandings rather than sampling the children themselves. In effect, Alderson (1995) is encouraging researchers to reflect on their theoretical models in terms of how they confirm and sustain particular social conceptions of childhood. Thus rather than focus on the discernible short-term impact of research on individual children, the effects of research are seen to be much broader in terms of the structural position of children.

One example of research that makes clear links between concept and methodology and has an impact on the social position of children is a project funded by Radda Barnen (Swedish Save the Children) concerning the lives of working children or the 'child labour problem' (Woodhead 1999a). A conventional approach within the dominant framework would draw on evidence to support the contention that child labour is a 'global evil', an increasingly visible aspect of child abuse or exploitation. Research here becomes part of a process of intervention that prioritises the rescue of 'child labourers' by taking them off the streets and out of the factories. We encountered this perspective in our discussion of crisis in Chapter 4. The Radda Barnem approach, on the other hand, is sceptical of an all-encompassing elimination of child labour. As Martin Woodhead, one of the researchers, notes:

> A first concern is about the outcome of interventions that target impoverished, vulnerable children, for whom work may be essential for survival and at the core of personal identity. At worst, such interventions risk inadvertently undermining their security unless followed through by sustained and comprehensive measures that they (the children) recognize as genuinely improving their long-term best interests. (Woodhead 1999a, p. 27)

The research is part of a project that works alongside the 'child labourers' in several different global contexts. The aim is to improve the conditions and positions of the children as they see things. Thus participatory research techniques become important in drawing out the children's understandings of their work and experiences. Woodhead (1999a) draws on what is called the 'Children's Perspectives Protocol', a framework of methods that accentuates children's perspectives. There are seven activities, ranging from children being given the opportunity to recount their 'life story' to being asked to evaluate the kinds of work that they do. The data is thus 'child-sensitive', allowing more general claims to be made about how working children can be supported.

Children as Researchers

Up until now I have concentrated on children as 'meaning-making' respondents within the research process. The broad thrust of child-focused research has been for adults to generate the ideas and the funding, manage the field work and bring children in as willing and capable respondents. I want now to turn to the more challenging notion of children as researchers. In principle there are different levels of involvement on the 'research' side. Hart's (1997) 'ladder of children's participation' sets out a hierarchy of children's involvement in a range of projects and activities. At the bottom we have forms of 'non-participation', claims made by adults about children's involvement that are in reality marginal, contrived and tokenistic. Thus very young children being taken to a street demonstration wearing T-shirts with political statements on them comes into the category of 'decorative participation'. At the upper end of the ladder, we have children initiating and controlling their affairs, with adults playing a lesser role. The further up the ladder we go, the more likely we are to find child-initiated projects. At this upper end, Hart (1997, p. 23) refers to the Earthnauts, a democratic structure for children's participation in local matters based in Austin, Texas. The board of directors is made up equally of adults and children, and the leadership of specific local projects is shared between the children and the adults.

Adapting the upper end of the ladder to the research context would mean children setting up their own project, conducting the research and publishing the results (Alderson 2000). The nearest we get to a situation where the children were instrumental from inception to publication is the 'Everybody In?' project involving young disabled people.[5] Three young male collaborators worked alongside the 'adult' researchers in examining the perceptions of disabled and non-disabled students on policies of inclusion (Roberts 2000). One of the material outcomes was a report co-written by the young people and the professional researchers (Ash et al. 1997). More recently the Open University in England has set up the Children's Research Centre where children generate the research topics, undertake the research and write up and publish their research on their own (childrens-research-centre.open.ac.uk). Examples of research papers found on the centre's website include:

- 'Hey I'm nine not six!' A small-scale investigation of looking younger than your age at school (Anna Carlini and Emma Berry, aged 10)

- How does death affect children? (Paul O'Brien, aged 12)

- Girls want to play too! Investigating the views of 9–11-year-old pupils about mixed-gender football (Ben Davies and Selena Ryan-Vig, aged 10).

It is in the middle range of the ladder of participation where we find most examples of children as researchers. Children's standpoints and life worlds are prioritised within these projects. Ethically, children who play a more 'collegiate' role in the research will have much fuller information about the aims and objectives of the research process. Thus the problem of informed consent becomes less of a problem, with children in a much better position to weigh up their involvement. Beyond these broad principles, children are playing different roles within the research enterprise as researchers.

Adults' Research Project, Children as Consultants

Here adults by and large determine the broad parameters of the research and play a more regulative role, but children have some influence over the methods used, the questions asked and the general conduct of the research. If we return to the research into children's perceptions of child abuse by Mason and Falloon (2001), their 'collaborative' approach meant that the small sample of children determined the form and membership of the 'focus groups' utilised, as well as the timing and location of the interviews. Interestingly, the researchers were keen to feed back the transcripts of the taped material and their interpretations to the children. The children, on the other hand, saw little value in this process and eschewed the feedback. The researchers speculate that one reason for this is that children have little sense of owning knowledge and are not used to being asked to comment on data. Being marginal to the production of knowledge in school, children's full involvement in the research process here comes up against a still-dominant culture of exclusion.

Adults' Research Project, Children as Fieldworkers

The recent ESRC-funded research initiative entitled 'Consulting Pupils about Teaching and Learning' set out to challenge the subordinate status of English schoolchildren and to encourage their involvement in decision-making processes at classroom and school levels (Rudduck and Flutter 2004). The 'Pupils as Co-Researchers' project, one of the six projects supported by the initiative, was a carefully adult-managed piece of research with a small group of Year 8 (age 13) pupils. The young respondents were selected on the basis of their popularity with staff and pupils and their 'good inter-personal skills' (Bragg 2001, p. 1).[6] Furthermore, as with most research in schools, there was an 'in-house' feel to this kind of research, with both researchers and respondents a 'captive audience'. Nevertheless, the project had three aims that went beyond the mere staging of pupil-centredness. First of all, the research was highlighting the possibility of including pupils as co-participants in the research process. In many ways, pupils were deploying many of the investigative skills that they are supposed to develop throughout their school careers (Alderson 2000). Here there was a more formalised 'adult' version, whereby teachers and pupils worked together in improving the culture within the schools. Rather than children's research skills simply being developed as a part of an individualised educational package, children's activities here contributed to broader school structures. In other words, an investigative approach among pupils was used to question the basis of their learning rather than simply as a means of learning. A second aim followed in that pupils were creating new identities for themselves within the school as researchers. Indirectly their subordinate positions were being challenged as teachers' worked alongside pupils in a more collaborative venture. A third aim was to contest a general teaching approach in schools that undervalues pupils' social competence. Pupils researched pupils on their teaching and learning; pupil voice was thus likely to be more audible, reinforcing the idea that children can take collective responsibility within school.

I have emphasised the principled involvement of children at various levels of the research process. There is also a more pragmatic basis to 'employing' child researchers. First of all, children are more actively involved in the research process because they may be the most effective observers of children's worlds within an educational context, what I referred to earlier as the hidden 'underworld' of schooling (Cullingford 1991, p. 58). Children may thus be employed as researchers in an attempt to solve Mandell's (1991) problem of the 'least-adult' role of the researcher. Secondly, where the research is problem-driven, for example work on bullying or sexism, children in school tend to consult with their peers first before approaching teaching staff (Cullingford 1991). Children as researchers or reporters of incidents may be more effective in that they bring to the surface a range of issues and problems that may remain hidden from adult purview. Thirdly, children who act as researchers are likely to develop a range of skills that improve their levels of self-esteem and commitment to schoolwork. The 'Consulting Pupils about Teaching and Learning' initiative took seriously the idea that pupils ought to play more formative and collective roles in all aspects of schooling. The broader political and social context currently in the UK is one of inclusion; the greater involvement of children in decision-making is one highly plausible way of creating a greater sense of pupil ownership of their education, which could have all sorts of spin-offs in terms of learning and behaviour.

If we take seriously the view that children can undertake research, we need to address the various legal restrictions (Masson 2000). One issue is whether child research assistants should be construed as employees in the same way as their adult counterparts. How are children to be rewarded for their work? Should child researchers be paid? Within the school context, research is normally subsumed within their education, and payment is rarely an issue. Nevertheless, the 'innovative' nature of employing child researchers needs to be set against the cost to the researcher of having to employ an adult research assistant in more conventional research. Another issue concerns the constraints placed on working children in, say, the UK where they are only allowed to work for a limited period of time per day. Thus children are allowed to work for no more than two hours per day on school days and Sundays, and no more than five hours on Saturdays (Masson 2000, p. 44).

'Employed' research in schools undertaken by children is more complex. Research is an ongoing, often quite mundane feature of school life; children are always being asked to 'investigate' or 'find out about things'. However, there is still an ethical issue as to when research in school counts as employment and how this squares with students' commitment to compulsory 'learning' in terms of both the time undertaken to do the research and any issue regarding payment. A third issue relates to the conditions of working children and the extent to which these come under special scrutiny from both employers and children. Thus, in the UK, regulations with regard to health and safety issues for young people under the age of 18 are tighter, with parents as well as children given full information on any risks involved in being employed. The protectionist nature of these regulations is obvious in the way that child researchers, who may be involved in interviewing 'strangers', may need to be chaperoned to and from interviews. The interviews may even have to be carried out with an adult guardian present (Masson 2000, p. 44). Finally, given that employers are legally required to train their employees, what kind of training should child researchers expect?

Conclusion

I have argued that, in line with a more child-focused sociology, 'working with children' signals an important shift in viewing children as research subjects rather than research objects. 'Working *with* children' rather than 'working *on* children' at a very basic level means drawing horizontal rather than vertical lines of interaction between researcher and researched. This might imply degrees of collegiality and equality in the way that researchers relate to the researched community. Researchers are now engaging with children in the research process as respondents and, to a limited extent, as co-researchers. In one sense equality means that children 'move up' in terms of ontology, agency and social competence. The binary divide between children and adults breaks down as both inhabit life worlds that generate social meaning. Researchers assume that these symbolic worlds are now open to both adults and children, which in turn produces a commitment on the part of the researcher to understand these symbolic worlds.

I referred to the way that researchers generate children's accounts of the social world through interviews. These accounts are important but they are abstracted from their everyday routines. Children tell us about their social worlds at a given time and place and, by virtue of our powerful positions, children, like adults, from time to time tell us what we want to hear. What the researcher misses is an interactive and collective component of children's worlds. In trying to capture this, equality with children necessitates a movement 'downwards' for many researchers. As we saw in the previous chapter, children are seen to be meaning-makers in their own terms, and within their own worlds and cultures. Ethnographers adopt various positions ranging from the empathetic to the 'least adult'. Understanding children's life worlds here means gaining access to children's worlds. Equality in these terms means being childlike, becoming an honorary member of a secret society or tribe where children routinely negotiate their own rules and relations. Whilst these movements among researchers and between researchers and researched could signify a change in the micropolitics of research, I argue that it is far from clear that there is any substantial shift in the power relationship between the adult researcher and the child respondent. As has been frequently mentioned in reviews and discussions of researching children and childhood, the macropolitics of research is dictated by conceptions of children as both socially and structurally vulnerable (James Jenks and Prout 1998; Morrow and Richards 1996). Methodologically, this can mean that attempts on the part of researchers to pass themselves off as 'least adult' invoke alarm and suspicion among the researched community, with researchers unable to shake off their power and authority. There is a certain necessary naivety to the research task as the researcher strives for insight, but this needs to be set against the equally plausible view, especially on the part of the children being researched, that the research is a form of surveillance, with control the primary objective. Moreover, researchers attempting to gain membership of the 'tribe' have to build up trusting, secret and confidential relationships, which are inevitably compromised by the ethical duty of researchers to regulate the respondents' wellbeing as children. One of the key ethical principles is the need to balance confidentiality with protection. To what extent can we maintain the view that children are competent social agents within the research process if we cannot ensure the integrity of the data generated by the child respondent? An associated issue is the appropriateness of conventional research techniques when working with children. In referring to the 'effects' of these kinds of methods on children, researchers have emphasised the intrusiveness, the resultant pressures and the alienating features of intensive observation and interviewing. I referred briefly to alternative 'child-friendly' methods which children are used to in school. Yet again this creates a dilemma for the researcher: do we protect children from the rigours of conventional research methods and risk patronising them as research respondents, or do we engage children fully in the research as competent actors and risk alienating them from the research by utilising what are seen by the child respondents to be adult methods? Whilst we cannot envision a wholly democratic relationship between researcher and researched, from within the new sociology of childhood we have identified the quintessentially reflexive nature of research with children.

Finally, in the third section of the chapter I tried to go beyond the adult as researcher/child as respondent relationship by examining a number of child-researcher initiatives. While this does not radically transform the adult/child relationship, there is an attempt to incorporate children more fully within research agendas.

10

Children: Their Rights and Politics

Introduction

In this final chapter I deal with two interrelated themes: the development of a children's rights agenda and the positioning of children and childhood in relation to the world of politics. In the first case, I report on the rather all-embracing and at times contradictory concept of rights as applied to children. Our first task is to draw out the ambiguities and tensions through an examination of the meaning of children's rights. Our second task is to locate the children's rights discourse at the global level, through an analysis of the United Nations Convention on the Rights of the Child instituted in 1989. I assess the convention as a possible charter for children and the implications it has for universalising a particular conception of childhood.

Whereas the UN convention acts as an important reference point for an increasingly vocal children's rights lobby, there is little sense in which children have a role to play in one of the areas that the rights discourse potentially opens up to children: the political realm. The 'political child' is seen as the 'unchild', a counter-stereotypical image of children that does not fit with the cultural norm of childhood (Stainton-Rogers and Stainton-Rogers 1992, pp. 32–3). In the second section of this chapter, I examine the basis for this political exclusion with reference to a dominant 'children's needs' discourse and, in the process, revisit several of the themes, discussed in earlier chapters, which underlie children's social exclusion. Yet, as with most aspects of contemporary children's lives, children are being pulled in different directions. I will argue that the children's needs discourse makes it difficult to think of children as political. At the same time, there are spaces for participation being opened up for children that position them closer to decision-making processes. Whilst children have little access to political centres, there are localised forums through which children can express their collective interests. I will look at some of these in the final section of the chapter. I will draw on cases studies of 'political' children from both a developing and a developed country, India and England, respectively.

Children's Rights

The Meaning of Children's Rights

Over the past few years children's rights has become a fairly contentious issue within the public sphere. Rights in general, as many lawyers and legal experts contend, are a central feature of Western democratic societies. Despite their abstract nature, they take on a 'thing-like' status within contemporary discourse, 'valuable commodities' according to Wasserstrom (cited in Freeman 1983, p. 32). Part of the contention around children's rights is the idea that children can own these rights as possessions in the same way that adults own rights. Some see this as a perfectly logical and reasonable outcome of viewing children as persons in their own right. Others are more sceptical: by giving children rights we put them on the same level as those who are supposed to be looking after them, compromising their authority and their child-care responsibilities. Children's rights in these terms become an all-or-nothing issue, with children automatically losing their 'childish' status once they take possession of rights. As I will set out later on in the section, there is a theoretical and philosophical standpoint that points to the liberation of children from childhood by granting them pretty much the same kinds of rights as adults. Whilst any analysis of children's rights needs to take account of these arguments, my contention here is that an all-or-nothing view of rights overly simplifies the meaning of children's rights. In analysing the meaning of children's rights, the issue is not so much the distinction between children having or not having rights but the way that political, moral and social discourses generate different types of children's rights. In essence, there are two types of children's rights that have very different implications for children and their relations with adults (Franklin and Franklin 1996). I will first of all discuss *welfare rights* which, I would argue, generate a consensus on the treatment of children and are therefore a central feature of the discourse around childhood. Secondly, there are what we might call children's rights to *self-determination*. These take two forms: rights that liberate children from childhood, and rights that emphasise a degree of self-determination through giving children a stronger voice. Whilst these kinds of rights, particularly the latter, are starting to gain a foothold in global and national child policy, there is much less support for them. A child's right to self-determination is still a peripheral feature of child policy and common discourse on childhood.

Welfare Rights

Several versions of this category of rights exist, such as Freeman's (1983) rights to welfare and protection, Franklin and Franklin's rights to protection and provision, and Archard's (1993) rights to welfare incorporated within his 'caretaker thesis'. They all have several things in common. First, in order for children to 'take possession' of these rights they require significant levels of support in the form of physical, emotional and moral resources; that is, they have a right to be provided for in terms of shelter, food, medical support and education. Secondly, these rights can be thought of in terms of freedom from a range of social and physical evils, such as starvation, abuse and exploitation. Welfare here extends into the realm of child protection. As we saw in Chapter 5, the problem of child abuse has brought to the fore the idea of a child's right to protection. Hence rights here take on the character of moral claims (see Freeman 1983). Thirdly, welfare rights are rights that are normally taken up by adults on behalf of children. The physical, moral and social wellbeing of children is the responsibility of adult caretakers rather than the children themselves. Adults ensure that children receive a range of common goods that support their physical and social development. To take one example: as we saw in Chapter 7, mass compulsory schooling was provided for the bulk of the child population in most Western countries by the late nineteenth century. Parents are charged with the responsibility for their children taking up this education. In most countries parents are legally obliged to ensure that their children attend school. Children have a right to attend school but it is parents who act on these rights by ensuring that children avail themselves of this common good. If we also refer to rights to protection, it is again adults who ensure that children do not experience any abuse or exploitation. As we saw in Chapter 5, the state intervenes in situations where children have been abused. Parents are assumed to be the protectors of children but, in situations where this does not take place, professional child workers will assume this role.

Rights to Self-determination

A casual perusal of the 'children's rights' literature reveals a conflict between rights to welfare and what are known as children's rights to *self-determination*: the former strengthens the hold that adults have over children because it works on the assumption that those in authority have an obligation to ensure that rights to health care, education and protection are met on the children's behalf. In an important sense, children never actually 'possess' welfare rights. Welfare implies that things are done to and for children. The invocation of children's rights in these terms is equated with adults acting in children's 'best interests', irrespective of children's own opinions and feelings. The latter, on the other hand, are far more controversial. Rights to self-determination take certain responsibilities and powers away from adults, as children have a right to make decisions for themselves that could potentially go against adults' claims that they are actually acting in the child's 'best interests'. These kinds of children's rights do threaten the protective and paternalistic roles of adults for they take seriously what children think and assume that children are self-determining agents (Alderson and Goodwin 1993). Franklin and Franklin (1996) set out the historical trajectory of the children's rights movement from around the early twentieth century onwards. One key moment in this development was the attempt by a group of American educationalists and philosophers to graft a children's agenda on to the civil rights movement in the USA in the 1970s. The key exponents, John Holt (1975) and Richard Farson (1978), take the line that if gender and race are illegitimate grounds for excluding people from their civil and political rights, then there is little justification for excluding children on the basis of their age.

There is here the transposition of dimensions of stratification into the political realm. As I discussed in Chapter 2, theories of gender and ethnicity have been used as part of a strategy of separation and integration. Liberationists are arguing that if age/generation can be thought of in the same way as gender and ethnicity, then there are grounds for positioning children as a minority group who can make claims on the state. These claims or entitlements need to be established in the same terms as the claims made by the majority population. If we are pushed to justify the rights of the adult population, this is usually couched in terms of rationality and competence. Holt (1975) uses these criteria for judging children's rights. If children are competent, age is no longer a barrier and children are in a position to make claims on the state. Holt (1975) counters the argument that children have an obligation to exercise their rights and at the same time challenges the caricatured version of children's rights as a mandate for 'baby power'. He asserts that 'the rights, privileges, duties and responsibilities of adult citizens be made available to any young person who wants to use them' (Holt 1975, p. 15). Thus just as adults do not always exercise their right to vote, children can choose not to take up their rights. Both Holt and Farson set out a blueprint for children's rights. Rights here range from a child's right to travel to having a choice over parents and guardians. In effect, children are not to be denied any of the rights that have accrued to adults over the past couple of centuries.

More recent proponents of children' rights to self-determination, such as Bob Franklin (1986, 1995) Gerison Lansdown (1994, 2000) and Priscilla

Alderson (1994), are less strident in tone, offering more modest possibilities for children. 'Rights' here revolve around improving children's access to decision-making processes and levels of participation, what has been referred to as the 'children's voice'. There is little attempt to liberate children here. At the same time, rights to welfare are viewed as insufficient in that adults do not have a monopoly over children's welfare. There is a much stronger sense here of children working alongside adults in providing for their development. Alderson's (1994) version of self-determination revolves around children's rights to integrity. There are three versions of this

- *Physical integrity*: a child's right to determine what is to be done to his or her body. This would include a right not to be physically abused or chastised and a right to be consulted in medical situations that directly affect them.

- *Mental integrity*: a right not to be mentally pressurised and coerced. This, for example, comes close to the notion of informed consent that was discussed in the previous chapter. Children's rights to mental integrity in a research context means that children can make up their own minds whether or not to take part in a research project and that they should not be unduly pressurised into participating.

- *Personal integrity*: this assumes that the children have fully formed and integrated personalities and that they have relatively clear conceptions of themselves as complete selves. Alderson (1994) argues that children are usually assumed not to have personal integrity in that their views are partial and that they are easily led or suggestible. Children thus have a weak sense of their identity and are seen as being less trustworthy than adults.

Alderson (1994) argues that adults are assumed to have a right to integrity and are expected to respect the right to integrity of other adults. She draws on the example of chronically ill children in hospital (see Chapter 6). In comparing the treatment of these children with equivalent adult patients, we expect the latter to be involved in their treatment at the very least at a consultative level. She examines cases of chronically ill children, the extent to which they are informed of their medical conditions, and their involvement in decisions affecting their treatment. She argues that children are not accorded the same rights as adults, with their rights to integrity routinely ignored. Thus just as we expect adults to be consulted over their medical treatment, a child's right to integrity would imply a similar consideration of children's views on any prospective treatment.

United Nations Convention on the Rights of the Child

The United Nations Convention on the Rights of the Child (UNCRC) has become a global frame of reference in legal, political and professional terms for the treatment of children. The convention was passed in 1989 and by the turn of the century most countries were signatories, with the exception of Somalia and the USA. In some respects the convention follows previous legal declarations made by international bodies throughout most of the twentieth century. These are summarised in Figure 10.1. The first half of the century was marked by two world wars separating many children from their families, making it difficult for them to receive the basic physical and psychological requirements for survival. Thus the early declarations were welfarist in character. Along with these trends came the development of supranational bodies such as the United Nations Children's Fund (UNICEF), an offshoot of the United Nations and the expansion of non-governmental organisations (NGOs) such as Catholic Action for Aid and Development (CAFOD), Oxfam and Save the Children, which work alongside supranational bodies. By the second half of the twentieth century, there was a complex organisational network of support for children at a global level, with the emphasis being on provision and protection.

It was not until the Polish government proposed a children's rights convention in 1978 that the United Nations broadened the conception of

---

Figure 10.1

Global developments in support for children

1924: **Declaration of the Rights of the Child** – (League of Nations) – post First World War, concerns over child hunger – emphasis on provision

1948: **Formation of United Nations Children's Fund** (UNICEF) the organisational wing of the United Nations that deals with child-related issues.

1959: **Declaration of the Rights of the Child** (United Nations) rights to welfare including development, protection and free education

1979: **International Year of the Child**: generating publicity through the media on the condition of the 'world's children'

1980: **Brandt Report** *Programme for Survival* – focus on infant mortality and global child poverty

1989 **United Nations Convention on the Rights of the Child**: combining provision, protection and participation

children's rights to include any notion of self-determination. This more or less coincided with the International Year of the Child, a campaign to focus attention on the plight of children at the global level. There is some continuity with earlier declarations, namely, a concern for the basic conditions of children: their health, their right to shelter and the right not to be abused or exploited. There are, though, several features of the convention that mark it out as different from the previous attempts to globalise children rights. Whilst there was little sense in which both the 1924 and 1959 declarations were legally binding, a body has been set up, the UN Committee on the Rights of the Child, to monitor the implementation of the convention in the various signatory countries. Independently of this, some countries such as the UK have set up their own bodies to oversee the convention's application (Children's Rights Development Unit 1994). More significantly, the UNCRC offers much more scope for children to have decision-making powers. Children's welfare rights were central to the 1924 and 1959 declarations. Franklin and Franklin (1996) argue that the UNCRC provides a framework for the three Ps: (children's rights to) protection, provision and participation. Broadly speaking, the first two correspond to welfare rights and the third corresponds to children's rights to self-determination or what Alderson (2000, p. 242) refers to as a 'moderate version of adult autonomy rights'.

Articles 12 to 15 of the convention (Figure 10.2) have frequently been discussed in terms of a charter for children, highlighting children's status as independent members of society. Most debate has centred around Article

Figure 10.2

Extracts from the United Nations Convention on the Rights of the Child

States Parties shall assure to the child who is capable of forming his or her own views the right to express those views freely in all matters affecting the child, the views of the child being given due weight in accordance with the age and maturity of the child. (Article 12)

The child shall have the right to freedom of expression; this right shall include freedom to seek, receive and impart information and ideas of all kinds, regardless of frontiers. (Article 13)

States Parties shall respect the right of the child to freedom of thought, conscience and religion. (Article 14)

States Parties recognise the rights of the child to freedom of association and to freedom of peaceful assembly. (Article 15)

12. Several authors have argued for the importance of the convention in terms of the autonomy and rights to self-determination that it bestows on children (Pinkerton 2001; Mayall 1996).

Yet if we look closely at Article 12, we find the conditional nature of children's agency. There is no automatic right for a child to be heard, for the article is carefully worded in terms of capabilities and competence. It cannot automatically be assumed that children are competent. There is no right, then, in the liberationist sense of children having choices; giving 'due weight' in effect means that children's agency is in the hands of responsible adults (Lee 2001). Parents and teachers are to make judgements on a child's abilities before that child can make any claims. I would argue that Articles 13 to 15 come close to Alderson's (1994) rights to integrity and that they merit at least equal attention. Children's right to information, right to be heard and to worship, and right to form their own social groupings in theory expand children's social frames of reference because they treat them as independent social actors. These articles also have implications for their schooling, their home life and their leisure time. They also have implications for the 'crisis' view of childhood discussed in Chapter 4. For example, the notion of children being out of place is challenged by Article 15 in that it suggests that children can occupy adult public spaces.

UNCRC and Cultural Ambiguity

There is a general consensus within academic and legal circles that the convention is a crucial step forward in establishing a social ontology for children. However, there have been some criticisms. In matters of aid and development, there has been some criticism of the way that international bodies have established a global standard of childhood from a predominantly Western, 'First-World' perspective. It is worth pointing out here that the lengthy process of drafting the convention between 1978 and 1989 can be put down to the disagreements, between states with quite different conceptions of childhood, over the content of the convention (Ennew 2000). The gist of these disagreements forms the basis of the following critique.

First of all, the convention seems to respect cultural differences, taking as it does 'due account of the importance and the traditions of the cultural values of each people for the protection and harmonious development of the child' (preamble). Yet there is an ambiguity in the way that children's interests are to be framed within the secluded borders of family and school. The family is seen here as 'the fundamental group of society' (preamble), with the emphasis on family as a naturalised and privatised entity where children are attached to their biological parents. According to Stephens (1995) and Boyden and Myers (1995), this is at odds with children's membership of more variegated kin and community networks and their involvement in more public, adult-oriented environments such as the workplace. It is also contrary to Article 15 that provides the grounds for children's collective representation. Boyden (1997) goes on to suggest that a dominant moral message running through the convention, that parents ought to prioritise school over work, oversimplifies the motives of both parents and children. As I argued in Chapters 2 and 4, poverty pushes some children into the labour market. Children in a variety of workplaces support greater regulation of their working lives, but this does not extend to the comprehensive removal of them from the street and any subsequent rehabilitation in school (Woodhead 1999a). In some cases, children are expected to pick up a trade and contribute to the local economy. We cannot automatically assume that school is always in the best interests of children, especially where economic and cultural imperatives favour children working.

Martin Woodhead (1997) states that broader patterns of support for children in developing countries are based on notions of need constructed around either the role of the mother or of the nuclear family. We can read a second cultural bias into the convention in the way that biologically based, two-parent families seem to be in the minds of the policy-makers, rather than more globally diverse patterns of child care. By emphasising the nuclear family, the convention ignores kinship and community as safe and acceptable spheres inhabited by children. Moreover, as I pointed out in the discussion of child abuse in Chapter 5, the nuclear family is no absolute guarantee of children's safety and security. In some cases, other care arrangements are more effective guarantors of a child's welfare. A third issue relates to the individualising tendencies of the convention, which potentially bring it into conflict with the rights of children to freedom of association in Article 15. Whilst the latter might hinge on the idea of children having collective interests or collective rights, the convention's focus on the 'rights of the child' implies the normal apprenticeship model of the individual child, a quintessentially Western notion.

Rachel Burr's (2004) research on the implementation of the convention in Vietnam reinforces the contradictory relationship between the convention and more local understandings and practice. Despite Vietnam being one of the first Asian countries to sign up to the convention, national policy and local practice contradict the privatism and individualism implicit in the convention. The latter's emphasis on the individual child's rights clashes with the way that Vietnamese legislation and child-care norms emphasise deference and communal obligations. The convention is exporting a welfare conception of childhood as part of a broader cultural project of global capitalism (Stephens 1995, p. 36). The demands made on developing countries by First-World economies extends into the cultural terrain, with children viewed as individualised bearers of human capital.

Children and Politics

In turning to the political realm, children have the same problems in claiming political status as they do in asserting any rights to self-determination. Children and young people in advanced Western societies do not ordinarily inhabit the civic or political spheres. In the USA and almost all European countries, voting is a political right enjoyed by those over the age of 18. In a few countries, children are represented at the political centre. For example, in Canada child advocates are appointed at provincial level to promote children's wellbeing within a range of contexts.[1] In Norway there is a well-established 'ombudsman' who has ministerial status and provides children with channels through which they are able to make claims on the state (Flekkoy 1988). More recently in the UK, children's commissioners and a minister for children have been appointed. There have also been some recent moves towards giving children a voice through the creation of youth parliaments at national and supranational levels, the European Youth Parliament and the Scottish Youth Parliament being notable examples (Wyness 2001). Despite these innovations, the general trend in developed countries is for children to be excluded from the political centre. Children and young people themselves are seldom given the opportunity to participate in agenda-setting, and the political establishment rarely seeks their views. It is worth noting at this juncture that the UNCRC seems to support this proposition with the drafters of the convention justifying children's political exclusion in a briefing paper on the grounds that 'the very status of a child means in principle that the child has no political rights' (cited in John 1995, p. 106).

As I have argued in earlier chapters, there are considerable obstacles to viewing children as full members of society. This poses difficulties for any idea of political inclusion. Two obstacles, in particular, are worth pursuing. First, we can refer again to childhood as a form of apprenticeship which, at least in Western societies, is characterised as a transitional phase. During this period, children are assumed to be developing the necessary abilities and understandings of the social world. In an important sense, children are apprentice citizens, rather than fully constituted members of the social world (Cockburn 1998). Children's lack of ontology rules them out from being viewed as fully 'social'. Full social status implies citizenship. Both are preconditions for political participation. Children are judged to arrive at a point of political maturity at around the time that they are supposed to be able to take advantage of the social, political and economic benefits and at the same time cope with the moral and social obligations of being a citizen. In other words, children are recognised as citizens at around the time that they leave childhood.

To put this idea of social apprenticeship another way, membership of a political community in Western societies is based on the idea of a social contract. Membership is based on the idea that any rights to participate and have a voice in the running of an institution or the governing of a territory bring with them obligations or responsibilities. Much of the recent political debate in Britain and the USA has revolved around the precise nature of the relationship between rights and obligations. But it now seems to be taken as read that both elements are required within a democratic polity (Roche 1992). Notions of respect, trust and tolerance are built into a network of mutual obligations such that the individual's political and social rights are intimately bound up with their obligations to the wider society. Children in this way do not figure within this network of mutual obligations. Children's lack of status equates with children not having a stake in society; to use the current political jargon in Britain, children are not 'stakeholders'. This is partly bound up with the privatisation of childhood discussed in Chapter 5, the general trend towards viewing children as part of the private realm of intimacy, emotion and family. Quite simply, children are not of the political world. Children also lack agency here because of their imputed incompetence, their inability to take moral or social responsibility. This becomes the basis for adults to act and talk on children's behalf. Adults assume the responsibilities that would be attributed to children were they to be recognised as citizens. In effect, Archard's (1993, pp. 51–7) 'caretaker thesis', discussed earlier in the chapter, excludes children from politics.

In some circumstances, children are politicised, for example in South Africa. The Soweto uprising in 1976 marked a turning-point for black South African children in that they became heavily involved in the struggle against apartheid. Njabulo Ndebele (1995) refers to the slogan 'Liberation now, education later', which became a popular expression of this involvement, with children forced to prioritise political participation over their schooling. Children became caught up in the political struggle owing to the overtly racist nature of the education system in South Africa. In his examination of the aftermath of Soweto, Ndebele talks of the young rejecting adult authority and, in some cases, attempting to run schools themselves. Children took control here because their educational interests were perceived by the children to have been neglected by the adult population. Ndebele refers more generally to the breakdown in adult/child relations, with adults unable or unwilling to offer children guidance and support. For Ndebele, the slogan 'Liberation now, education later' symbolised a loss of childhood. His rejection of 'pupil power' is not based on the idea that children are incapable or incompetent, but on their lack of experience: 'By assuming adult responsibilities, they have striven after wisdom without the foundation of growth. They shed their childhood without having the pains and joys of learning from it' (1995, p. 331). Thus, as with children in relatively peaceful settings, the commentator here views child-hood as a period free from political responsibilities.

Children's Interests?

We might return to Qvortup's distinction between children's needs and children's interests, which I considered in Chapter 2. The key point to make here is that 'needs' is part of a discourse that individualises children and assumes that things need to be done to and for them as they go through childhood. 'Interests', on the other hand, is a quintessentially political concept. Members of a social group find themselves in similar situations with respect to a governing or superior political class. Their common inter-ests push them into a separate social category. There are parallels here with the tensions within the children's rights discourse. Rights to welfare are bound up with the idea of needs in that adults take control of a child's welfare, bringing the child 'in need' up to a global standard of normality. Rights to self-determination, on the other hand, can be associated with chil-dren's interests in that they underpin the demands children make to be heard. This may mean that children make demands on adults to provide for their welfare, as in the case of the South African children mentioned earlier. The point that we want to make here is not that children make claims on the state, the school or the family to maintain a conception of childhood that privileges adults over children. What is significant is that children are in a position to make these claims in the first place. Irrespective of the substance of these claims, children are in a different position with regard to their abil-ity to be heard and taken seriously.

The tension between welfare and self-determination and needs and interests is evident when examining child-related political initiatives at a global level. One recent example of children's global 'needs' is the problem of child labour. Media coverage has concentrated on children being exploited in 'Third World sweatshops' (*Observer*, 7 November 1999, p. 13). Economic and moral arguments are deployed in comparing the defi-cient status of child labourers in Nepal and Venezuela with the way that compulsory full-time education meets the developmental needs of the majority of children from developed countries. Just as with the UNCRC, some account is taken of indigenous cultural norms. For example, the afore-mentioned newspaper article goes on: 'Surveys in Nicaragua and Mali have suggested that children in rural areas accept work as part of normal life and enjoy the company, if they are not forced into heavy labour or beaten'. Yet the broad thrust of media coverage has been to attack child labour per se: to expose the exploitation of child labourers and emphasise their needs in terms of schooling. Drawing on the language of rights, there is a strong tendency towards child-saving, with children's rights to provision and protection having priority over their rights to participation.

A more promising statement from the United Nations on children's interests is Local Agenda 21, a blueprint on the global environment drawn up as a result of the United Nations Conference on Environment and Development of 1992. Chapter 25, entitled 'Children and Youth in Sustainable Development', deals with 'children and youth' as a significant political community: 'Governments . . . should take measures to . . . establish procedures allowing for consultation and possible participation of youth of both genders, by 1993, in decision-making processes with regard to the environment involving youth at the local national and regional levels.' Agenda 21 stipulates that national governments should establish procedures to incorporate children's concerns into all relevant policies and strategies for environment and development at the local, regional and national levels' (http://soc-info.soc.titech.ac.jp/ngo/agenda21/ch-25).

At the European level there is a similar tension between children's needs and interests. European Community policy rarely targets those under the age of 15. What has been done relates more to their needs than their interests. In part this is the result of long-standing tensions between EC social-policy makers and the national sovereignty concerns of some member states. Yet the social policy that does exist at this level is protectionist in nature, with resources being directed towards tackling child exploitation in the form of sex tourism and child pornography. However, throughout the 1990s some attempts were made to introduce participatory structures for young people. In 1992 the Council of Europe set up the European Charter on the Participation of Young People in Municipal and Regional Life. In 1997 the Council of Europe made further commitments to participation through the Committee of Ministers on Youth Participation and the Future of Civil Society. A report commissioned by the European Union calls for a substantive European children's policy. The author of the report, Sandy Ruxton (1999), is quite clear in positioning children as separate political entities: child-focused issues are to be dealt with in their own terms rather than subsumed within 'family, youth or gender policy' (1999, p. 2). The report emphasises the need to improve children's political status and sets out a range of proposals from the general: 'the extension of citizenship and participation' and giving 'children the right to participate in the democratic process' (1999, Preface), to the more specific, such as the reduction of the age of majority to 16 in member countries. If we take this along with the European Youth Parliament established in the mid-1990s, and the attempts to incorporate the voices of those under the age of 18 across European towns and cities, there are some grounds for optimism with respect to children's interests (Casman 1996).

Children's Views on Politics

Given the low priority placed on associating childhood with politics, there is a limited amount of research in this field. What I can say is that there are few positive associations between young people and the political mainstream. In the USA scholars have been testing the notion that 'Generation Xers', those aged between 16 and 30, are disengaged and disaffected from the political mainstream (Craig and Earl Bennett 1997). Whilst there is little conclusive evidence, research findings range from viewing young people as politically ambivalent to them having a greater distrust of politics, putting young people in the same category as older political cynics. If we look at the UK, and a slightly younger cohort, there seem to be similar levels of distrust. The Joseph Rowntree Foundation commissioned the National Centre for Social Research's (2000) survey of young people's political views. According to the data drawn from 24 focus groups made up of young people aged between 14 and 24, there is some interest in and commitment to social and political issues. Yet, the main finding of the research is that young people express a mixture of indifference and cynicism towards mainstream politics, what has been referred to as the 'democratic deficit'. As the Economic and Social Research Council, the key research body in the UK, sets out in a recent briefing paper:

> The low turnout at the 2001 General Election [in the United Kingdom], particularly by young people, seems to confirm the view that there is a widening gulf between the citizen, disengaged from traditional forms of democratic involvement and government with its commitment to a more inclusive and participatory democracy and citizenship education. (ESRC 2001, p. 1)

Roker, Player and Coleman's (1999) survey of 1160 teenagers aged between 14 and 16 is more positive in suggesting that children and young people are political in the sense that there are varying degrees of commitment to voluntary organisations and single-issue groups. Importantly, they argue that, with reference to actions such as signing petitions and taking part in demonstrations, their sample indicates that young people are likely to be more political than the adult population.

Whilst the point is not explicitly made, the authors seem to be concurring with another common theme within this research field and one shared by US research (Craig and Earl Bennett 1997): young people's energy and commitment to single-issue campaigns and one-off political actions are a consequence of their disillusionment with conventional party politics. Reference is made to young people's alienation from party politics, as compared with their greater commitment to single-issue politics. This seems to bear out the general shift in young people's affiliations from youth wings of the main political parties to single-issue organisations such as Greenpeace and Amnesty International (Matthews et al. 1999, p. 17).

The Joseph Rowntree study links levels of youthful commitment and interest to politics with levels of understanding of politics. The more committed young people appear to have a more sophisticated and informed understanding of politics. By the same token, those who are bored and disillusioned are less likely to know about the political world. One of the main findings of an earlier piece of research carried out by Barnardos with a sample of 12–19-year-olds is that young people are not particularly well-informed, with only a small minority having what Walker calls a 'fact-formed consciousness' of politics (1996, p. 127). There are two important caveats here. First, we would not want to see this lack of knowledge as a product of some innate cognitive incompetence. I have already argued that children and young people are skilled users of the mass media and acutely aware of the range of information available to them. Walker seems to be arguing that there is an element of choice here, with young people 'switching off' from the kinds of media that provide informed opinion and debate about politics. Secondly, in England and Wales we might put this ignorance down to a lack of political preparation. Rather ironically, the idea of childhood as an apprenticeship excludes any notion of learning about the political world. Historically in England and Wales, educationalists have been either indifferent to or suspicious of anything to do with 'political education' (Davies 1999). This can be linked to the notions of innocence discussed in Chapter 1, with children's minds apparently incapable of taking in knowledge of the political world. There is also a general fear that children's lack of worldliness and rationality opens them up to exploitation from teachers, schools or local education authorities whose interests are in the form of political indoctrination (Harber and Meighan 1989). Children are thus expected to become political more or less once they leave childhood at 18. Those older children within touching distance of formal adult status are infantilised. As Hodgkin and Newell argue (cited in Matthews et al. 1999, p. 17), 'society assumes (here) an incapacity long past the date when they are more capable'. Children's social apprenticeship is largely an apolitical experience. This is not to deny that political socialisation takes place; children pick up ideas and possibly experiences through family, friends and media about the political world. However, there is little formal structure to this knowledge, little sense in which children can collectively inquire about the political world.

It is important not to overstate the case here in relation to political education. Citizenship education was brought into the National Curriculum in England and Wales as a compulsory component in September 2002. A proportion of the curriculum is given over to making young people more politically literate, encouraging children to discuss 'controversial issues' and introducing concepts relating to political systems. Secondly, whilst there is a weak tradition for political and citizenship education in England and Wales, the picture is quite different in countries such as Germany, Denmark and the USA. If we take Denmark, for instance, children aged from 6 up to 16 regularly take part in discussions on civic and political issues. These discussions take place within what Hahn (1999, p. 237) calls a 'supportive communal environment'.

Case Studies of Political Participation

In this final section I explore the possibilities for viewing children as a more constituent element within the world of politics. I will do this by exploring a series of localised initiatives in quite different cultural contexts that demonstrate children's political involvement:

- working children's trade unions in Bangalore, India

- children's parliaments in Rajasthan, India

- young people's town councils in England.

Bhima Sangha: Working Children's Union Activities

Bhima Sangha was set up by child workers in the Indian city of Bangalore in an attempt to strengthen their lowly economic and social positions. Organised action and political voice are features of the adult population, particularly with respect to the workplace. Bhima Sangha act on one of the fundamentals of economic and political life, that individual workers need to group together collectively in an effort to articulate and improve their economic positions.[2] Whilst economic, social and political circumstances can make this a hazardous and arduous process in the contemporary adult world, Bhima Sangha has grown in size and influence and now represents the interests of 16,000 children in the Indian state of Karnataka (Reddy 2000, p. 53).

The union activists here have three clear sets of interests. First, there is the issue of exploitation and the need to promote the interests of child workers inherently economically vulnerable. The fragmented location of child workers, the hidden nature of their activities, and the temporary, part-time and seasonal nature of their work puts them in a very weak bargaining position with reference to controlling the work process, their rates of pay and their general working conditions. A second issue relates to the very idea of child work. As I discussed earlier in the chapter, the dominance of

Western conceptions of childhood render child work a contradiction in terms. The general political trend at global and to some extent national levels is to get children off the street and into families and schools.[3] Bhima Sangha is challenging the popular idea that child labourers are at best always going to be exploited because of their 'childish' natures and at worst are children 'out of position'. As Nandana Reddy, an advocate of child workers, argues, the union is heavily involved in both abolishing the worst excesses of employer exploitation *and* 'preserving and increasing the benefits' of children working (Reddy 2000, p. 52).

Children's interests are strengthened in a third way. To be more specific, we are referring to the interests of female child workers. Reddy (2000) draws on the example of a group of girls, aged between 10 and 12, who foraged in the forest for fuel. These girls encountered a range of problems from their employers, ranging from excessively long hours, lack of transport to the forest, which was 12 kilometres from their village and the loss of income earned through fines. They had put up with this because it gave them some financial freedom, but, more importantly, it allowed them a degree of social freedom to meet other girls, which by convention they would have been denied. Through negotiation with employers and the mediating skills of a local NGO, the girls were able to gain access to schooling in place of their irregular income and at the same time they were allowed the same levels of autonomy conventionally enjoyed by young male workers.

Bal Sansad: A Children's Parliament

This second case study concerns the Bal Sansad, a children's parliament based in Rajasthan, one of the poorest and largest states in north-west India. In 1993 a local social work centre (SWRC) set up the Bal Sansad to focus on local children's interests. There are three aims: to involve children more in local politics, to give children decision-making powers in areas that directly affect them, and to encourage the population 'to respect children's and opinions and capabilities' (Bernard van Leer Foundation 1999, p. 1). There is an important educational role in that children are being prepared for responsible adult positions in their respective villages. There is also an emphasis on them becoming aware of 'their rights as equal members' (1999, p. 1). Children aged between 6 and 14 become members of parliament (MPs) by being directly elected by their peers. The electorate consists of around 1700 children with between 15 and 20 MPs elected. The current parliament, for instance, consists of 5 boys and 11 girls. The SWRC mediates between the electorate (acting as a 'civil service', according to Parry-Williams 1998, p. 33) and the elected, providing training courses and general support for those with little experience of the political process. The Bal Sansad is also made up of two competing parties: Ujala, which means Light, and Gauval, which means Shepherd. Both have their own logos. Prospective candidates can choose to join either party.

A lengthy election process takes place, culminating in votes being cast by secret ballot. Representatives from both parties scrupulously oversee the counting of the votes, with problems being dealt with by an election commissioner. The party with the largest number of votes forms the government. Parliament meets on a monthly basis. Government is directly accountable to parliament with the appointed prime minister having to account for her actions to MPs of both sides (the current prime minister is a 13-year-old girl). Ministers are appointed and are expected to attend all parliamentary sittings. Sanctions are imposed on those who fail to attend. Regular contact is kept between the ministers, the MPs and children from the local communities. The Bernard van Leer Foundation refers to a series of achievements and focal points.

- *Improving school attendance*: One of the key problems in the area is the poor attendance of both children and teachers at school. The ministers are charged with the responsibility of persuading parents and children of the benefits of schooling. MPs have also been asked by parents to monitor the problem of teachers 'skipping' evening classes (United News of India 1999).

- *School closures*: Ministers are also influential in keeping schools open and in making routes to school safer for pupils. One notable example of this was the pressure that MPs put on a local 'liquor lord' to close down one of his shops which was situated directly opposite a local school.

- *Changing the attitudes of adults*: One important issue that the Bal Sansad regularly faces is the lack of support from some groups of parents. MPs from both parties often mediate here with some success. In particular, through the work of the MPs, some orthodox parents are now allowing their daughters to go to school and take part in elections.

- *Broadening children's collective interests:* The Bal Sansad brings children together from different villages where common issues and problems are collectively expressed and dealt with. Moreover, the origins of Bal Sansad are in the work that SWRC did with children attending night school. The initial focal points were, therefore, school-related. Work with the parliament over time has widened children's concerns to all aspects of village life. This has meant that elected representatives of the Bal Sansad now take an active role in adult bodies.

Marylebone Borough Student Council (MBSC)[4]

This third case study is drawn from a research project recently completed by the author.[5] The background to the student and youth councils in England follows the general pattern in Western societies of children's exclusion from public and civic affairs. However, in recent years there has been some consideration given to the voice of young people at the local political level, not least because of the aforementioned global initiatives such as Agenda 21 and the UN convention. In Britain at the national level a youth parliament was set up in 2001. Moreover, the regeneration of British cities and the greater emphasis on 'democratic renewal' has focused attention on the possibilities for political inclusion of previously marginalised groups such as the disabled, the elderly and the young (Duncan and Thomas 2000). Currently there are a variety of local youth organisations, from ad hoc groups that meet on the street to more formally constituted young people's town councils. Some are more established and formalised than others, but the general aim is to strengthen the voice of young people in local matters.

Drawing on the model provided by civic youth councils in France, the Association Nationale des Conseils d' Enfants et des Jeunes (ANACEJ), the Marylebone Borough Student Council was set up in 1994 to improve the involvement of young people in local issues.[6] Located in a medium-sized town in central England, the MBSC shadows the adult council in the way that it is structured and constituted. The council is made up of 24 members, four from each of the six secondary schools in the area. Years 9 and 10 (ages 13–15) provide the council with four members elected from both years per school. Elections are an important characteristic of the MBSC. In the six participating secondary schools, candidates for council office put themselves forward and present their policies to their school year group. After a period of canvassing, elections take place on a given day, normally coordinated across the six schools. The setting of meetings and procedures follows pretty closely the activities of the adult councils. For example, meetings take place in the council chambers, the setting for the adult councils, agendas are sent out in advance to members by adult council officers, minutes are taken at the meetings by council officials, issues are formally proposed and votes are taken on key decisions made. As with the Bhima Sangha and Bal Sansad, the student council has an adult mediator who acts as an adviser to the council, the current adviser being employed by the local council.

A more detailed outline of the different ways in which children's interests are conceptualised is discussed in more detail elsewhere (Wyness 2001). For the purposes of this brief exposition, I will concentrate on two elements of those 'interests', concepts which emerged as key themes in the young counsellors' thinking about their roles: the idea of *representation*, and the extent to which the young councillors are attempting to have an *influence* locally.

Children's interests are usually represented by those with some sort of mandate to act on behalf of sectors of the child population. In the case of Bhima Sangha and the Bal Sansad, we have the union representatives and the MPs respectively who act on behalf of a constituency of children and young people. In the case of the MBSC, we are talking about the student councillors. These representatives participate in political structures where they can exert a degree of influence over decisions at both individual and general levels. This involves children having a voice in decisions that directly affect them as individuals. This is more likely to happen where children are in a position to influence the way that they are received and perceived by the adult population.

Representation

In turning first to representation, the formal documentation emphasises the representative position of the councils. In the constitution one of the key aims of the MBSC is 'to represent young people in the Borough, to comment on public services, in particular those that impinge on the lives of young people, and to initiate discussion with service providers on the development or changes to public services' (Members' Handbook, p. 7).

Some students mentioned the council as a preparation for the adult world, as a means of developing levels of self-confidence and powers of expression – there was an element of 'self-interest' here. They were also keen to confirm their roles as representatives of young people at some level. In some cases this was quite general, with a focus on students and young people:

> I think it's to get across students' views because it's always normally adults saying what they want all the time and kids don't get a say in what they want. So it's really just to say what we want and if anything gets done about it which does now, now we've got this [the council]. (Lindsay, Year 9)

> I heard it might be something that I'd enjoy and something that I believed in that young people's views should be heard rather than just the older members of the area voting on what they believed. (James, Year 9)

Some councillors were more specific when discussing the aims of the council, referring to either the locale or their age-related peers who voted in the class election:

> To provide better things for students around the Marylebone borough. To make their voices heard and just generally bring up any issues they want to get heard and try and resolve them. (Andrew, Year 10)

I wanted to have a say for our age group, what we could do in Marylebone. (Emily, Year 10)

The councillors were also asked about how representative they thought their roles were. There were mixed responses. Given that the councillors' constituencies are determined by school age-gradings, many of the issues picked up by councillors work their way through informal networks. On the positive side, their peers will ask them to bring up specific problems:

If we're coming up to a meeting, I have a word with some of my mates, 'Is there anything on the bus passes?' We keep bringing them up at meetings. The big problem is they ask, say, the Odeon [people who run the local cinema] to come in and we've being asking them for a year and they haven't turned up. (James, Year 10)

MBSC links with the six schools within a variegated geographical area meant that there were formal as well as informal networks through which the student voice could be expressed and heard:

Interviewer: Do you think that the council gives young people in Marylebone more of a say?
Alan: Yes it does because by having it from every school, having four from every school, you do get the view of Marylebone and the surrounding area because people in my school tell me stuff that they want sorting like the bus problems and all that.
Interviewer: So do you get people coming up to you saying you're the student councillor?
Alan: Yeah, we can then bring it up in any other business and we can put it in the agenda for next time (Year 10).

On the other hand, some of the younger councillors are critical of the older members' 'self-interests'. A couple of first-year councillors were asked about how the council could be improved.

I don't know. I think maybe the older councillors should probably go out and talk to people more rather than they seem to put their own views forward more. (Hayley and Janine, Year 9)

Influence

The issue of influence is also a significant feature of the councillors' accounts of their roles. When discussing both Bhima Sangha and the Bal Sansad, I made reference to the way that members were trying to change local adult opinion on their capabilities as children. With respect to the

English student council, the influence that young people aim to have here over the adult population is couched in terms of challenging the needs model of childhood discussed earlier, the assumption that children necessarily have to be kept in line by adult authority figures:

> At the time there wasn't a lot for teenagers to do and they were always criticised, stereotyped, so I just wanted to, if everyone was complaining about having nothing to do and they hadn't heard of the student council, so I thought that I could go forward and put their points of view forward. (Alan, Year 9)

This comment suggests that the MBSC is challenging the 'youth as social problem' theme discussed in Chapter 4. One instance of MBSC trying to change attitudes came up at a council meeting. Representatives from the local bus companies involved in transporting pupils to schools within the borough were invited to attend. There had been four recurring problems with school transport: the cost of travelling to school, the safety of pupils on the buses, the poor physical state of the buses, and the attitudes of the bus drivers.[7] The bus company representatives were ushered into the meeting at the appropriate point on the agenda and the councillors set out the problems as they saw them. With reference to the problems of safety, the state of the buses and the drivers' attitudes, they presented anecdotal evidence of incidents that had taken place and set out the general perception that pupils had of the way they were treated by the drivers. Many of the claims made by councillors were countered by the bus representatives asserting that the state of the buses and the 'strict' attitude of the drivers was due to the lack of respect that many young people had for the company's property, often resulting in the buses being vandalised. The councillors were courteous in their manner and organised and articulate in putting their points across. Yet the message from the bus companies seemed to be that if the young people wanted respect, they had to earn it. Some of the councillors were interviewed a couple of weeks after this meeting. Some felt that the important thing was to make their point, which they felt they had done. Others were more critical, referring to the 'youth as problem' stereotype:

> **Interviewer:** What do you think of that debate that you had with the bus companies?
> **Lindsay:** I disliked some of their attitudes. A lot of adults see the council as just some little organisation, which shouldn't actually do anything.
> **James:** I find them patronising. I felt patronised at one point. It really annoyed me because they were talking down on me because I was a kid or something.
> **Lindsay:** That's the problem, some adults don't actually have much respect for us. All they see is a bunch of teenagers sitting around shouting.

Conclusion

I return to a dominant theme within the book: the tensions between adult-driven conceptions of childhood and children's practices, between the general and the particular. This tension runs through our discussions of children's rights and children's politics. In the first place, the discourse on children's rights presents us with a dilemma: how to underwrite children's welfare without negating or marginalising children's abilities as self-determining agents. Are children's rights to welfare and their rights to self-determination irrevocably conflictual? For many there is no conflict. Care and control come before liberation. The liberal Western model provides a framework within which children gradually *become* self-determining agents. As I have argued in this book, this lack of ontology is often used to deny children unconditional involvement within society. For advocates of moderate degrees of self-determination, the search is for a middle way. The question here is whether we can construct a basic structure, some sort of physical and moral bottom line upon which children simply *are* competent social agents.

We might fruitfully explore a middle way by incorporating children into the political realm. In the second section of the chapter I discussed the tension between the general and the particular with reference to children's political exclusion. I drew a parallel between the children's rights discourse and children's needs and interests. To think in terms of children's politics is to move away from a crude, but still-dominant needs conception of childhood towards the idea of children as members of a minority group with distinct collective political interests (James, Jenks and Prout 1998). The case studies in Part Three hopefully provide illustrations of children's localised practices that challenge the needs discourse. Whilst cultural differences generate different ways of seeing young people, in all three case studies children saw themselves as counter-stereotypes, who, through good works and persuasion, are attempting to alter the perceptions that adults have of young people. In previous chapters I discussed the literal and metaphorical positioning of children, such that those who do not conform to the dominant subordinate model of childhood are rendered deviant, often taken to be 'out of place'. In the case of Bhima Sangha, working children with a degree of control over the work process contradicts the care/control and schooled versions of childhood. Their commitment to better working conditions does not invalidate their desire to be schooled. Nevertheless, Bhima Sangha demonstrates that children as well as adults are capable of making the best of economic conditions. The younger representatives demonstrate that children are of the social and political world rather than being on the cusp of society.

Similarly, a key aim of the young English town councillors was to controvert the 'youth as problem' stereotype. Children here, in a manner of speaking, invade adult territory. The aim is to shift adult thinking so that children in public spaces are not necessarily viewed as a threat or a menace. The means to this end, the council structures, are themselves a challenge in that political structures, like public territory, are often defined as adult spaces. A second aim of the case studies appears to be the need to articulate the interests of young people based on either formal democratic principles or through more informal networks and friendships. The very idea of representation here implies levels of responsibility, involvement and participation not normally attributed to children and young people. One other shared aim of the young people from the case studies is the desire to establish social status and recognition. The data from the town council project reveal that the councillors want to be recognised as young adults, with life or social experience rather than age the main criterion for judging their worth. In referring to the idea of children's interests, we might speculate that this takes us closer to Lee's (2001) point that children and adults are more or less agentic depending on context and experience.

Conclusion

In this book I have outlined the importance of children and childhood as topics of sociological concern. In the past, sociologists have tended to subsume children and childhood within the fields of family, education, gender, social policy and youth. Social scientists have discussed children in relation to what were seen as more significant categories, institutions and practices. Researchers with an interest in late modernity or postmodernity identified children as the projects of adults and states; socialisation, development and education signify analyses of large structures and the work of significant adult others such as parents and teachers. Children simply did not count within the social sciences. Moreover, this lack of social status was reflected in the marginal position accorded the study of childhood. Those with an interest in childhood have been accused of being 'childish', both in the treatment of work that foregrounds children within the research process and in the micropolitics of academic departments where status has traditionally been accorded to those whose interests are in theory, social class or gender.

However, as we saw in Chapter 9, in the last decade or so childhood has been a growth area within sociology. University departments are creating courses, modules and degrees in childhood studies, with sociology the prominent discipline; research centres specialise in research with children, and academic journals on childhood have sprung up as researchers foreground children's lives and challenge the dominant assumptions about childhood. In Chapter 2 I referred to the development of a 'grown-up' theory of childhood through the notion of generation (Alanen 2001b; Mayall 2002). Whilst there are difficulties in singling out children's structural location as children from other dimensions of social difference, this approach has strategic significance for the sociology of childhood. The promotion of the child as an agent, the voices of children as research subjects and the discourse on children's rights attest to the need to take childhood seriously within the sociological community. By bringing age/generation into the theoretical mainstream, the importance of childhood as a branch of sociology is more likely to be taken seriously.

Just as the trivialising and marginalising of childhood in academia reflected children's invisibility in the past, the current developments within a new sociology of childhood are probably linked to attempts within the wider society to take children more seriously. We can view this as a dialectical relationship between the social and the sociological. In one direction, researchers foreground children's perspectives, leading to the implicit questioning of their subordinate social positions and the extent of adults' responsibilities as caretakers. One scenario at the local level is that researchers within childhood studies have been able to persuade adult gatekeepers such as teachers and social workers that children can be treated as research collaborators, resulting in more research being done with children. One effect or by-product of this might be that children are perceived by child professionals to be more competent.

Another scenario is that researchers are able to work with children now because in the wider society children are more likely to be viewed as competent. There is less need for researchers to persuade child professionals that children are capable of playing a proactive role within the research process. Given the pressures on child professionals to protect children, we remain to be convinced that the majority of gatekeepers take this view of children and childhood. Nevertheless, there is undoubtedly a sense that children are now much more visible members of society, which, at the very least, generates ambiguous responses from the adult population as to the status of children. It is ambiguity that forms a key theme running through the chapters of this book. Paradoxically, in the process of foregrounding conceptual and empirical work on childhood, throughout this book I have identified its elusive, ambiguous and inconsistent nature.

Childhood and Ambiguity

Competing Discourses

In Chapter 1 I started off by emphasising childhood as a meaning system: children's lives, the actions of adults towards children and, to some extent, the sense that adults have of their own identities are governed by understandings we have of childhood. Sociologists delineate these understandings as discourses that position children as both cherished and demonised (Jenks 1996). In the former case, children are represented as pure and innocent, originating in the work of the eighteenth- and nineteenth-century romantics. This purity needs to be nurtured and protected. In these terms, adults are to support children's development, channel their energies and in general create an environment within which children are 'encouraged, enabled and facilitated' (Jenks 1996, p. 73). In the latter case, the sporadic influence of the Puritans from the seventeenth century onwards and, in some respect, the assumptions made by the dominant figures in sociology in the first half of the twentieth century view children as anarchic and demonic, as corrupting influences. Agencies of socialisation and control are activated to bring children into line. Rather than simply act as supportive props in children's natural development, adults are more interventionist, more overtly controlling and regulatory.

As discussed in Chapter 3 late modern society has the potential to keep these conflicting ideas about childhood in check through the notions of control and self-realisation (Prout 2000a). However, Chapters 4 and 5 identify a contemporary crisis of childhood in the way that the media and social commentators have difficulty reconciling these images of the conflicting fears that adults have of children as being in need of both protection and control. The pressures to protect and nurture arise out of the problems of abuse and economic exploitation; a concern for discipline and control comes from the equally pressing need to impose order in the lives of wayward children because of a perceived rise in youthful disorder.

Children and the State

In part the ambiguous management of children by the state follows on from the demonised/romanticised tension within contemporary conceptions of Western childhood. I referred in Chapter 5 to the conflicting theory and practice of delinquency. In addressing the treatment of young criminals in England and Wales over the past 200 years, notions of 'welfare' and 'justice' have been sharply counterposed. Whilst the reality is a messy compromise of the two, the significance of age and the assumptions about children's competence have helped us to formulate criminal justice policy. Yet the tension between care and control is partially resolved if we address the different ways in which the treatment of victims and offenders overlap. As I argued in Chapter 5, the state tends to elide these conflicting constructions of childhood. This is nicely illustrated in a recent book on incarcerated children by Barry Goldson (2002). Here the author examines the experiences of two distinct categories of children dealt with by the state: those children placed in secure accommodation through welfare statutes, those in need of protection, and those held in remand in both youth offender institutions and adult prisons through the criminal justice system. Goldson generates several critical themes on the treatment of both child populations. Two are pertinent here.

First, the recent trend in England and Wales towards punishing rather than treating youngsters who break the law has led to a rise in the numbers of children being imprisoned. In some cases, this has meant children being remanded in adult prisons. Moreover, the shift towards a more punitive regime has focused government attention on how to make prisons and youth offender institutions more effective forms of accommodation for young people. Policy-makers are thus less likely to question the appropriateness of prison for children in the first place. Secondly, there is a more punitive approach in the case of those children who have taken the protectionist welfare route into 'secure accommodation'. Goldson (2002, p. 122) refers to this as the 'criminalisation of vulnerable children'. This emphasis on control rather than care is brought out in the way that the children are treated within secure accommodation, with staff being more concerned with regulating behaviour than with tending to their emotional and social needs. The emphasis on control in both forms of secure accommodation creates a paradox: 'the locked institution can be seen as *relief from vulnerability* for one identifiable group of children, and as a *source of vulnerability* for another' (author's emphasis) (2002, p. 2). Thus abused and sexually exploited children are taken out of the community for their own protection, whereas the 'excluded' delinquent is exposed to all sorts of psychological and physical threats once placed in prison. To complicate matters further, recent high-profile cases of abuse in children's homes have given the impression that children in care or secure accommodation are being exposed to similar threats as children in prison.[1]

Children's Rights

Ambiguity is also prevalent in debates on children's rights. Whilst political capital has been made through the caricaturing of children's rights in terms of child liberation, a more careful consideration of children's rights reveals a tension between children's right to welfare and children's right to self-determination. I argued in Chapter 10 that these forms of children's rights have quite distinct implications for adult/child relations and children's institutional treatment. However, whether we are talking about doing things for children or giving them the space to do things for themselves, the rights agenda has repositioned children as central figures within child policy at both global and national levels. The UNCRC has established children as 'beings', albeit of the dependent variety, and thus goes some way to seeing children as an important social minority group (Lee 2001). At the national level, if we take the case of the UK, recent pressure on central government to take children more seriously has resulted in the creation of a more integrated political structure for children. In June 2003 the UK Labour government introduced a ministry for children to oversee a range of services for children as well as to provide more direct channels of accountability. Whilst this was a direct response to a series of high-profile cases of child abuse, with a remit that was almost exclusively protectionist, government for the first time was recognising children as a population with distinct needs that went beyond the proprietorial interests of either parents or child professionals.

As I discussed in Chapter 10, progress has been made in developing participatory structures for children within the public realm, However, as yet there is little sense of children being accorded similar degrees of respect and autonomy within the education system. In Chapter 7 I argued that children's lives are over-determined in schools in most Western societies. Schooling presents us with something of a paradox: children numerically are a majority population in schools but lack any means through which this numerical superiority has any clout politically. Thus, whilst schools are quintessentially children's places, there is little sense of children owning these places or having any control over how they are organised, run or structured. Despite their numerical supremacy, children in this sense conform most clearly to a social minority group, as discussed in Chapter 2. In conceptualising school students in this way, they become more visible in political and social terms; that is, bringing children into view as a minority group directs us towards asking questions about their lack of rights, their limited degrees of autonomy and their exclusion from a range of decision-making processes. This lack of voice or rights is particularly marked in secondary schools, particularly in relation to older students within touching distance of gaining formal political rights.

Again, following the emphasis on children's 'voice' within the UNCRC, there are modest gains being made with regards to the participatory rights of schoolchildren (Rudduck and Flutter 2004). Whilst the regulatory demands of the curriculum and the system of education provision continue to bear down on children, there is a growing recognition that the social, political and educational interests of schools, educational administrators and policy-makers are better served by a more inclusive student population.

Children as Structurally Marginal and Situationally Competent

What I think I have shown in this book is that children in the research process, as in other contexts, are now ambiguously placed as structurally marginal and situationally competent. That is to say, there is a much greater awareness of children's minority status with respect to their access to political and cultural resources. At the same time, we are now beginning to move beyond the idea that children are passive recipients of the work of significant adult others; we are starting to view children as having a formative involvement in a range of social contexts. Viewing children as part of a broader social whole, we become aware of a range of obstacles that limit the capacity of children to play full social roles. In Chapter 2 I discussed this with reference to the work of Qvortrup and his European colleagues in the project, Childhood as a Social Phenomenon, where children were located as a constituent element within the social structure as incomplete social actors. Whilst I would not completely dismiss the biological nature of some of these obstacles, the political, social and cultural restrictions needed to be treated separately rather than being inferred from children's physical size.

If we view children within a range of more localised contexts, we start to see things differently. In among the adult-defined proscriptions and constraints, children in their everyday settings at home, school and play actively create and renew social relations. Some of these contexts are hidden. The home remains the dominant site for shaping children's social identities. In many Western cultures since the nineteenth century this has always been seen as a private matter, with parents having responsibility for socialisation. In Chapter 4 I discussed a small group of children who, due to a combination of disability, poverty and distrust of the social services, were the primary carers within the home, tending to the physical and emotional needs of their disabled parents. Whilst most commentators have seen child carers as an exceptional and aberrant category of childhood, a recent study locates 'child carers' along a spectrum of domestic tasks and responsibilities undertaken by children within the home (Chambers 2003). The idea of a 'home responsibility continuum' is useful here for it breaks down the distinction between the deviant 'child carer' and the 'domesti-cated child', suggesting that children in general are more competent within the home, involved in a range of activities that often belie their chronological status.

The tension between situational competence and structural marginality is also a useful way of characterising the research relationship between researcher and child discussed in Chapter 9. In Chapter 6, children were worked upon by researchers in the pursuit of measurement and normalisation. In moving to a situation where children work with adult researchers, we are introducing a relatively recent participatory context for children. I discussed a range of roles for children within the research context, but we were effectively bringing children into focus as research collaborators. The equitable treatment of children here brings into play a range of ethical questions with which researchers are faced when working with adult respondents. In Chapter 9 I argued that children's structural marginality manifests itself as the adult researcher's imperative to protect and nurture, reminding us that children are special cases and that issues such as informed consent and confidentiality are not so easily ensured within the research process. Thus we are brought back to the 'exceptional' status of children, with researchers erring on the side of exclusion. The notion of informed consent applied to research with children is more likely to lead to children being consulted, but this is usually after the parent or guardian has been consulted first. Whilst there is little point in persisting with child respondents who are unhappy at taking part in the research, the key informant is still the responsible adult; agreement has to be reached at this stage before the research can move on.

Children's Agency

In this final section I want to reflect a little on one of the key concepts deployed within the sociology of childhood: children's agency. I have argued throughout the book that the sociologists of childhood take it as read that children can be understood as competent social actors. Just as we ascribe to adults an ability to make sense of their social worlds, so we impute agency to children in a variety of social contexts. The idea of children's agency is sometimes rather vaguely articulated as anything from children having full control over their social environments, the liberationist position, to a weaker sense of children making some contribution within their social environments. Mayall's (2002, p. 21) distinction between 'actor' and 'agency' is instructive here. The former implies that children are of the social world: beings rather than becomings. The latter takes 'action' forward and implies that children make a difference. Children have an influence; their views are taken seriously, and there is some recognition of this within the political as well as the social sphere.

One question that has to be faced by advocates of children's agency in the more liberationist sense is whether children would always want to be treated as agents. I hinted at this issue in the last chapter when I discussed children's interests. Here I discussed the case of the Soweto schoolchildren demanding that adults take more responsibility and exercise more authority and leadership within the home and the classroom. In one sense, children are making demands on the adult population to return to a state of social and cultural normality, with adults assuming their positions as arbiters of children's best interests. One way of resolving this issue is to highlight the notion of children's voice. Soweto children did not want to be treated as if they were adults, but the very fact that they were in a position to make these claims or express a preference implies that there can probably be no return to an earlier state where adults simply acted on behalf of children. As I argued in Chapter 3, children are likely to have more 'space' within the home now, with parents having to earn their children's respect. Children's voice implies here an intermediate state. Agency does not simply liberate children. It opens up possibilities for hearing children, consulting and working with children, and creating new spaces for children's contributions, even if this means children appealing to the 'natural' authority of adults. To all intents and purposes, the liberationist moment has gone, but the residual effects are notable: children want respect, they want to be heard and, in conjunction with adults, they want a degree of self-determination.

A related problem, which I referred to in Chapters 4 and 8, is the adult fear of the third party. Children's lives are now increasingly mediated by technology, inducing fears within the adult population. Whilst this fear often relates to the compromise of a modernist conception of childhood innocence, some commentators have suggested that these fears reflect deeper concerns for a perceived shift in balance of power away from adults towards children. If we come back to the notion of 'children's place', the displacement of children generates fears for their physical and moral safety. It might also relate to the repositioning of children within the generational hierarchy. Thus if we were to reframe children's agency in a relational sense with an emphasis on the exercise of authority and power, then a part of the adults' 'fragmentation of self' is the dispersal of control, a perceived inability to regulate the lives of children, particularly those children for whom they have responsibility.

For some, this dispersal of control misses the point. In referring to agency we are implicitly suggesting that in some respects children should emulate adults in terms of politics and rights. Yet in Chapter 3 I alluded to a paradox when examining the relationship between childhood studies and sociological theory. The sociology of childhood is attempting to establish the child as a fully constituted social subject just at the point where late modernity pulls the ontological ground from under the individual. Nick Lee (2001) brings this out clearly in a recent book. He argues that the focus on the child as a competent social actor rather than a trainee citizen or citizen-in-waiting does not sit that well next to the fragmented social identity of the adult subject (Lee 2001). Agency appears to be a less significant frame of reference within the 'grown-up' world of social theory.

One final associated point concerns the 'sentimentalisation' of children's voice: in some respects the sociology of childhood has concentrated on affirming children's right to be heard in social and sociological terms. To some extent, the establishing of children's agency has meant that locating children within the research community becomes an end in itself rather than a strategy for making sense of children's lives and their relations with others. In research terms, is it enough to say that we now hear children's voices, we take children seriously? Whilst this may have been an early strategy for establishing children's social ontology, a new sociology of childhood has to move on and evaluate what children say; in research terms we need to do something with the child data. As Prout (2000b, p. 16) comments, '[t]he observation that children can exercise agency should be a point of analytical embarkation rather than its terminus'. Thus rather than romanticising child agency, we need to start from the basic assumption that children are of the social world and are, in a number of complex and not always readily visible ways, socially competent. We might start to see this happening as the process of researching with children is normalised.

Notes

Chapter 1

1. See Roche's (1992) analysis of how the political culture in the USA and the UK in the 1980s marginalised the poor in this way.
2. In 1986 the British government increased the age at which young people can claim an income from the state from 16 to 18.
3. That is not to say that all children from non-developed countries have economic responsibilities. Margaret Mead (1930, p. 73), in her study of New Guinean society in the 1920s, sums up the nature of childhood in this society: 'The whole convention of the child's world is a play convention.'
4. See Firestone (1971) and Gittins (1998) for the gendered nature of Ariès's conception; Archard (1993) and Pollock (1983) for a critique of his assumptions and methods; Fuller (1979) for a psychoanalytic critique.
5. The Sexual Offences Act became law in 2001, bringing the homosexual age of consent in line with the heterosexual age of consent.

Chapter 2

1. The analysis here concentrates on the social structure rather than cultural or linguistic structures found in the work of Levi-Strauss (1978) and Barthes (1973).
2. Qvortrup goes on to argue that this is still an underestimate, as the child-focused statistics do not include 'single' children with younger not-yet-born siblings and older siblings living away from home.
3. This was one of the aims set out at the World Education Forum, held in Dakar in April 2000.
4. The same age-related analysis could apply to the elderly here.

Chapter 4

1. In the UK the pregnancy rate of girls under the age of 18 has fallen since early 2004, with the current UK Labour government aiming to halve the rate by the year 2010. See the Social Exclusion Unit website (www.socialexclusion.gov.uk).
2. Corsaro (1997) offers an interesting critique of Murray. Murray's imputation of blame obscures the vulnerability of many single teenage mothers: in the USA the majority of teenage mothers are the victims of 'sexual molestation, rape and sexual assault' (p. 204). The majority of teenage mothers had children by much older adult men.
3. Some have argued that the latter is a misnomer. Child carers may take on some caring tasks but the great majority of disabled adult recipients are still in control (Keith and Morris 1995).

4. In 1999 the International Labour Organisation (ILO) passed a convention which called for the elimination of child soldiers as 'one of the worst forms of child labour'. In 2000 the United Nations drafted the 'optional protocol' on to the 1989 convention, prohibiting states from the compulsory recruitment of those under the age of 18 into the armed forces. While the UK has signed the agreement, it still exercises 'an interpretative declaration' on its application (Moszynski 2001).

Chapter 5

1. Incest was a public issue in the early part of the twentieth century. See La Fontaine (1990).
2. Dr Marietta Higgs, a local paediatrician, was singled out – her diagnoses led to the Cleveland parents being arrested.
3. For other features of this laissez-faire perspective, see Fox-Harding (1991).
4. The emphasis on 'his' is significant here.
5. Harder and Pringle (1997, pp. 148–9) refer to the dynamic nature of these national systems: '[T]he development of child protection services in almost all of them [European countries] represents an oscillation between approaches to families which we might characterise as punitive/judicial on the one hand and welfare-oriented on the other.' Nevertheless, these internal tensions cannot obscure a general trend towards one approach in each European country.
6. In the past few years in the UK there have been a number of scandals involving cases of child abuse in state-funded residential homes.
7. See the first survey of juvenile delinquency in London (1815–16), *The Report of the Committee for Investigating the Causes of the Alarming Increase of Juvenile Delinquency in the Metropolis*, reviewed in Shore (1999).
8. The boys' lawyers took their cases to the European Court of Human Rights and had their sentences reduced to eight years.
9. See the *Guardian*, 29 August 1997, 21 October 1997. There have also been isolated cases of girls raping boys (see also *Guardian*, 26 October 1997).
10. We need to be careful when associating competence and reliability. One could just as easily argue that there is an inverse relationship between the competent child and the reliable child. Younger children are arguably more reliable than older children in that they do not have the competence to lie in court. Older children, on the other hand, are less reliable precisely because they are more competent: capable of covering their tracks and providing plausible reasons; more simply, older children are competent at lying.

Chapter 6

1. In more recent years, following criticism of the 'strangeness' of these conditions, psychological experiments have been naturalised, with the observation of children taking place within more familiar surroundings. See Smith and Cowie (2003, p. 4).
2. Yet the influence of other children did become a source of discontent among some sociologists in the mid- to late twentieth century. Riesman (1950) and Lasch (1979) were prominent critics of other children in that they saw the peer group as a social and moral threat to the stability of the nuclear family.
3. And yet in some non-Western countries, psychology textbooks abound with developmental ideas. See Woodhead (1999b).
4. Elements of this approach appear in most sociological theories of delinquency. See Muncie (2004) for a summary.
5. Mayall (2002, pp: 140–58) makes similar points about Finnish children in her comparison of Finnish and English children's lives.

6. I turn to non-Western examples in Chapter 10 in the discussion of the political compe-
    tence of groups of Indian children.

Chapter 7

1. David Buckingham (1994) illustrates this point in his analysis of children watching tele-
    vision.
2. Some would see performance as antithetical to teaching and learning. See Watkins
    (2001).
3. Ofsted, the Office for Standards in Education introduced in 1992, was the new school
    inspectorate answerable directly to central government (DES, 1992).
4. Whilst we need to treat crime statistics with caution, US figures point to a close rela-
    tionship between school absence and crime. In San Diego, for example, 44 per cent of
    violent juvenile crime takes place between 8.30 a.m. and 1.30 p.m. (www.unomaha.edu).
5. Thomas's sample (1998) was small and unrepresentative. However, what we can glean
    from his home-schooling families is that they were predominantly middle class, with
    around a third containing at least one parent as a qualified teacher. We might also spec-
    ulate from the research that home education is a female occupation, with 83 per cent of
    the sample of mothers having responsibility for their children's education at home.
6. An example of this approach can be found in Haralambos and Holborn (2000), a popu-
    lar textbook for 'A' level (final-year) school students and first-year university students.
7. See Illich (1971, p. 20) on the importance of incidental learning.
8. In the USA a recent newspaper report cited three reasons for the rise in popularity of
    home education: poor teaching in school, lack of moral direction in the classroom and
    fear of playground shootings. See T. Rhodes (2000), 'US parents switch to home-school-
    ing', *Sunday Times*, 10 September, p. 26.
9. I will discuss this research in the chapter on children's cultures.
10. The World Education Forum organised by UNESCO, for example, stated at one of its
    regional conferences in Dakar, Senegal, that compulsory elementary education should
    be available to all the world's children.
11. See Moss and Petrie (2002) for an interesting discussion of this.

Chapter 8

1. Davies (1982, p. 68) cites Homans in astutely commenting, 'an increase of interaction
    between persons is accompanied by an increase of sentiments of friendliness between
    them . . . You can get to like some pretty queer customers if you go around with them
    long enough. Their queerness becomes irrelevant.' Despite adults' 'higher-level' intel-
    lectualising of likeability, most of us become friends after we have been associates.

Chapter 9

1. Mahon et al. (1996) refer to a third 'therapeutic' role.
2. But see Finch (1984) for some of the drawbacks to this approach.
3. Within childhood geography, for example, researchers utilise the 'walking interview',
    whereby children can be interviewed on the move with the children determining the
    physical direction of the interview and in many cases its content. See Driskell (2002).
4. One recent commentary suggests that we should always err on the side of the guardian
    (France, Bendelow and Williams 2000).

5. The collaborators were over 18.
6. The full title is 'Involving Pupils as (Co-)Researchers in the Process of Teaching and Learning in Ways that Enable them to Manage Learning more Effectively', Project Four of the ESRC-funded Teaching and Learning Research Programme (Phase 1 Network Project).

Chapter 10

1. See the federal government's response to the United Nations Special Session on Children). Canada's Response to UN Special Session on Children (2002), *A Canada fit for Children*, http://www11.sdc.gc.ca/en/cs/sp/socpol/publications, consulted September 2004.
2. There is no historical precedent being set here. Corsaro (1997), for example, refers to the way that the late nineteenth-century American child newspaper vendors, the 'newsies', formed a union to counter their employers cutting their wages.
3. The Indian government, for example, is ambivalent in its support for anti-child-labour policies. Compulsory education, which would succeed child labour, can only be realistically considered once the most serious poverty has been reduced (Boyden and Myers 1995).
4. The names of the town and the councillors have been changed in order to maintain the anonymity of the sample.
5. The project, funded by the British Academy (Project No. SG 31775), examines children and young people's representation in four geographical areas at local government and school levels. Methods of research consist of (a) group and individual interviews with young councillors, local authority personnel, adult councillors and teachers, and (b) non-participant observation of council meetings.
6. See Matthews and Limb (1998) for a review of the French model.
7. Transport was free to pupils who went to the designated schools. Where parents had chosen to send their children to other schools outside of their immediate vicinity, parents and pupils had to pay.

Conclusion

1. One of the more recent scandals involved systematic abuse in children's homes in North Wales throughout the 1980s and 1990s. A report was commissioned by the government to investigate the allegations of abuse. See Home Office (2004).

References

Alanen, L. (1998) 'Children and the Family Order: Constraints and Competencies', in I. Hutchby and J. Moran-Ellis (eds) *Children and Social Competence*, London: Falmer Press.

Alanen, L. (2001a) 'Childhood as a Generational Condition: Children's Daily Lives in a Central Finland Town', in L. Alanen and B. Mayall (eds) *Conceptualising Child–Adult Relations*, London: RoutledgeFalmer.

Alanen, L. (2001b) 'Explorations in Generational Analysis', in L. Alanen and B. Mayall (eds) *Conceptualising Adult–Child Relations*, London: RoutledgeFalmer.

Alderson, P. (1994) 'Researching Children's Rights to Integrity', in B. Mayall (ed) *Children's Childhoods Observed and Experienced*, London: Falmer.

Alderson, P. (1995) *Listening to Children: Ethics and Social Research*, Barkingside: Essex.

Alderson, P. (2000) 'Children as Researchers: The Effects of Participation Rights on Research Methodology', in P. Christensen and A. James (eds) *Research with Children: Perspectives and Practices*, London: Falmer.

Alderson, P. and Goodwin, M. (1993) 'Contradictions within Concepts of Children's Competence', *International Journal of Children's Rights*, 1, 3/4, pp. 303–12.

Aldridge, J. and Becker, S. (1993) *Children Who Care*, Loughborough: Loughborough University.

Allan, G. and Crow, G. (2001) *Families, Households and Society*, Basingstoke: Palgrave.

Archard, D. (1993) *Children: Rights and Childhood*, London: Routledge.

Ariès, P. (1960) *Centuries of Childhood*, Harmondsworth: Penguin.

Armstrong, D. and Galloway, D. (1996) 'Children's Perceptions of Professionals in SEN', in R. Davie and D. Galloway (eds) *Listening to Children in Education*, London: David Fulton.

Arnot, M., David, M. and Weiner, G. (1999) *Closing the Gender Gap*, Cambridge: Polity.

Ash, A., Bellew, J., Davies, M., Newman, T. and Richardson, M. (1997) 'Everybody in? The Experience of Disabled Students in Colleges of Further Education', *Disability and Society*, 12, 4, pp. 605–21.

Asquith, S. (1996) 'When Children Kill Children: The Search for Justice', *Childhood: A Global Journal of Child Research*, 3, 1, pp. 99–116.

Astill, J. (2001) 'Children Fight on in Congo's War', *The Guardian*, 25 February.

Ball, S. (1994) *Education Reform*, Buckingham: Open University Press.

Ball, S., Bowe, R. and Gewirtz, S. (1995) 'Circuits of Schooling: A Sociological Exploration of Parental Choice of School in Social Class Contexts', *Sociological Review*, 43, 1, pp. 52–78.

Barber, B. (1995) *Jihad vs McWorld*, New York: Ballantine Books.

Barber, M. (1992) 'An Entitlement Curriculum: A Strategy for the Nineties', *Journal of Curriculum Studies*, 24, 5, pp. 449–55.

Barrett, H. (1998) 'Protest–Despair–Attachment: Questioning the Myth', in I. Hutchby and J. Moran-Ellis (eds) *Children and Social Competence*, London: Falmer.

Barrett, M. and McIntosh, M. (1982) *The Anti-Social Family*, London: Verso.

Barthes, R. (1973) *Mythologies*, London: Jonathan Cape.

Baumrind, D. (1964) 'Some Thoughts on Ethics of Research: After Reading Milgram's "Behavioural Study of Obedience" ', *American Psychologist*, 19, pp. 421–3.

BBC News (2000) 'Tweenagers Rule the High Street', *BBC News Homepage*, www.news.bbc.co.uk

Beck, U. (1998) *Democracy without Enemies*, Cambridge: Polity.

Beck, U. (1992) *Risk Society*, London: Sage.

Becker, S. Aldridge, J. and Dearden, C. (1998) *Young Carers and their Families*, Oxford: Blackwell.

Becker, S., Dearden, C. and Aldridge, J. (2001) 'Children's Labour of Love: Young Carers and Care Work', in P. Mizen, C. Pole and A. Bolton (eds) *Hidden Hands: International Perspectives on Children's Work and Labour*, London: RoutledgeFalmer.

Beirens, H. (2001) 'Child Soldiers: A Contradiction in Terms?', paper presented at Children in their Places Conference, University of Brunel, 22 July.

Bernard van Leer Foundation (1999) India: Bal Sansad – Children's Parliaments, *Early Childhood Matters*, February, 91, pp. 37–41.

Bernard Van Leer Foundation (2001) 'Rights from the Start: ECD and the Convention of the Rights of the Child', *Early Childhood Matters*, June, 98, pp. 8–11.

Bernardes, J. (1985) 'Do We Really Know what "the Family" is?', in P. Close and R. Collins (eds) *Family and Economy in Modern Society*, Basingstoke: Macmillan.

Bernstein, B. (1971) *Class Codes and Control*, vol. 1, London: Paladin.

Blasco, M. (2005) 'Mobilising Family Solidarity: Rights, Responsibilities and Secondary Schooling in Urban Mexico', in J Goddard et al. (eds) *The Politics of Childhood: International Perspectives, Contemporary Developments*, Basingstoke: Palgrave Macmillan.

Bourdieu, P. (1984) *Distinction: A Social Critique of the Judgement of Taste*, London: Routledge and Kegan Paul.

Bowlby, J. (1952) *Childcare and the Growth of Love*, Harmondsworth: Penguin.

Bowles, S. and Gintis, H. (1976) *Schooling in Capitalist America*, London: Routledge.

Boyden, J. (1997) 'Childhood and Policy Makers: A Comparative Perspective on the Globalization of Childhood', in A. James and A. Prout (eds) *Constructing and Reconstructing Childhood*, Basingstoke: Falmer.

Boyden, J. (2003) 'The Moral Development of Child Soldiers: What do Adults have to Fear?', *Peace and Conflict: Journal of Peace Psychology*, 9, 4, pp. 343–62.

Boyden, J. and Myers, W. (1995) *Exploring Alternative Approaches to Combating Child Labour: Case Studies from Developing Countries*, Florence: UNICEF.

Bradshaw, J. (2003) 'Poor Children', *Children and Society*, 17, 3, pp. 162–72.

Bragg, S. (2001) 'Is "As" the Most Important Word?', *ESRC Network Project Newsletter*, 3, p. 2.

Brake, M. (1995) *Comparative Youth Culture: The Sociology of Youth Cultures and Youth Subcultures*, London: Routledge.

Brett, R. and McCallin, M. (1998) *Children: The Invisible Soldiers*, Vaxjo: Radda Barnen.

British Sociological Association, *Ethical Guidelines*, www.britsoc.co.uk, consulted August 2003.

Brown, P. (1990) 'The "Third Wave": Education and the Ideology of the Parentocracy', *British Journal of Sociology of Education*, 11, 1, pp. 65–85.

Buchner, P. (1990) 'Growing up in the Eighties: Changes in the Social Biography of Childhood in the FRG', in L. Chisholm, P. Buchner, H-H. Kruger and P. Brown (eds) *Childhood, Youth and Social Change*, London: Falmer.

Buckingham, D. (1994) 'Television and the Definition of Childhood', in B. Mayall (ed) *Children's Childhoods Observed and Experienced*, London: Falmer.

Buckingham, D. (2001) *After the Death of Childhood: Growing up in the Age of Electronic Media*, Cambridge: Polity.

Bunting, M. (2004) 'Reasons to be Cheerless', *Guardian*, 1 March (http://www.guardian.co.uk/comment/story).

Burke, J. (2000) 'Children Suffer Stress over their "Love Lives" ', *Observer*, 29 October (http://www.observer. guardian.co.uk/uk_news).

Burman, E. (1994) *Deconstructing Developmental Psychology*, London: Routledge.

Burr, R. (2004) 'Children's Rights: International Policy and Lived Practice', in M. J. Kehily (ed) *An Introduction to Childhood Studies*, Buckingham: Open University Press.

Carlen, P., Gleeson, D. and Wardhaugh, J. (1992) *Truancy: The Politics of Compulsory Schooling*, Buckingham: Open University Press.

Carroll, S. and Walford, G. (1997) 'The Child's Voice in School Choice', *Educational Management and Administration*, 25, 2, pp. 169–80.

Casman, P. (1996) 'Children's Participation: Children's City Councils', in E. Verhellen (ed) *Understanding Children's Rights*, Ghent: Children's Rights Centre.

Chambers, V. (2003) 'Helping at Home and Informal Care: An Examination of Children's Contribution to Family Life', unpublished Ph.D., University College, Northampton.

Channel 4 (2003) *Kids on Porn*, televised 19 November.

Cheal, D. (1991) *Family and the State of Theory*, London: Harvester Wheatsheaf.

Cheal, D. (2003) *Sociology of Family Life*, Basingstoke: Palgrave Macmillan.

Children's Rights Development Unit (1994) *UK Agenda for United Nations Convention on the Rights of the Child*, London: CRDU.

Chitty, C. and Dunford, J. (eds) (1999) *State Schools: New Labour and the Conservative Legacy*, London: Frank Cass.

Christensen, P. and James, A. (2000) 'Introduction: Researching Children and Childhood: Cultures of Communication', in P. Christensen and A. James (eds) *Research with Children: Perspectives and Practices*, London: Falmer.

Cockburn, T. (1998) 'Children and Citizenship in Britain: A Case for a Socially Interdependent Model', *Childhood*, 5, 1, pp. 99–117.

Cohen, R. and Kennedy, P. (2000) *Global Sociology*, Basingstoke: Palgrave.

Connell, R. (1987) *Gender and Power*, Cambridge: Polity.

Connolly, P. (1995) 'Boys will be Boys? Racism, Sexuality and the Construction of Masculine Identities among Infant Boys', in J. Holland, M. Blair and S. Sheldon (eds) *Debates and Issues in Feminist Research and Pedagogy*, Clevedon: Multilingual Matters in Association with Open University Press.

Corsaro, W. (1997) *The Sociology of Childhood*, California: Pine Forest.

Corsaro, W. and Molinaro, L. (2000) 'Entering and Observing Children's Worlds: A Reflection on a Longitudinal Ethnography of Early Education in Italy', in P. Christensen and A. James (eds) *Research with Children: Perspectives and Practices*, London: Falmer.

Craig, S. and Earl Bennett, S. (eds) (1997) *After the Boom: The Politics of Generation X*, Maryland: Rowman and Littlefield.

Cullingford, C. (1991) *The Inner World of the School*, London: Cassell.

Cunningham, H. (1995) *Children and Childhood in Western Society since 1500*, London: Longman.

Cunningham, S. and Lavalette, M. (2004) ' "Active Citizens" or "Irresponsible Truants"? School Student Strikes against the War', *Critical Social Policy*, 24, 2, pp. 255–79.

Dallos, R. and Sapsford, R. (1995) 'Patterns of Diversity and Lived Realities', in J. Muncie, M. Wetherell, R. Dallos and A. Cochrane (eds) *Understanding the Family*, London: Sage.

Davies, B. (1982) *Life in the Classroom and Playground: The Accounts of School Children*, London: Routledge.

Davies, I. (1999) 'What has Happened in the Teaching of Politics in Schools in the Last Three Decades and Why?', *Oxford Review of Education*, 25, 1 and 2, pp. 125–41.

Davis, J., Watson, N. and Cunningham-Burley, S. (2000) 'Learning the Lives of Disabled Children: Developing a Reflexive Approach', in P. Christensen and A. James (eds) *Research with Children: Perspectives and Practices*, London: Falmer.

Dearden, C. and Becker, S. (2000) *Growing Up Caring: Vulnerability and Transition to Adulthood*, Leicester: Joseph Rowntree Foundation.

Delphy, C. (1984) *Close to Home: A Materialist Analysis of Women's Oppression*, London: Hutchinson.

Dennis, N. and Erdos, G. (1992) *Families without Fatherhood*. London: Institute of Economic Affairs.

DES (Department of Education and Science) (1992) *Education (Schools) Act*, London: HMSO.

DfE (Department for Education) (2001) *Schools Achieving Success*, London: HMSO.

DfSS (Department for Social Services) (1988) *Report of the Inquiry into Child Abuse in Cleveland 1987*, London: HMSO.

Dingwall, R., Eekelaar, J. and Murray, T. (1995) *The Protection of Children: State Intervention and Family Life*, 2nd edn, Oxford: Blackwell.

Dixon, A. (2000) 'Too Much too Young', *Forum*, 42, 3, p. 113.

DoH (Department of Health) (1995) *Child Protection: Messages from Research*, London: HMSO.

Donzelot, J. (1979) *The Policing of Families*, London: Hutchinson.

Driskell, R. (2002) *Creating Better Cities with Children*, London: Earthscan.

Dubet, F. (2000) 'The Sociology of Pupils', *Journal of Education Policy*, 15, 1, pp. 93–104.

Duncan, P. and Thomas, S. (2000) *Neighbourhood Regeneration: Resourcing Community Involvement*, Cambridge: Polity.

Durkheim, E. (1961) *Moral Education: A Study in the Theory and Application of the Sociology of Education*, London: Collier Macmillan.

Durkheim, E. (1982) 'Childhood', in C. Jenks (ed) *The Sociology of Childhood: Essential Readings*, London: Batsford.

Eberstadt, M. (2001) 'Home-Alone America', Policy Review, www.policyreview.org, consulted August 2004.

Edwards, R. and Alldred, P. (2000) 'A Typology of Parental Involvement in Education Centring on Children and Young People: Negotiating Familialisation, Institutionalisation and Individualisation', *British Journal of Sociology of Education*, 21, 3, pp. 435–55.

Elkin, F. (1960) *The Child in Society: The Process of Socialisation*, New York: Random House.

Elliott, M. (1989) *Dealing with Child Abuse: The Kidscape Training Guide*, London: Kidscape.

Engels, F. (1958) *The Condition of the Working Class in England*, Oxford: Blackwell.

Ennew, J (2000) 'The History of Children's Rights: Whose Story?', *Cultural Survival Quarterly*, 24, 2, pp. 44–8.

Epstein, D. (1993) 'Too Small to Notice? Constructions of Childhood and Discourses of "Race" in Predominantly White Contexts', *Curriculum Studies*, 1, 3, pp. 317–34.

ESRC (Economic and Social Research Council) (2001) *Mind the Gap: The Democratic Deficit*, ESRC Fifth National Social Science Conference, www.esrc.ac.uk/esrccontent/connect

Facer, K., Furlong, J., Furlong, R. and Sutherland, R. (2001) 'Home is where the Hardware is: Young People, the Domestic Environment, and "Access" to New Technologies', in I. Hutchby and J. Moran-Ellis (eds) *Children, Technology and Culture*, London: RoutledgeFalmer.

Farson, R. (1978) *Birthrights*, New York: Penguin.

Fielding, M. (2001) 'Target Setting, Policy Pathology and Student Perspectives', in M. Fielding (ed) *Taking Education Really Seriously: Four Years' Hard Labour*, London: RoutledgeFalmer.

Fine, M. (1997) '[Ap]parent Involvement: Reflections on Parents, Power and Urban Public Schools', in A. H. Halsey et al. (eds) *Education: Culture, Economy, Society*. Oxford: Oxford University Press.

Firestone, S. (1971) *The Dialectic of Sex: The Case for Feminist Revolution*, London: Jonathan Cape.

Flekkoy, M. (1988) 'Child Advocacy in Norway', *Children and Society*, 4, pp. 307–18.

Flowerdew, J. and Neale, B (2003) 'Trying to Stay Apace: Children with Multiple Challenges in their Post-divorce Family Lives', *Childhood*, 10, 2, pp. 147–62.

Foley, P., Roche, J. and Tucker, S. (2001) 'Foreword', in P. Foley, J. Roche and S. Tucker (eds) *Children in Society: Contemporary Theory, Policy and Practice*, Basingstoke: Palgrave.

Foucault, M. (1980) *Power/Knowledge: Selected Interviews and Other Writings, 1972–77*, London: Harvester Wheatsheaf.

Fox-Harding, L. (1991) *Perspectives in Child Care Policy*, London: Longman.

France, A., Bendelow, G. and Williams, S. (2000) 'A Risky Business: Researching the Health Beliefs of Children and Young People', in A. Lewis and G. Lindsay (eds) *Researching Children's Perspectives*, Buckingham: Open University Press.

Franklin, A. and Franklin, B. (1996) 'Growing Pains: The Developing Children's Rights Movement in the UK', in J. Pilcher and S. Wagg (eds) *Thatcher's Children?*, London: Falmer.

Franklin, B. (1986) *The Rights of Children*, Oxford: Blackwell.

Franklin, B. (1995) (ed) *Handbook of Children's Rights*, London: Routledge.

Franklin, B. and Petley, J. (1996) 'Killing the Age of Innocence: Newspaper Reporting of the Death of James Bulger', in J. Pilcher and S. Wagg (eds) *Thatcher's Children?*, London: Falmer.

Freeman, C. (1996) 'Local Agenda 21 as a Vehicle for Encouraging Children's Participation in Environmental Planning', *Local Government Policy Making*, 23, 1, pp. 41–51.

Freeman, M. (1983) *The Rights and Wrongs of Children*, London: Frances Pinter.

Freeman, M. (1992) *Children, their Families and the Law*, Basingstoke: Macmillan.

Fuller, P. (1979) 'Uncovering Childhood', in M. Hoyles (ed) *Changing Childhood*, London: Writer's Coop.

Garbarino, J., Kostelny, K. and Dubrow, N. (1991) *No Place to Be a Child: Growing up in a War Zone*, Lexington, MA: Lexington Books.

Garfinkel, H. (1967) *Studies in Ethnomethodology*, Englewood Cliffs: Prentice-Hall.

Giddens, A. (1971) *Capitalism and Modern Social Theory*, Cambridge: Cambridge University Press.

Giddens, A. (1984) *The Constitution of Society*, Cambridge: Polity.

Giddens, A. (1991) *Modernity and Self-identity*, Cambridge: Polity.

Gittins, D. (1998) *The Child in Question*, Basingstoke: Macmillan.

Glauser, B. (1997) 'Street Children: Deconstructing a Construct', in A. James and A. Prout (eds) *Constructing and Reconstructing Childhood*, 2nd edn, Basingstoke: Falmer.

Goldson, B. (2001) 'The Demonisation of Childhood: From the Symbolic to the Institutional', in P. Foley, J. Roche and S. Tucker (eds) *Children in Society: Contemporary Theory, Policy and Practice*, Basingstoke: Palgrave, pp. 34–41.

Goldson, B. (2002) *Vulnerable Inside: Children in Secure and Penal Settings*, London: The Children's Society.

Goldstein, J., Freud, A. and Solnit, J. (1980) *Before the Best Interests of the Child*, London: Burnett.

Goodwin-Gill, G. and Cohn, I. (1994) *Child Soldiers*, Oxford: Clarendon.

Gorard, S. (1996) 'Three Steps to "Heaven"? The Family and School Choice', *Educational Review*, 48, 3, 237–51.

Gordon, L. (1985) 'Child Abuse: Gender and the Myth of Family Independence', *Child Welfare*, 64, 3, pp. 213–24.

Hacking, I. (1991) 'The Making and Moulding of Child Abuse', *Critical Inquiry*, 17, Winter, pp. 253–88.

Hahn, C. (1999) 'Citizenship Education: An Empirical Study of Policy, Practice and Outcomes', *Oxford Review of Education*, 25, 1 and 2, pp. 231–50.

Hall, K. (1995) ' "There's a Time to Act English and a Time to Act Indian": The Politics of Identity among British-Sikh Teenagers', in S. Stephens (ed) *Children and the Politics of Culture*, Princeton, NJ: Princeton University Press.

Hall, S. (1983) 'The Great Moving Right Show', in S. Hall and M. Jacques (eds) *The Politics of Thatcherism*, London: Lawrence and Wishart.

Hall, S. and Jefferson, T. (eds) (1976) *Resistance through Rituals*, London: Hutchinson.

Hanawalt, B. (1993) *Growing up in Medieval London*, New York: Oxford University Press.

Haralambos, M. and Holborn, S. (2000) *Sociology: Themes and Perspectives*, 5th edn, London: Collins.

Harber, C. and Meighan, R. (1989), 'Preface', in C. Harber and R. Meighan (eds) *The Democratic School*, Derbyshire: Ticknell.

Harder, M. and Pringle, K. (eds) (1997) *Protecting Children in Europe: Towards a New Millennium*, Aalborg; Aalborg University Press.

Hargreaves, A. and Reynolds, D. (1990) 'Decomprehensivisation', in A. Hargreaves and D. Reynolds (eds) *Educational Policies: Controversies and Critiques*, Basingstoke: Falmer.

Hargreaves, D. (1990) *The Challenge for the Comprehensive School: Culture, Curriculum and Community*, London: Routledge.

Harre, R. (1986) 'The Step to Social Constructionism', in M. Richards and P. Light (eds) *Children of Social Worlds*, Cambridge: Polity.

Harris, C. C. (1983) *The Family and Industrial Society*, London: Routledge.

Hart, R. (1997) *Children's Participation: The Theory and Practice of Involving Young Citizens in Community Development and Environmental Care*, London: Earthscan.

Hartmann, H. (1980) 'The Unhappy Marriage of Marxism and Feminism: Towards a More Progressive Union', in L. Sergent (ed) *Women and Revolution*, New York: Monthly Review.

Harvey, D. (1989) *The Condition of Postmodernity*, Oxford: Blackwell.

Harvey, R. (2000) 'Child Soldiers: The Beginning of the End?', *ChildRight*, 164, pp. 18–19.

Hatcher, R. (2000) 'Social Class and School: Relationships to Knowledge', in M. Cole (ed) *Education, Equality and Human Rights*, London: Routledge.

Hendrick, H. (1997) 'Constructions and Re-constructions of British Childhood: An Interpretive Survey, 1800 to the Present', in A. James and A. Prout (eds) *Constructing and Reconstructing Childhood*, 2nd edn, London: Falmer.

Hendrick, H. (2000) 'The Child as a Social Actor in Historical Sources: Problems of Identification and Interpretation', in P. Christensen and A. James (eds) *Research with Children: Perspectives and Practices*, London: Falmer.

Hetherington, E. M. (2003) 'Social Support and the Adjustment of Children in Divorced and Remarried Families', *Childhood*, 10, 2, pp. 217–36

Hill, M., Davis, J., Prout, A. and Tisdall, K. (2004) Moving the Participation Agenda Forward, *Children and Society*, 18, 2, pp. 77–96.

Hill, M., Laybourn, A. and Borland, M. (1996) 'Engaging with Primary-aged Children about their Emotions and Well-being: Methodological Considerations', *Children and Society*, 10, 2, pp. 129–44.

Hobbs, S., Lavalette, M. and McKechnie, J. (1992) 'The Emerging Problem of Child Labour', *Critical Social Policy*, 34, pp. 93–105.

Holloway, S. and Valentine, G. (2003) *Cyberkids: Children in the Information Age*, London: RoutledgeFalmer.

Holt, J. (1975) *Escape from Childhood*, Harmondsworth: Penguin.

Home Office (1988) *Report of the Inquiry into Child Abuse in Cleveland 1987*, London: HMSO.

Home Office (1998) *Crime and Disorder Act*, London: HMSO.

Home Office (2004) *The Waterhouse Report*, London: HMSO.

Hood, S., Kelley, P. and Mayall, B. (1996) 'Children as Research Subjects: A Risky Enterprise', *Children and Society*, 10, 2, pp. 117–28.

Hood-Williams, J (1990) ' Patriarchy for Children: On the Stability of Power Relations in Children's Lives', in L. Chisholm, P. Buchner, H-H. Kruger and P. Brown (eds) *Childhood, Youth and Social Change*, London: Falmer.

Humphries, S. (1981) *Hooligans or Rebels?* Oxford: Blackwell.

Illich, I. (1971) *Deschooling Society*, Harmondsworth: Penguin.

James, A. (1993) *Childhood Identities: Self and Social Relationships in the Experience of the Child*, Edinburgh: Edinburgh University Press.

James, A., Jenks, C. and Prout, A. (1998) *Theorising Childhood*, Cambridge: Polity.

James A. and Prout A. (1997) 'Re-presenting Childhood: Time and Transition in the Study of Childhood', in A. James and A. Prout (eds) *Constructing and Reconstructing Childhood*, 2nd edn, London: Falmer.

James, A. L. and James, A. (2001) 'Tightening the Net: Children, Community and Control', *British Journal of Sociology*, 52, 2, pp. 211–28.

James, A. L. and. James A. (2004) *Constructing Childhood: Theory, Policy and Social Practice*, Basingstoke: Palgrave.

Jenks, C. (1982) 'Introduction: Constituting the Child', in C. Jenks (ed) *The Sociology of Childhood: Essential Readings*, London: Batsford.

Jenks, C. (1996) 'The Post-modern Child', in J. Brannan and M. O'Brien (eds) *Children in Families: Research and Policy*, London: Falmer.

John, M. (1995) 'Children's Rights in a Free Market Culture', in S. Stephens (ed) *Children and the Politics of Culture*, Princeton, NJ: Princeton University Press.

Keith, L. and Morris, J. (1995) 'Easy Targets: A Disability Rights Perspective on the ' "Children as Carers" Debate', *Critical Social Policy*, 44/45, Autumn, pp. 36–57.

Kelly, A. V. (1994) *The National Curriculum: A Critical Review*, London: Paul Chapman.

Kenway, J. and Bullen, E. (2001) *Consuming Children: Education–Entertainment–Advertising*, Buckingham: Open University Press.

Kitzinger, J. (1997) 'Who Are You Kidding? Children, Power and the Struggle Against Sexual Abuse', in A. James and A. Prout (eds) *Constructing and Reconstructing Childhood*, London: Falmer.

Kline, S. (1993) *Out of the Garden: Toys and Children's Culture in the Age of TV Marketing*, London: Verso.

Koss, F. (2001) 'Children Falling into the Digital Divide', *Journal of International Affairs*, 55, 1, pp. 75–90.

La Fontaine, J. (1990) *Child Sex Abuse*, Cambridge: Cambridge University Press.

Langford, W., Lewis, C., Solomon, Y. and Warren, J. (2001) *Closeness, Authority and Independence in Families with Teenagers*, York: Joseph Rowntree Foundation.

Lansdown, G. (1994) 'Children's Rights', in B. Mayall (ed) *Children's Childhoods Observed and Experienced*, London: Falmer.

Lansdown, G. (2000) 'Children's Welfare and Children's Rights', in P. Foley, J. Roche and S. Tucker (eds) *Children in Society: Contemporary Theory, Policy and Practice*, Basingstoke: Palgrave, pp. 87–97.

Lasch, C. (1979) *The Culture of Narcissism*, New York: Norton.

Latour, B. (1993) *We Have Never Been Modern*, Hemel Hempstead: Harvester Wheatsheaf.

Lavalette, M. (1996) 'Thatcher's Working Children: Contemporary Issues of Child Labour', in J. Pilcher and S. Wagg (eds) *Thatcher's Children?*, London: Falmer.

Lee, N. (2001) *Childhood and Society: Growing up in an Age of Uncertainty*, Buckingham: Open University Press.

Lévi-Strauss, C. (1978) *Myth and Meaning*, London: Routledge and Kegan Paul.

Lightburn, A. (1992) 'Participant Observation in Special Needs Adoptive Families', in J. Gilgun, K. Daly and G. Handel (eds) (1992) *Qualitative Methods in Family Research*, London: Sage.

Livingstone, S. (2003) 'Children's Use of the Internet: Reflections on the Emerging Research Agenda', *New Media and Society*, 5, 2, pp. 147–66.

Lowden, S. and Bennett, S. (1995) 'State, Private or DIY? The Challenge of Home-based Education', *British Journal of Curriculum and Assessment*, 6, 1, pp. 40–5.

Lyotard, J-F. (1984) *The Post-Modern Condition: A Report on Knowledge*, Manchester: Manchester University Press.

MacDonell, H. (2004) 'Paedophile Laws to Tackle Grooming', news.scotsman.com, 27 September.

Mclean, M. (1990) *Britain and a Single Market Europe: Prospects for a Common School Curriculum*, London: Kogan Page.

McRobbie, A. (1991) *Feminism and Youth Culture*, Basingstoke: Macmillan.

Mahon, A., Glendinning, C., Clarke, K. and Craig, C. (1996) 'Researching Children: Methods and Ethics', *Children and Society*, 10, 2, pp. 145–54.

Maitles, H. (2004) 'Why are they Bombing Innocent Iraqis? Political Literacy among Primary Pupils', *Improving Schools*, 7, 1, pp. 97–105.

Mandel, R. (1995) 'Second-generation Noncitizens: Children of the Turkish Migrant Diaspora in Germany', in S. Stephens (ed) *Childhood and the Politics of Culture*, Princeton, NJ: Princeton University Press.

Mandell, N. (1991) 'The Least Adult Role in Studying Children', in F. Waksler (ed) *Studying the Social Worlds of Children*, London: Falmer Press.

Mann, G. and Ledward, A. (2000) 'The Best Interests of "Separated" Children in Rwanda', *Cultural Survival Quarterly*, 24, 2, pp. 59–61.

Mason, J. and Falloon, J. (2001) 'Some Sydney Children Define Abuse: Implications for Agency in Childhood', in L. Alanen and B. Mayall (eds) *Conceptualising Child–Adult Relations*, London: RoutledgeFalmer.

Masson, J. (2000) 'Researching Children's Perspectives: Legal Issues', in A. Lewis and G. Lindsay (eds) *Researching Children's Perspectives*, Buckingham: Open University Press.

Matthews, H. and Limb, M. (1998) 'The Right to Say: The Development of Youth Councils/Forums within the UK', *Area*, 30, 1, pp. 66–78.

Matthews, H., Limb, M., Harrison, L. and Taylor, M. (1999). 'Local Places and the Political Engagement of Young People: Youth Councils as Participatory Structures', *Youth and Policy*, Winter, 62, pp. 6–30.

Mayall, B. (1996) *Children, Health and the Social Order*, Buckingham: University Press.

Mayall, B. (2000) 'Conversations with Children: Working with Generational Issues', in P. Christensen and A. James (eds) *Research with Children: Perspectives and Practices*, London: Falmer.

Mayall, B. (2002) *Towards a Sociology of Childhood: Thinking from Children's Lives*, Buckingham: Open University.

Mead, M. (1930) *Growing up in New Guinea*, Harmondsworth: Penguin.

Meighan, R. (1995) 'Home-based Education Effectiveness Research and Some of its Implications', *Educational Review*, 47, 3, pp. 275–86.

Melucci, A. (1992) 'Youth Silence and Voice: Selfhood and Commitment in the Everyday Experiences of Adolescents', in J. Fornas and G. Bolin (eds) *Moves in Modernity*, Stockholm: Almqvist and Wiksell.

Miles, S. (2000) *Youth Cultures in a Changing World*, Buckingham: Open University Press.

Moorehead, C. (1987) *School Age Workers in Britain Today*, London: Anti-Slavery Society.

Moran-Ellis, J. and Cooper, G. (2000) 'Making Connections: Children, Technology and the National Grid for Learning', *Sociological Research Online*, 5, 3, http://www.socresonline.org.uk

Morgan, D. H. J. (1996) *Family Connections*, Cambridge: Polity.

Morrow, V. (1994) 'Responsible Children: Aspects of Children's Work and Employment Outside School in Contemporary UK', in B. Mayall (ed) *Children's Childhoods Observed and Experienced*, London: Falmer.

Morrow, V. (1996) 'Rethinking Childhood Dependency: Children's Contributions to the Domestic Economy', *Sociological Review*, 44, 1, pp. 58–77.

Morrow, V. and Richards, M. (1996) 'The Ethics of Social Research with Children: An Overview', *Children and Society* 10, 2, pp. 90–105.

Morss, J. (1996) *Growing Critical: Alternatives to Developmental Psychology*, London: Routledge.

Moss, P. and Petrie, P. (2002) *From Children's Services to Children's Spaces*, London: RoutledgeFalmer.

Moszynski, P. (2001) '41 Countries Send Children into War', *Guardian*, 13 June, p. 13.

Moxnes, K. (2003) 'Risk Factors in Divorce: Perceptions by the Children Involved', *Childhood*, 10, 2, pp. 131–46.

Muncie, J. (2004) *Youth and Crime*, 2nd edn, London: Sage.

Murray, C. (1994) *Underclass: The Crisis Deepens*, London: Institute of Economic Affairs.

National Centre for Social Research (2000) *Young People's Politics: Political Interest and Engagement amongst 14- to 24-Year-Olds*, York: YPS.

National Children's Bureau, *Guidelines for Research*, www.ncb.org.uk/resguide, consulted August 2003.

National Curriculum Council (1992) *Starting out with the National Curriculum*, York: NCC.

Ndebele, N. (1995) 'Recovering Childhood: Children in South African Reconstruction', in S. Stephens (ed) *Childhood and the Politics of Culture*, Princeton, NJ: Princeton University Press.

Neill, A. S. (1968) *Summerhill*, Harmondsworth: Penguin.

Newson, J. and Newson, E. (1976) *Seven Years Old in the Home Environment*, Harmondsworth: Penguin.

Oakley, A. (1972) *Sex, Gender and Society*, London: Maurice Temple Smith.

Oakley, A. (1981a) 'Interviewing Women: A Contradiction in Terms', in H. Roberts (ed) *Doing Feminist Research*, London: Routledge and Kegan Paul.

Oakley, A. (1981b) *Sex, Gender and Society*, 2nd edn, London: Maurice Temple Smith.

Oakley, A. (1994) 'Women and Children First and Last: Parallels and Differences between Children's and Women's Studies', in B. Mayall (ed) *Children's Childhoods Observed and Experienced*, London: Falmer.

O'Brien, M., Alldred, P. and Jones, D. (1996) 'Children's Constructions of Family and Kinship', in J. Brannen and M. O'Brien (eds) *Children in Families*, London: Falmer.

O'Keeffe, D. (1994) *Truancy in English Secondary Schools*, London: HMSO.

Oldman, D. (1994) 'Adult/Child Relations as Class Relations', in J. Qvortrup, M. Bardy, G. Sgritta and. H. Wintersberger (eds) *Childhood Matters: Social Theory, Practice and Politics*, Aldershot: Avebury.

Oswell, D. (1998) 'The Place of "Childhood" in Internet Content Regulation', *International Journal of Cultural Studies*, 1, 2, pp. 271–91.

Parry-Williams, J. (1998) 'Child-sensitive Local Government Structures in Synergy with Children's Representative Bodies', in V. Johnson, E. Ivan-Smith, G. Gordon, P. Pridmore and P. Scott (eds) *Stepping Forward: Children and Young People's Participation in the Development Process*, London: IT Publications.

Parsons, C. (1999) *Education, Exclusion and Citizenship*, London: Routledge.

Parsons, T. (1951) *The Social System*, London: Routledge and Kegan Paul.

Parsons, T. (1961) 'The School Class as a Social System: Some of its Functions in American Society', in A. Halsey, J. Floud and A. Anderson (eds) *Education, Economy, and Society: A Reader in the Sociology of Education*. New York: Free Press of Glencoe.

Parton, N. (1985) *The Politics of Child Abuse*, Basingstoke: Macmillan.

Parton, N. (1996) 'The New Politics of Child Protection', in J. Pilcher and S. Wagg (eds) *Thatcher's Children?*, London: Falmer.

Parton, N., Thorpe D. and Wattan, C. (1997) *Child Protection: Risk and the Moral Order*, Basingstoke: Macmillan.

Pascall, G. (1997) *Social Policy: A New Feminist Reader*, London: Routledge.

Paterson, F. (1989) *Out of Place: Public Policy and the Emergence of Truancy*, London: Falmer.

Pearce, D. (1993) 'Children Having Children: Teenage Pregnancy and Public Policy from the Woman's Perspective', in A. Lawson and D. Rhodes (eds) *Politics of Teenage Pregnancy*, New Haven, CT: Yale University Press.

Pearson, G. (1983) *Hooligan: A History of Respectable Fears*, Basingstoke: Macmillan.

Petrie, A. (1995) 'Home Educators and the Law within Europe', *International Review of Education*, 41, 3–4, pp. 285–96.

Phillips, M. (1996) *All Must Have Prizes*, London: Little, Brown.

Piaget, J. (1932) *The Language and Thought of the Child*, London: Routledge and Kegan Paul.

Pike, L. (2003) 'The Adjustment of Australian Children Growing up in Single Parent Families as Measured by their Competence and Self-esteem', *Childhood*, 10, 2, pp. 181–200.

Pinkerton, J. (2001) 'Developing Partnership Practice', in P. Foley, J. Roche and S. Tucker (eds) *Children in Society: Contemporary Theory, Policy and Practice*, Basingstoke: Palgrave.

Pollard, A. (1996) 'Playing the System? Pupil Perspectives on Curriculum, Pedagogy and Assessment in Primary Schools', in P. Croll (ed) *Teachers, Pupils and Primary Schooling*, London: Cassell.

Pollard, A. and Filer, A. (1999) *The Social World of the Pupil Career: Strategic Biographies Through Primary School*, London: Cassell.

Pollard, A. and Trigg, P. (2000) *What Pupils Think*, London: Cassell.

Pollock, L. (1983) *Forgotten Children: Parent–Child Relations from 1500 to 1900*, Cambridge: Cambridge University Press.

Postman, N. (1982) *The Disappearance of Childhood*, London: Comet.

Pringle, K. (1998) *Children and Social Welfare in Europe*, Buckingham: Open University Press.

Prout, A. (2000a) 'Childhood Bodies: Construction, Agency and Hybridity', in A. Prout (ed) *The Body, Childhood and Society*, London: Macmillan.

Prout, A. (2000b), 'Children's Participation: Control and Self-Realisation in British Late Modernity', *Children and Society*, 14, 4, pp. 304–15.

Prout, A. and James, A. (1997) 'A New Paradigm for the Sociology of Childhood? Provenance, Promise and Problems', in A. James and A. Prout (eds) *Constructing and Reconstructing Childhood*, 2nd edn, London: Falmer.

Punamaki, R. (1996) 'Can Ideological Commitment Protect Children's Psychological Wellbeing in Situations of Political Violence?', *Child Development*, 67, pp. 55–69.

Punch, S. (2002) 'Interviewing Strategies with Young People: The "Secret Box", Stimulus Material and Task-based Activities', *Children and Society*, 16, 1, pp. 45–56.

Qvortrup, J. (1994) 'Childhood Matters: An Introduction', in J. Qvortrup et al. (eds) *Childhood Matters: Social Theory, Practice and Politics*, Aldershot: Avebury.

Qvortrup, J. (1997) ' A Voice for Children in Statistical and Social Accounting: A Plea for Children's Right to be Heard', in A. James and A. Prout (eds) *Constructing and Reconstructing Childhood*, 2nd edn, London: Falmer.

Qvortrup, J. (2000) 'Macro-analysis of Childhood', in P. Christensen and A. James (eds) *Research with Children: Perspectives and Practices*, London: Falmer.

Reddy, N. (2000) 'The Right to Organise: The Children's Movement in India', *Cultural Survival Quarterly*, 24, 2, pp. 52–5.

Riesman, D. (1950) *The Lonely Crowd*, New Haven, CT: Yale University Press.

Rizzini, I. (1996) 'Street Children: An Excluded Generation in Latin America', *Childhood: A Global Journal of Child Research*, 3, pp. 215–33.

Roberts, H. (2000) 'Listening to Children: And Hearing Them', in P. Christensen and A. James (eds) *Research with Children: Perspectives and Practices*, London: Falmer.

Roberts, K. (1997) 'Same Activities, Different Meanings: British Youth Cultures in the 1990s', *Leisure Studies*, 16, 1, pp. 1–16.

Roche, M. (1992) *Rethinking Citizenship*, Cambridge: Polity.

Roker, D., Player, K. and Coleman, J. (1999) 'Young People's Voluntary and Campaigning Activities as Sources of Political Education', *Oxford Review of Education*, 25, 1 and 2, pp. 185–98.

Rose, N. (1992) *Governing the Soul*, London: Routledge.

Rudduck, J., Chaplain, R. and Wallace, G. (1996) 'Introduction', in J. Rudduck, R. Chaplain and G. Wallace (eds) *School Improvement: What Can Pupils Tell Us?* London: David Fulton.

Rudduck, J. and Flutter, J. (2004) *How to Improve your School*, London: Continuum.

Rudduck. J., Wallace, G. and Day, J. (1997) 'Students' Voices; What Can They Tell Us as Partners in Change?', in K. Scott and V. Trafford (eds) *Partners in Change: Shaping the Future* London: Middlesex University Press.

Ruxton, S. (1999) *A Child's Policy for 21st Century Europe: First Steps*, Euronet http://eurochild.gla.ac.uk

Saraga, E. (1993) 'The Abuse of Children', in R. Dallos and E. McLaughlin (eds) *Social Problems and the Family*, London: Sage.

Scott, J. (2000) 'Children as Respondents: The Challenge for Quantitative Methods', in P. Christensen and A. James (eds) *Research with Children: Perspectives and Practices*, London: Falmer.

Scott, S., Jackson, S. and Backett-Millburn, K. (1998) 'Swings and Roundabouts: Risk Anxiety and the Everyday Worlds of Children', *Sociology*, 32, 4, pp. 689–705.

Seabrook, J. (1982) *Working Class Childhood*, London: Golancz.

Seiter, E. (1995) *Sold Separately: Children and Parents in Consumer Culture*, New Brunswick, NJ: Rutgers University Press.

Selwyn, N. (2001) 'Children, Computers and the Discursive Construction of the Information Society', paper presented at European Sociological Association Conference, Helsinki.

Sharp, R. and Green, A. (1975) *Education and Social Control*, London: Routledge.

Shore, H. (1999) *Artful Dodgers: Youth and Crime in Early Nineteenth Century Britain*, London: Royal Historical Society.

Shorter, E. (1976) *The Making of the Modern Family*, Harmondsworth: Penguin.

Smith, P. and Cowie, H. (2003) *Understanding Children's Development*, 4th edn, Oxford: Blackwell.

Social Trends (2000) London: HMSO.

Solberg, A. (1996) 'The Challenge in Child Research: From "Being" to "Doing" ', in J. Brannen and M. O'Brien (eds) *Children in Families: Research and Policy*, London: Falmer.

Solberg, A. (1997) 'Negotiating Childhood: Changing Constructions of Age for Norwegian Children', in A. James and A. Prout (eds) *Constructing and Reconstructing Childhood*, London: Falmer.

Somekh, B. (2000) 'New Technology and Learning: Policy and Practice in the UK, 1980–2010', *Education and Information Technologies*, 5, 1, pp. 19–38.

Song, M. (1996) ' "Helping Out": Children's Labour Participation in Chinese Take-away Business in Britain', in J. Brannen and M. O'Brien (eds) *Children in Families*, London: Falmer.

Song, Y. and Lu, H-H. (2002) 'Early Childhood Poverty: A Statistical Profile', National Center for Children in Poverty, http://cpmcnet.columbia.edu/dept/nccp

Spencer, J. and Flyn, R. (1993) *The Evidence of Children*, London: Blackstone.

Stainton-Rogers, R. (1989) 'The Social Construction of Childhood', in W. Stainton-Rogers, D. Harvey, and E. Ash (eds) *Child Abuse and Neglect*, London: Open University Press.

Stainton-Rogers, W. and Stainton-Rogers, R. (1992) *Stories of Childhood*, London: Harvester Wheatsheaf.

Stanley, L. and Wise, S. (1983) *Breaking Out: Feminist Consciousness and Feminist Research*, London: Routledge and Kegan Paul.

Stephens, S. (1995) 'Children and the Politics of Culture in "Late Capitalism" ', in S. Stephens (ed) *Childhood and the Politics of Culture*, Princeton, NJ: Princeton University Press.

Suss, D. et al. (2001) 'Media Childhood in Three European Countries', in I. Hutchby and J. Moran-Ellis (eds) *Children, Technology and Culture*, London: RoutledgeFalmer.

Taal, M. and Edelaar, M. (1997) 'Positive and Negative Effects of a Child Sexual Abuse Prevention Programme', *Child Abuse and Neglect*, 21, 4, pp. 399–410.

Thorne, B. (1987) 'Re-visioning Women', *Gender and Society*, March, pp. 85–109.

Thorne, B. (1993) *Gender Play: Girls and Boys in School*, Milton Keynes: Open University Press.

Thomas, A. (1998) *Educating Children at Home*, London: Cassell.

Thomas, N. (2001) 'Listening to Children', in P. Foley, J. Roche, and S. Tucker (eds) *Children in Society: Contemporary Theory, Policy and Practice*, Basingstoke: Palgrave Macmillan.

Townsend, M. (2004) 'Exam Fears Driving Teenagers to Prozac', *Observer*, 6 June, p. 1.

Townsend, P. (1996) *A Poor Future: Can We Counter Growing Poverty in Britain and Across the World?* London: Lemos and Crane.

Troyna, B. (1993) *Racism and Education*, London: Routledge.

UNICEF (1997) *Children at Risk in Central and Eastern Europe: The Monee Report*, Florence: Innocenti Papers.

United Nations (1989) *Convention on the Rights of the Child*, Geneva: United Nations.

United News of India (1999) 'Child "Legislators" Wrest Welfare Benefits', *Indian Express*, 13 December, www.indian-express.com/ie/daily

Vasquez, A. and Martinez, I. (1992) 'Paris–Barcelona: Invisible Interactions in the Classroom', *Anthropology and Education Quarterly*, 23, pp. 219–312.

Wainwright, M. (1994) 'Call for a National Childcare System', *Guardian*, 6 January, p. 7.

Walker, A. (1996) *Young Carers and their Families*, London: HMSO.

Walker, D. (1996) 'Young People, Politics and the Media', in H. Robertson and D. Sarchev (eds) *Young People's Social Attitudes*, Essex: Barnardo's.

Walkerdine, V. (1983) 'Developmental Psychology and the Child Centred Pedagogy: The Insertion of Piaget into Early Education', in J. Henriques et al. (eds) *Changing the Subject: Psychology, Social Regulation and Subjectivity*, London: Methuen.

Watkins, C. (2001) 'Developing a Language for Talking about Learning: Towards a Narrative View', paper delivered at the ESRC Teaching and Learning Research Programme meta-seminar, Homerton College, University of Cambridge, 10 May.

Wexler, J. et al. (1992) *Becoming Somebody: Toward a Social Psychology of School*, London: Falmer.

Widdicombe, S. (1995) *The Language of Youth Subcultures*, London: Harvester Wheatsheaf.

Williams, C. (1993) 'Who are "Street Children?" A Hierarchy of Street Use and Appropriate Responses', *Child Abuse and Neglect*, 17, pp. 831–41.

Willis, P. (1977) *Learning to Labour*, Aldershot: Avebury.

Wilson, R. (2002) 'Is a Child Soldier a "Child" in the Eyes of the Law?', *Times Higher Education Supplement*, 25 January, p. 23.

Wintersberger, H. (1994) 'Costs and Benefits: The Economics of Childhood', in J. Qvortrup, M. Bardy, G. Sgritta and. H. Wintersberger (eds) *Childhood Matters: Social Theory, Practice and Politics*, Aldershot: Avebury.

Woodhead, M. (1990) 'Psychology and the Cultural Construction of Children's Needs', in A. James and A. Prout (eds) *Constructing and Reconstructing Childhood*, 1st edn, London: Falmer.

Woodhead, M. (1997) 'Psychology and the Cultural Construction of Children's Needs', in A. James and A. Prout (eds) *Constructing and Reconstructing Childhood*, 2nd edn, London: Falmer.

Woodhead, M. (1999a) 'Combating Child Labour: Listen to what the Children Say', *Childhood*, 6, 1, pp. 27–50.

Woodhead, M. (1999b) 'Reconstructing Developmental Psychology – Some First Steps', *Children and Society*, 13, 1, pp. 3–19.

Wrong, D. (1961) 'The Over-socialised Conception of Man in Modern Sociology', *American Sociological Review*, 26, pp. 183–93.

Wyness, M. (1994) 'Keeping Tabs on an Uncivil Society: Positive Parental Control', *Sociology*, 28, 1, pp. 193–209.

Wyness, M. (2000) *Contesting Childhood*, London: Falmer.
Wyness, M. (2001) 'Children, Citizenship and Political Participation: English Case Studies of Young People's Councils', *International Journal of Children's Rights*, 9, pp. 193–212.
Wyness, M. and Silcock, P. (1999) 'Market Values, Primary Schooling and the Pupils' Perspective', in D. Lawton, J. Cairns and R. Gardner (eds) *Values and the Curriculum: The School Context*, Occasional Paper, London: Institute of Education.
Zelitzer, V. (1985) *Pricing the Priceless Child: The Changing Social Value of Children*, New York: Basic Books.

Useful websites

British Council – http://www.britcoun.org/governance/jusrig/human/childrig/index.htm
British Youth Council – http://www.byc.org.uk
ESRC 'Children 5–16, Growing into the 21st Century' Research Programme – www.regard.ac.uk/cgi-bin/regardng/getProgrammes.pl
ESRC 'Consulting Pupils about Teaching and Learning' Research Programme – www.consultingpupils.co.uk
The Glasgow Centre for the Child and Society – www.gccs.gla.ac.uk
On child workers – http://www.workingchild.org
Social Exclusion Unit, www.socialexclusion.gov.uk
www.datamonitor.com/consumer
www.warchild.org

Index